MEIC STEPHENS
My Shoulder to the Wheel

Happy Birthday Dad!
Love Dave ♂ 2018.

MEIC STEPHENS

My Shoulder to the Wheel

AN AUTOBIOGRAPHY

First impression: 2015

© Copyright Meic Stephens and Y Lolfa Cyf., 2015

The contents of this book are subject to copyright, and may
not be reproduced by any means, mechanical or electronic,
without the prior, written consent of the publishers.

The publishers wish to acknowledge the support of
Cyngor Llyfrau Cymru

Cover photograph: Ben Hussain

ISBN: 978 1 78461 074 6

Published and printed in Wales
on paper from well-maintained forests by
Y Lolfa Cyf., Talybont, Ceredigion SY24 5HE
website www.ylolfa.com
e-mail ylolfa@ylolfa.com
tel 01970 832 304
fax 832 782

Contents

Author's Note

THIS BOOK IS the English-language version of my autobiography *Cofnodion* (Y Lolfa, 2012), which was one of three books short-listed for Llyfr y Flwyddyn / Book of the Year in the creative non-fiction category for 2013. I have made no attempt to reproduce here the rich flavour of the Gwentian dialect, once widely spoken in upland Gwent and Glamorgan, in which the original text was written. I have, however, tried to put on record some of the more significant events and people in my life and the affairs of Wales since the book was first published. The other changes are that I have compressed Chapter 9, which in *Cofnodion* described my attempts to win the Crown at the National Eisteddfod, for I think they would not have been all that interesting for English-speaking readers unfamiliar with eisteddfodic culture, and I have expanded Chapter 10, which deals mainly with recent political, personal and family matters which I have felt able to share with strangers. For these reasons, and because I have made a number of other emendations here and there, I should like *My Shoulder to the Wheel* to be considered a different book from *Cofnodion*.

One point in particular remains unaltered: I dedicated the Welsh text to my wife Ruth, thanking her for being sensible, generous, steadfast and cheerful in all things; that much has not changed.

Meic Stephens
Whitchurch, Cardiff
May 2015

1

A Small House in Meadow Street

I WAS BORN in industrial south Wales, English-speaking but Welsh in character and outlook, and into the working class. Brought up in the village of Trefforest, near Pontypridd, in the heart of the old county of Glamorgan, as a boy I was familiar with foundry, pit, furnace, tip, siding, gulley, chimney stack, tramway, canal, feeder, terrace, hooter, railway, factory, chapel, cinema and a river thick with coal dust – the main features of the urban scene hereabouts. From our kitchen window we set our clock by the trains going up to the Rhondda, Aberdare and Merthyr, and down to the docks in Cardiff and Barry, day and night.

The village had grown into a place for the working of tinplate early in the nineteenth century and took its name from Fforest Isaf, a farm on the lower slopes of a wooded hill, Coed Berthlwyd. Trefforest was a community of some importance in those days, long before the growth of Newbridge, the name first given to Pontypridd. The enormous ruins of the Fforest tinworks, including a rolling-mill, still stood at the bottom of our street, beyond the Bute, a wooded embankment named after the Marquis whose wealth built Cardiff. Another site with its Egyptian furnaces was situated near the northern gate of what later became the University of Glamorgan. The Taff Vale Railway ran along the Bute before crossing the Taff on a viaduct on its way down the valley, and another line to the docks in Barry that had been built for David Davies, Llandinam, to rival those of the Marquis, and for that reason Coed Berthlwyd was known locally as the Barry Mountain. Seeing trucks with the names of famous pits painted in large white letters on their sides going past our house every day was proof, for us, that Trefforest lay at one of the busy hubs of the south Wales coalfield in those days; quite right, too.

When I was a boy the house once owned by Francis Crawshay, the eccentric son of William Crawshay, the Merthyr ironmaster, which we could see from our kitchen, was well known as the South Wales and Monmouthshire School of Mines, although local people called it the Mining School, or even The School. It was maintained by the mineowners and its original purpose had been to train skilled workers for the heavy industries, and this in the days before nationalization. In due course the School grew into the Glamorgan Technical College, the Glamorgan Polytechnic and the Polytechnic of Wales, and then, in 1992, it became the University of Glamorgan; it is now one of the sites of the University of South Wales. One of the things we used to do as boys was sneak across the line, the better to bring the windows of Crawshay's house within range of our catapults, and then let fly. There is nothing so satisfying to a boy as the sound of shattering glass. Once across, we would play among the limestone tips, the white waste from the Fforest furnaces, where some of the main buildings of the University stand today. Little did I know at the time that I would one day have a closer association with the place.

As the poet Thomas Hood reminds us, a man doesn't easily forget the house where he was born, and I remember 50 Meadow Street in all its detail. I have read, moreover, that a child isn't aware of his home and family until he's at least nine or ten years old. If that's true, I think I can call to mind the moment when this happened in my case. It must have been one evening during the winter of 1947, one of the severest on record, when I would have been nine, because it had been snowing for weeks and the drifts were up over the top of our kitchen window, so that it felt like living in an igloo. The coal fire was burning brightly in the grate, the wireless was on, Nan and Gramp (my mother's parents) were sitting each side of the hearth, my father was busy with his Union papers, my mother sewing in her armchair, and my brother Lloyd, four at the time, was playing with his lead soldiers, when I happened to look up and see them all clearly, as if in a living tableau, for the first time ever. This picture remains in my memory to this day as one of the epiphanies of my childhood.

Wherever else I have lived since then, it's from that small house in Meadow Street that my earliest memories spring and there, as I grow old, especially in the minutes before sleep, that my mind usually returns, to a time, place and people that left an indelible mark on me. It's a pleasure and a privilege to be able to write about them now.

I saw the light of day for the first time on the 23rd of July 1938. I came into the world in my parents' bed, the window wide open on account of the warm weather, so that my mother's pains could be heard in the street outside. Soon afterwards, Gramp, who was a bit of a tippler, went to invite the neighbours in to wet the baby's head from a barrel of cider he'd been keeping for that purpose. I was christened Michael because Nan was a great fan of Michael Wilding, whose birthday was on the 23rd of July. I was lucky not to be called Haile Selassie, who also shared the birth date.

Our house had three bedrooms. My parents slept in the front, my grandparents at the back, and my brother and I in the box room, which was barely big enough to take a single bed, a wardrobe and a chair. In fact, the room was so cramped that we had to take it in turns to undress while the other got into bed. But we didn't take off our shirts: the room was so cold in winter, before the days of central heating, that we had to keep our flannel shirts on, since we had no pyjamas. One of my small pleasures nowadays is to wear my shirt in bed on cold winter nights, if my wife Ruth doesn't object too much;

it's not always easy to give up the habits of childhood, I tell her, to which she replies, 'Gertcha!' The famous madeleine may have had its effect on Marcel Proust, but it's the memory of wearing my shirt in that little room so long ago that does it for me.

If the box room was tiny, the rest of 50 Meadow Street was not much bigger. The house had been built in a *gwli*, a gap between the houses, and so it was smaller than the others in the row. Even so, I didn't fully appreciate quite how small it was until I saw a description of it in the legal documents setting out their tenants' rights for Nan and Gramp. The house had been owned by the sons of Francis Crawshay, Tudor and De Barri Crawshay, gentlemen with posh addresses in the Home Counties. This was how it was described: 'All that piece or parcel of land on which the said messuage or dwelling-house stands measures thereat some two hundred and five square yards or thereabouts...' Our living room in Whitchurch today is bigger than that.

At the same time, the crafty Crawshays had inserted in the contract a number of clauses making sure they were giving nothing away. One laid claim to any coal that might be found under Number 50, without compensation, and another prevented the occupants from letting the house to 'tanners, soap-makers, farriers, knackers, blacksmiths, inn-keepers or wine-merchants...' This last seemed to me preposterous, since Charlie and Lilian Symes intended only to live quietly in the house and call it home – and that's precisely what they did for the rest of their lives. Their only child, Alma, my mother, was born there in 1910, in the same bed as me, and in 1936 her husband Arthur, my father, came to live there too. The house was bought in the 1950s for the terrifying sum of £500, after the Crawshays had at last relinquished the freehold.

What did my parents get for their money? A small house in fairly good condition and in a pleasant neighbourhood not far from the power station at Upper Boat, a few miles down the valley, where my father trudged on his bike to work as a turbine-driver. From the front room there wasn't much to see: only the houses on the other side of the street, every one in Pennant stone with red and yellow trimming, just like ours. Inside, the furniture and decor were quite plain and of indifferent quality. There was a gas jet in the passage and another in the front room which we kept for visitors and special occasions such as Christmas. In the *cwtsh* under the stairs, a dark space with a musty smell to it, there was a jumble of household goods, mostly broken or worn out, which Gramp, a sesquipedalian whose fondness for fancy words I seem to have inherited, insisted on calling the lazaretto, which I now know to be another word for storeroom. Here, during the war, when German aeroplanes came droning up the valley looking for places to drop their bombs, we would huddle for nights on end until the hooters sounded the all clear. The wail of a siren, such as the one heard at the end of *Dad's Army*, gives me the creeps to this day.

I have a faint recollection of Lord Haw-Haw (William Joyce) announcing on the wireless that the Germans were going to bomb Meadow Street, Long Row and Raymond Terrace, though I think now it was talk of the threat rather than the broadcast itself that I heard. Even so, a few bombs fell on the hills around Trefforest in places where people had lit bonfires in a bid to mislead the Luftwaffe, and one demolished the wall of a school in Pontypridd. The iron railings in front of houses were taken away as scrap metal to be used as part of the war effort. When the small enamel plate disappeared from our back door, my father told me it had gone to make a bullet to shoot a German, and I was glad about that. I used my experience of growing up in Trefforest during the war in a sequence of poems that came close to winning the Crown at the National Eisteddfod in 2005.

At the rear of the house, in the scullery, there was a tap which dispensed cold water, a bosh (our word for a sink which I assume had been brought to Trefforest by the tin-workers of Llanelli), and a flagstone floor, where we kept foodstuffs and kitchen equipment. I have no recollection of the occasion but it was here, according to my mother, that Dr Gwyn Evans, the family GP, stuck a needle in my spine when I was one year old, as a precaution against meningitis, or so I was later given to understand. In the scullery, too, we performed our weekly ablutions in a tin tub filled with water heated on the kitchen fire. Outside in the yard there was a lavatory or dubs, as we called it, with whitewashed walls and square pieces of the *South Wales Echo* hanging neatly on the back of the door from a large nail, and a patch of earth in which a row of asters, loganberries and a privet hedge made valiant attempts to grow with help from the leaves of the family teapot. In the shed my father kept his push-bike and my grandfather his tools. There was also a mangle for the weekly wash, a clothes line and, atop the pole, a money-box in the shape of a golliwog's head. Over the low wall we would chat with Tom and Blodwen Jones from number 49, Welsh-speakers from the Vale, the salt of the earth and good neighbours down the years. On the other side, at number 51, lived the Smiths, with their daughters Joan and Eileen.

Through the back-lane door we went out to the eponymous meadow to help with the hay and to trap rabbits on the Bute and, with night-lines, catch small trout in Nant y Fforest, all of which was quite unusual in a district as heavily industrialised as ours. It was on the Bute I saw a fox, a badger, a squirrel and an owl for the first time and, I'm ashamed to say now, took birds' eggs which I blew with a pin and kept in a shoe-box padded with wool gathered on the sheep-walks of Coed Berthlwyd. To this day I can't see a copse or railway embankment, even from a distance, without wanting to check it for nests. In the evenings, summer and winter, I was free to roam the village and play whatever games were popular among children at the time, each in its season. On long summer evenings when I wasn't building bivouacs in the Bute woods, I spent many hours on my roller-skates, sometimes even coming in for my tea without taking them off; I often think my long legs are attributable to the fact that I was a champion skater. The only time I came near to danger was when one of my playmates fell from the girders of the Glyn-taf weir, and drowned – an accident recorded in my poem 'Elegy for Wiffin'.

Not much changed in our house during my childhood. In the kitchen, which was our living room, there was a black-leaded grate with a thick brass rail and fender, a pair of candlesticks, a clock and a large iron kettle that always stood simmering on the hob. This room, about four yards by four, was where the six of us lived happily enough from day to day, eating, playing, talking, reading and listening to the wireless, in front of a fire that was never allowed to go out because we had no other means of drying clothes. On the stone floor there were mats made with pegs from sackcloth in patterns that were, I like to think, a traditional craft among people like us. The best china was kept in a glass-fronted wall-cupboard and in the sideboard there was a drawer for the best cutlery.

On another wall there was a stuffed squirrel and woodpecker, and three cases of moths and butterflies, slightly faded by sunlight, that had come from Gramp's home in London: his father, James Symes, whom I never met, was a cabinet-maker and taxidermist in the King's Cross area. After Gramp died at the age of 77 in 1957, my second year at university, Nan burnt the whole lot because, she said, she had always loathed these dead creatures pretending, as it were, to be still alive. As a result, the only example of my great-grandfather's craft that has survived, as far as I know, are the pair of toucans that roost quietly in our sun lounge, which I was given by one of my mother's cousins. This woman, whose name is Hilda Clarke, lives in Somerset and, having seen me on S4C talking about Trefforest, she somehow found my number and, in due course invited Ruth and me to visit her and bring away the two birds. They still have their colours, as in an advertisement for Guinness, and we call them Ronech and Echni, the Welsh names for Flatholm and Steepholm.

Things were sure to change in number 50 eventually, of course. The biggest changes occurred during my last year at the Boys' Grammar School in Pontypridd and my first year at university. The old iron grate was taken out and a new one with modern tiles put in its place, and a carpet was laid down in the kitchen for the first time ever. Talk about luxury! The wall-cupboard was removed to make room for a television set and the wireless lost its place of honour under the window sill. After Gramp died the process went on apace. The scullery was extended to make a bathroom and indoor toilet, and a hot water system was installed. I think this happened because I'd begun bringing schoolfriends home and my parents were embarrassed whenever one of them asked to use the toilet and was directed to the dubs in the yard outside.

Be that as it may, over the years, each time I came home, I noticed the house had been improved in some way. My parents had been busy painting and refurbishing it, and there were appliances everywhere – a gas fire, a Hoover, a washing machine, an electric oven – so that the place was cleaner and more comfortable than before. Furthermore, new materials such as chrome, Perspex, Formica, Artex, polyvinyl, plastic and Dralon had begun to transform the tastes of the working class and my parents, obviously, were keeping up with the times.

We were never poor, as far as I know. Indeed, in comparison with some families in the terrace (Meadow Street was known as Meadow Terrace before the houses opposite were built), we were quite comfortably off. After all, although Gramp and my father earned only a few pounds a week, the family had two wages coming in, until my grandfather retired from his work as a cableman with the Pontypridd Urban District Council in 1945. Neither man had ever been unemployed, not even during the General Strike of 1926 and the Depression of the inter-war years. Their status as men in reserved occupations in the electricity industry kept them out of the war, although my father joined the Home Guard and Gramp served as an air-raid warden during the blackout. That explains why there was a telephone in the passage that rang shrilly in the middle of the night every time the Luftwaffe came up the valley. The phone gave us a certain status among our neighbours, I think, and they often used it for emergencies.

My mother didn't go out to work, as many Trefforest women did after the opening of the industrial estate between Upper Boat and Nantgarw. Despite the fact that she'd been to a secondary school, her parents' wish was that she should stay at home to help her mother keep house. A kind of working-class pride was responsible for this, I think, something to do with my grandfather's status as a skilled artisan who could earn enough to keep his family on his own wages. My mother was a good-looking blonde, quite tall and with blue eyes, and she dressed well all her life. She didn't use cosmetics of any kind but on VJ Day in 1945, when there was a party the length of our street, I saw her dancing with my father, and her face was made up, an unsettling experience for a seven-year-old boy for reasons about which Freud would no doubt have had something to say. This much I can confirm: I have never enjoyed dancing and I don't like too much lipstick on a woman. Little wonder I prefer the Scandinavian type such as Ingrid Bergman, Isabelle Huppert, Emma Thompson and Liv Ullmann, and that I married a blue-eyed blonde, too.

My mother's place, for good or ill, was at home. There was plenty for her to do about the house: lay sticks and paper for the fire each morning, polish the fender, wash and dry my father's overalls, do the weekly wash, scrub the pavement outside the front door, do the shopping, prepare meals, deal with the tradesmen who came down our street such as the grocer, milkman and baker, keep an eye on the family's finances, and so on. There was always enough to eat, even during the war and shortly afterwards when the ration book ruled our lives. Among the food I remember were pigs' trotters, blood pudding, cockles, winkles, rissoles, brawn, poloni,

17

junket, chutney, tapioca and semolina. Every Friday, on my way home from Parc Lewis Junior School, I had to call at a house on the Broadway to collect a blood-stained parcel from one of Gramp's friends who worked in the slaughter-house, though in my innocence I never connected this errand with the meat that appeared regularly on our table. I remember seeing a coconut, a banana, a pomegranate and a pineapple for the first time, soon after the end of the war; Gramp said they'd fallen off the back of a lorry and that was good enough for me.

It was a matter of principle with my parents never to run into debt: if we needed something we couldn't afford, we had to do without, because buying something on tick or hire purchase was anathema in their view. Even so, I didn't have to go to elementary school on an empty stomach, nor have cardboard soles fitted in my shoes, like some boys in my class, although I do remember patches in my trousers and large darns in my woollen jersey: better than a hole, every time, especially in the days when coupons were needed to buy new clothes. Very seldom did we go away on holiday. The only time I remember was a wet fortnight in a caravan among the sand dunes of Porthcawl, and I was only too glad to come home after that.

My father's idea of a holiday was to spend a Sunday with his people in Merthyr or go for a picnic on the Beacons – he was too self-conscious to eat in a café or any kind of public place such as the beach at Barry Island. That's one reason why I can identify with Alan Bennett, who comes from a similar background and whose work I greatly admire, when he writes about his own parents and their lack of basic social skills. During these visits I first became aware of that dreadful thing, social class, which was rife among people like us. Uncle Enoch worked as a blacksmith and farrier underground, but his wife, Auntie Annie, kept a grocer's shop known as Sunclad Stores that stood opposite the war memorial in the High Street, Cefncoedycymmer, a little to the north of Merthyr. The

Chappells (for that was their surname) were very kind to us, and yet I sensed a patronising attitude at times, as if we were the poor relations. As things turned out, there was no blood connection between Auntie Annie and my father, despite their having been brought up together in Heolgerrig. But I didn't know that at the time and so I thought of her, and her sister Auntie Gwen Leyshon, a well-to-do grocer's widow who lived in The Walk, off the Brecon Road, as my aunts. Even so, I wasn't wholly comfortable in their homes on account of this feeling of a difference in our standard of living, although the difference was quite small in fact. There were always doilies and napkins, and salt butter from Carmarthenshire on their tables, and thinly-cut cucumber sandwiches, and nutmeg on their biscuits, and of course, an abundance of fruit from the shop. Another thing: we boys had to be on our best behaviour when we went up to Cefn. The only way to escape the monotony of those long Sunday afternoons was to go down to the Blue Pool, where I learned to swim in the icy water with local boys, or walk over to Vaynor.

In short, we were a tidy family, and we had to remember it. Our neighbours, too, were ordinary – in the Raymond Williams sense: hard-working, law-abiding, warm-hearted, neighbourly and long-suffering. I have never viewed the working class through rose-tinted spectacles, as some left-wingers tend to do, because I'm only too well aware of the proletariat's shortcomings. Nevertheless, whatever interests I've had over the years, and notwithstanding the middle-class comforts of our home in Whitchurch nowadays, it's among ordinary people that I feel most comfortable, and I have never lost sight of them in forming my view of society and politics.

After my father's death in 1984, my mother went on living at the house in Meadow Street until the time came for her to cross the river to Glyn-taf at the age of 84. She had been faithful to her chapel until the very end but as her neighbours died off and younger couples moved out to places such as Ton-teg or Church Village, and Meadow Street begin to fill up with students from the University of Glamorgan, she grew more and more socially isolated and was content to spend her last days in her sons' homes, often for months at a time. The end came in St David's Hospital in Pontypridd with Ruth and me at her bedside. She left the house to her sons, of course, but as my brother had no interest in it, I bought his half to avoid putting it up for sale and thus losing possession of a house that had been in our family for the better part of a hundred years. The only way of doing that was to rent the house to students.

My brother Lloyd made it perfectly clear that he didn't want to know what might happen to 50 Meadow Street after our mother's days. He lives in a thatched cottage in Binton, near Stratford-upon-Avon, and has no intention of ever coming back to Wales. We've never been close, my brother and I. With five years between us, his school friends weren't mine and we had different interests from the start. While he was kicking a football I usually had my nose in a book. He left school at the age of sixteen to work as a clerk with the Gas Board in Pontypridd, and then as a policeman in Penarth, where he met his future wife, Patricia Morris, an auctioneer's daughter. He later joined a pharmaceuticals company and had several good jobs in the commercial world in various parts of England. Fair play – and without being patronising – he has done well for himself.

The bone of contention between Lloyd and me may be the Welsh language, a subject on which my brother can be emotional and querulous. Let me give one example. At the wedding breakfast of one of my daughters, he had the bad manners to say a few heated words in English after complaining that the chapel service had been entirely in Welsh, as the bride and groom had wished. He is, too, very quick to refer to the fact that I went to university and he didn't. There's no point trying to reason with him on these scores, as I've found on more than one occasion.

I haven't seen my brother, or spoken to him, in many a

year, and that's of his choosing: he refused to come to another daughter's wedding in 2001, but wouldn't say why, not even to his wife or children. Every attempt of mine to discuss this with him has failed, and the whole thing remains a mystery. Sibling rivalry, perhaps; ill feeling towards me on account of my being able to speak Welsh and having brought up four children to speak it; something I've said or not said; an inferiority complex of some kind; a dark little corner in his psychological make-up? I have no idea and he refuses to say what's bugging him. Although he has offended my family – we sometimes half-jokingly refer to him as the Binton Poisoner – I only hope my brother is happy playing golf in the leafy parts of Warwickshire where he's lived for decades. But I don't expect to see him at my funeral.

I wonder whether he thinks sometimes of 50 Meadow Street? In fact, the old house has become a bit of an albatross round my neck. Although I don't enjoy being a landlord, and although some of the tenants have behaved badly, letting it has worked fairly well until quite recently. But I'm now too old to look after it properly, and so I've decided to sell it. I'd much prefer to keep it and leave it to my children, because it's part of our family's history, like a photo album or a piece of furniture, and I can't remember my childhood without it – 'There are ghosts and voices about the place,' as T. H. Parry-Williams said. But although selling the house would feel like an insult to Nan and Gramp, and to my parents, and akin to turning my back on my own past in a manner of speaking, I'm afraid the time is not far off when 50 Meadow Street will belong to strangers.

2

The Square Mile

I'VE ALWAYS TAKEN the view that the ways in which Welsh people discover and define their national identity are many and various, and that there isn't just one way of doing it and one alone. Ours is a small country but it has great variety. Even so, we have to come to an understanding of Wales and its people based on our own background and experience, whatever they may be. There's no point in falling out over this because everyone's viewpoint is equally valid. Much more important, in my opinion, is to recognize and accept one another's ways of being Welsh and come to some agreement about how we can work together, for the good of Wales. As my late friend Glyn Jones once remarked, anyone can be Welsh who chooses to be – as long as he or she is prepared to take the consequences. Appreciating our country in all its rich variety, and contradictions, is the first step towards seeing it whole. It's not at all helpful to say, 'Oh no, that's not Wales' or 'Oh no, she or he isn't Welsh', if that person considers themselves to be Welsh. Nationality is not something to be denied or challenged or even queried by others. That is equally true of English people, and of people from other countries, who choose to live and work among us, and who wish to contribute to life in Wales, as far as I'm concerned. I don't accept that nationality is based on 'blood' – that way leads to racism of the worst kind.

However that may be, by the time I was seventeen I knew for certain I wasn't English. This perception didn't have anything to do with the Welsh language, at least at first. After all, there wasn't much Welsh spoken in Trefforest, except in the chapels, and I had only a few words of it anyway. Although some of our neighbours, such as Tom and Blodwen Jones next door, had a smattering of the language, I had no real experience of Welsh-speakers.

'On n'est pas sérieux quand on a dix-sept ans,' said Rimbaud, but hold on, Arthur, that wasn't true of me: I was quite a serious lad at seventeen. I didn't spend my pocket money on pop records, or sit for hours in cafés, or play snooker for money in the YMCA, or go to hops in the Catholic Hall and take part in fights afterwards, or smoke behind the school laboratories, or drink scrumpy in the pub at Eglwys Ilan on the Meio mountain, like some of my schoolmates. I was no goodie-goodie but if I had hobbies, they were innocent boyish ones: collecting stamps, making aeroplanes out of balsa wood, playing with my Meccano set, fishing for roach and perch at Abercwmboi, and taking part in activities organized by the Scouts. My only cultural pursuit was going to the cinema: the Cecil in Trefforest and the County and White Palace in Ponty, where I saw films such as *The Lavender Hill Mob*, *The Robe*, *Mrs Miniver*, *The Third Man* and *The Cruel Sea*. By the time I was seventeen I was venturing as far as The Globe in Cardiff, where I saw *Le jour se lève*, *Le mouton à cinq pattes*, the Monsieur Hulot comedies and anything with Brigitte Bardot in it – they all helped me improve my grasp of French. Cinema is among my chief interests to this day.

At home we had a wireless set around which we gathered every evening to listen to the Welsh Home Service (Tommy Trouble was one of my favourite programmes), as well as popular shows from London such as *In Town Tonight*. I was a keen fan of *The Goon Show* and I can't help smiling now as I recall the names of the characters: Neddie Seagoon, Eccles, Bluebottle, Major Bloodnok, Minnie Bannister, Henry Crun, Grytpype-Thynne and Moriarty. We sang along with Bing Crosby, Vera Lynn and Gracie Fields, and laughed with Tony

Hancock. Some of the big bands entertained us nightly – Billy Cotton, Henry Hall, Glenn Miller, Joe Loss and Bert Ambrose – on the wireless and on some of the LP records that Gramp brought home from time to time. We didn't have a television set until 1958, though I do remember going to a neighbour's to watch the Coronation in 1953 – we didn't have any particular regard for the Queen but we were short on ceremony and pageantry. My only experience of the theatre was accompanying Gramp to the music hall in Pontypridd: I still know the words of old favourites such as 'The Man who Broke the Bank at Monte Carlo', 'If You Were the Only Girl in the World', 'A Nightingale Sang in Berkeley Square', 'Roses are Blooming in Picardy', and many other gems from the Edwardian era.

There was another difference between me and most of my schoolfriends: by 1951 I was becoming a real book-worm. I'd learned to read at a very young age; according to my mother, the first words I mastered were 'El-y Al-es, best in Wal-es', on the wall of a pub in Trefforest. There weren't many books in the house, however, apart from the detective and cowboy paperbacks that my father swopped with his workmates. But I had a fistful of tickets from the Public Library in Pontypridd where I used to go twice, sometimes three times a week, on my way home from school. After reading children's classics such as *Black Beauty*, *Treasure Island*, *Tom Sawyer* and *Huckleberry Finn*, I moved on to the Nordic and Greek myths. But this is the strange thing: for reasons I'm at a loss to explain, I started borrowing books in Welsh, regarding them as something mysterious and wanting to know about their contents. I suppose I must have been able to understand a few words of Welsh, at least enough to know what sort of book I'd selected. Perhaps there was something going on in my sub-conscious, a yearning to understand my square mile and, eventually, myself. Anyway, Welsh became an integral part of the process of growing up, just out of reach but very alluring.

But where could I turn to hear the language? I had a chance to listen to Siân Yeoman, my first sweetheart, talking to her mother at their home in Cadoxton, near Barry, where I spent the occasional Saturday, but I wasn't ready to use the few words at my disposal with them. I remember feeling uncomfortable when Mrs Yeoman took us to visit Aneirin Talfan Davies, one of the BBC mandarins to whom she was in some way related, and his charming wife Mari, at their home in Pencisely Road, Llandaf, and the conversation over the teacups turning to English for my sake, I think (unless they habitually conversed with the Yeomans in English). Owen Talfan was there, too, a most sophisticated young man, I thought, and his younger brother Geraint and jolly sister Elinor. I was shown a cheque made out to Aneirin by Dylan Thomas, uncashed and neatly framed on the wall of their sitting room. Siân's parents, Olwen and Tom Yeoman, elementary school teachers and stalwarts of the Labour Party in Barry, were invariably kind to me but I was a very callow youth in those days, and inordinately bashful. I'd met their daughter on a sixth-form course at Dyffryn House in the Vale of Glamorgan, and this immature relationship was to drag on unsatisfactorily until I was at university.

The few words of Welsh I had in 1955 I'd picked up in chapel. Libanus (the Welsh for Lebanon) belonged to the Welsh Baptists, and there I went every Sunday as a boy. The hymns were all in Welsh, and some of the sermons, too. My mother sang the hymns perfectly and sat through the sermons, like most of the congregation, without understanding much. I remember seeing copies of a newspaper, almost certainly *Seren Gomer*, being handed out among some of the older members, but I don't recall anyone actually speaking the language – not in my hearing anyway.

We were living through the twilight years of the Welsh Baptist cause, I suppose; indeed, through a very late phase of chapel culture in the village. Although I enjoyed singing the hymns and learning to recite verses from the Bible (I was once given a shilling by Mrs Ferris, the organist, for my rendering of 'O, for the wings of a dove'), it was harder to have to listen to the preaching. I'm still unable to sit through a sermon in Welsh without suffering again the ennui that I first felt at Libanus. At least in those days I could amuse myself by heating coins on the vestry stove and pressing them into the sizzling varnish of the pew; I could hardly do that at Crwys nowadays. Although I'm happy to see Ruth going to chapel, where all our children also went, and despite my respect for the Reverends Cynwil Williams and Glyn Tudwal Jones, I never go near the place myself. There's no point in pretending or going through the motions, as I suspect some do. Even so, I wouldn't dare to argue with anyone on account of their religious convictions: like nationality, religious faith should be beyond questioning by others.

The minister at Libanus was the splendidy-named Washington Owen who preached eloquently but mostly way over our heads. He could be at it loudly and terrifyingly for an hour without stop, a splendid example of the old-school preachers who went in for that incantatory rhetoric known as the *hwyl*. He wore a 'come-to-Jesus' collar and spats and his hair was white and abundantly bardic. He had a son called Peredur, who took a class in the Sunday school, and that's where my spiritual pilgrimage ran into trouble. One Sunday afternoon, while Peredur was taking his class in the Big Seat, as we called the place where the deacons usually sat, and in full view of the rest of the congregation, I must have said or done something naughty, because our teacher gave me a wallop with his copy of the Holy Bible that made me fall out of my seat with a clatter.

At once, there was hullabaloo and over the next few weeks there emerged two opposing camps that would in due course set one half of the congregation at loggerheads with the other. Talk about a split chapel! In the end, Peredur ran off with a pretty girl whose family was in the opposing camp. The Welsh inscription in Gothic letters on the wall above the pulpit read *Cerwch eich gilydd*, ('Love one another'), and in a chapel where there was quite a bit of backbiting over such vital matters as which hymns were to be chosen for the next singing festival, it became obvious to me that there were some who took this commandment rather more lightly than others. The connection between the Bible and the use of physical force wasn't lost on me. By the way, there's a portrait of Libanus in the book by David Davies, *Reminiscences of my Country and People* (1925), which reflects the same chapel's schismatic nature in the early years of the twentieth century. Things hadn't changed much by my time.

That wasn't the end of the story as far as I was concerned. When I was sixteen, and of an age to be baptized in the huge bosh under the big seat, we were practising for the ceremony one evening when the hot-water system broke down. The pipes juddered and hissed under the floorboards, there was the grinding of wheels and pistons, the clanking of chains, the chapel filled up with steam, and the whole thing had to be postponed. By the time the system had been repaired some months later, my mother had half-hinted that I didn't really have to attend Sunday school, or the Band of Hope, unless I wanted to, and soon thereafter, when I was in the lower sixth, I decided not to go to chapel any more.

Having had enough of the bad blood at Libanus, my mother took her membership to Castle Square, which belonged to the Independents, where she'd been married. Neither my father nor grandfather ever went to a place of worship and I don't recall either of them ever saying anything that was at all religious in my hearing. My grandmother claimed to be a Churchwoman but I'm pretty sure that was something deferential she'd picked up, like her disgusting smoking habit, during the years she was in service in Cardiff before her marriage. Gramp would pull her leg on this score and call her Matilda, the name she'd been given by a family of shipowners who lived in Cathedral Road and with whom she'd been in service. I don't know why I was christened at St Mary's Church in Glyn-taf – my only contact with the Church in Wales – unless my grandmother saw this as 'the middle way' between the Roman Catholicism of her people, which she had in fact abandoned, and the Nonconformity of most of our neighbours, which held no appeal for her. She was, however, extremely superstitious. Every mirror had to have a cloth put over it during a thunderstorm, opening an umbrella in the house would bring bad luck and whistling on the hearth would attract the Devil. At her insistence, and in deference to her Catholic background, we always had fish on Fridays. Even so, if I was spoiled, it was Nan who spoiled me. She and Gramp had their own sugar-basin, their own milk-jug, their own loaf of bread, and I was often invited to help myself from their side of the table after I'd eaten my fill of my mother's provisions.

Not every activity in Libanus was boring. The Sunday school used to go by train to Barry Island twice a year and to Creigiau, a village on the Barry line at the edge of the Vale, to pick primroses for dressing the chapel for Easter. We also used to walk in procession through the streets of Trefforest at Whitsun with banners and gazookas and drums, followed by a picnic in the Little Park near the Machine Bridge, and that was great fun. We also played games in the vestry, although I didn't enjoy them much, not being a team-player. Everything at Libanus was in English, apart from the hymns which we sang not only in chapel but in the concrete shelters at Barry Island, where we'd sit in a circle to entertain ourselves when it was raining, as it often was. But unfortunately, there wasn't the slightest attempt by the chapel elders to teach us even the simplest vocabulary which would have served as the basis of our Welsh identity later on. By today Libanus belongs to the Pentecostals.

For all that, I learned some Welsh in the small burial-ground at the side of the chapel: *er cof am, yr hwn a fu farw, er serchus cof, gynt o'r plwyf hwn, hefyd ei annwyl briod, hedd perffaith hedd*, and so on – the usual phrases seen on monumental masonry. Soon I was taking pleasure in reading passages from the Bible aloud, just to hear words that were music to my ears and which affected me in a way that I didn't understand at the time. They had an incantatory quality rather like the Latin mass has for some people or Italian for opera buffs.

I was able to proceed to the next stage of acquiring some Welsh while working as a grave-digger at the cemetery in Glyn-taf. Every Christmas, when I was a student, I worked as a postman but in the summer holidays I earned good money digging graves. A grave had to be dug in an afternoon and filled in again as soon as the mourners were back in their cars. This was the healthiest work I ever did as a student, especially when the weather was fine, and I was physically fit. We'd take off our shirts, dig frantically for half an hour like demented terriers, and then take ten minutes off to get our wind back. The grave had to be seven feet long and four across and six deep, no more and no less. We kept a bottle of cider under the 'patient yew' where we had an hour off to eat our sandwiches; during these breaks I tried to teach the illiterate Reg, a champion digger, how to tell the time and read from the *Daily Mirror*, but to no avail. The phrase 'the man with the spade', meaning Death, has always had special significance for me.

Every now and then we were required to wheel the coffins on their trolleys across to the incinerators. I remember doing this with the coffin of the poet Huw Menai (Williams) in 1961. The occasion was memorable for another reason, too, for I saw, among the handful of mourners, 'the three Jones boys', namely Gwyn, Jack and Glyn, walking into the crematorium, my old English Professor sporting a canary-yellow pullover and Glyn in a green corduroy jacket. When someone asks me nowadays which is preferable, burial or cremation, I answer with a grin and with some authority in these matters, that there's not much difference really, but that out of respect for Dr William Price of Llantrisant, the pioneer of cremation and one of my boyhood heroes, I tend to favour cremation, and I leave the matter there – unless pressed to say more.

If it wasn't the chapel, I often wonder what was responsible for nurturing a consciousness of being Welsh in the growing boy. I should like to say it was the time I spent as a pupil at the Pontypridd Boys' Grammar School between 1949 and 1956, but that wouldn't be true. The school was considered to be among the best of its kind in south Wales during the post-war years. Most people can say something favourable about their schooldays, as they should, and most of their memories, like Tolstoy's happy families, resemble one another. But mine aren't altogether happy.

I enjoyed my English lessons with Mr Ken Davies, who introduced me to Yeats, Eliot and Auden, and with Mr Dennis Clare, who gave me his own dog-eared copy of *The Oxford Book of English Verse* as a prize for winning at the school eisteddfod with a poem about a Welsh win against England at Cardiff Arms Park. I also won a prize for an essay and a short story. I learned quite a useful bit of Latin from Mr Herbie Taylor: *Sagittae barbarorum nostros non terrebunt* (The arrows of the barbarians will not frighten our men), and pearls of that sort. Our Art lessons could be great fun, too, because Mr John Whitehead, a man the same dap as the comedian Jimmy Edwards ('Whack-O!'), would often leave the class to its own devices while he read the sports pages and drank tea in his cubby-hole at the back of the classroom. It was in his classes, but without supervision from him, that I discovered an interest in calligraphy. Teachers of this kind stick out in most reminiscences about schooldays. And yet I can put names to only a handful of the teachers who stare dully out of the pages of the official school history.

Thanks to Mr Don Herbert, my teacher at Parc Lewis School, I was second out of the 120 boys in my year who passed the 11+ examination in 1949. Thanks, too, to the Butler Act of 1944, my generation was the first to receive free secondary education. And because of my coming second

I was put in the B stream from the start (strangely, there was no A stream), that is to say, the class for boys considered to be the brightest. I hasten to add that I never reached such academic heights again, although in due course I did get my Central Welsh Board certificate (the equivalent of today's GCSE) in eight subjects, failing only Chemistry in which I was given a mark of nine per cent for what I thought was a very decent drawing of a Bunsen burner.

But by the time I was in my fourth year I had to choose between Welsh and French, like most of my contemporaries in Wales in those days. What a rotten, execrable old system! And there was no one to advise me, especially not my parents because they had no experience on which to base a view. I'd done well in French with Mr Jack Reynolds and indifferently in Welsh with Mr William Lewis, and for that reason alone, quite naturally, I tended to favour French. I remember the headmaster Mr E. R. Thomas (Piggy to us boys) addressing the class on the subject: only boys at the top of the class, he explained, should think of doing French and, unless our parents objected, the rest would do Welsh. None objected.

Looking back, we had to listen to all sorts of guff in justification of this choice: French, announced the headmaster in his pseudo-English accent, was the language of the diplomatic service, the language of culture, a language with a great literature, and he was *so* glad he'd taken an Honours degree in French. Welsh, on the other hand, this Welsh-speaker from Porth informed us, was only the language of the home and was confined to Wales, especially among farmers, in short an inferior language in every respect. So the choice was clear: I had no inclination to be a farmer!

Although it's difficult to imagine now, it must be borne in mind that secondary school teachers in those days belonged to the same professional class as doctors, solicitors and bank managers, with a status based on salary, education and a middle-class lifestyle that was completely alien to the working class. These men wore three-piece suits under their academic gowns and drove cars and lived in houses with bay-windows, front gardens and nameplates on the gates rather than numbers. Their wives went to coffee-mornings, played golf and dressed in the latest fashions and went shopping in London. Inevitably, my parents were prepared to accept the headmaster's advice, and so it was: I chose French and dropped Welsh altogether, a decision I've regretted ever since.

The school motto, by the way, was 'Ymdrech a lwydda' (Perseverance will succeed), and this was interpreted to mean 'Work hard and turn your back on your community and country'. If a boy showed even a smick of academic ability the words 'For export only' were stamped in bold letters on his forehead. I can put names to all the lads who stand with me in the photograph of the school's prefects in 1956, and of these only two now live in Wales, as far as I know. This is an example of Patrick Pearse's 'murder machine' in action! It's no wonder the Valleys of south Wales have lost generation after generation of their ablest people, with dire results.

Other unpleasant memories well up now, and I must try to staunch the flow. I remember especially being thrashed by the woodwork master, a vicious thug by the name of Owen, for failing to put my name on a miserable piece of wood that was meant to be a toothbrush-rack. He hit me on my backside with the edge of a steel ruler a yard long and the blows were so severe I was unable to sit down for days. I shall never forget the experience of standing, with my trousers around my knees, in the presence of the new headmaster, Mr P. R. Jones (or Nap, as he was known), another Welsh-speaker and a pillar of the Baptist cause in Pontypridd, so that he could see the bruises and weals for himself, and how my father doffed his cap before going into his study – only in chapel had I seen anyone doing that. In the end, my father was fobbed off with an assurance that Owen would be cautioned, and he probably was because ever after the lout would smirk at me as he flung my wood at me at the start of the lesson.

The only other time I was in trouble with Nap was when he caught me entertaining my classmates by impersonating Al Jolson just before class began one afternoon, but on that occasion he chose to discuss films with me rather than use the cane. I had a chance to go into the headmaster's study while teaching at my old school in the 1990s, and a strange experience it was to see how small and nondescript the place actually was.

There were other teachers who were quite as brutish as Owen. Take Mr William Lewis (Willie Woodbine), for example, the Welsh teacher, who came from Merthyr Tydfil. From this man I learned, in four years, almost nothing except how to count to twenty and a few nonsensical rhymes such as the one about Siôn and Siân and Siencyn going to buy chickens in Aberdare, and then only because he clipped me about the ears as an aid to learning the words by rote. The tribute to him in *The Pontypriddian*, the school magazine, reads: 'He has toiled and he has spun in the classroom with undiminished energy and unflagging zeal. He is a very ardent Welshman. The urgencies and exigencies of his native land impregnate every fibre of his being.' Scarcely believe! And that's why, years later, I paid my own tribute to the old bully in my poem 'Elegy for Mr Lewis (Welsh)'.

Despite all this, some good came of my French lessons with Mr Jack Reynolds. I learned the language's grammar very thoroughly indeed and this, with my grasp of Latin, served as the basis of my understanding the syntax of other languages later on. When I started having Welsh lessons in Bangor with Islwyn Ffowc Elis and in Merthyr with Chris Rees, I already knew the difference between verb and adjective, noun and pronoun, preposition and participle, and this was a great advantage later on. I still know how to conjugate the French verbs in the preterite tense and the subjunctive mood.

I also learned about the work of Symbolist and Romantic poets such as Hugo, Lamartine, Alfred de Vigny, Leconte de Lisle, Verlaine, Rimbaud, and Baudelaire, and this gave me a good grounding when I came to study French in Aberystwyth. There are, by the way, two syllables to the name Baude-laire, not three as is sometimes heard when 'experts' are discussing French poetry. Because he taught me such things, Mr Jack Reynolds is the only one who lives on in my memory as a good teacher, and although he died quite a while ago, and was an out-and-out Tory, I'm glad to be able to pay him tribute now. Even so, I very much regret that I wasn't taught Welsh properly when I was at school: if I had been I would perhaps have at least mastered the mutations, which still give me trouble!

If I'd hoped to learn something of my country's history at the Grammar School, I was disappointed again, alas. Our History lessons were dominated by the luminaries of the Methodist Revival week after week. We heard not a word about Caratacus, Llywelyn, Rhodri Mawr, Hywel Dda, Glyndŵr, William Morgan, Iolo Morganwg, the Chartists, Dic Penderyn, Henry Richard, the Penrhyn Strike, Keir Hardie, the Tonypandy Riots, Lloyd George, the fire at Penyberth, and Aneurin Bevan. The lessons were all about Griffith Jones, Howell Harris, Williams Pantycelyn, Ann Griffiths, Thomas Charles and the like, *ad nauseam*. We weren't even taught the words of '*Hen Wlad Fy Nhadau*' – in the town where the national anthem was composed! We heard a little Welsh at the school eisteddfod on St David's Day, mostly when boys such as Euros Miles, Gareth Edwards and Geraint Stanley Jones, who'd been brought up Welsh-speaking, were ushered on to the stage to sing and recite, but for the rest of the year the school might just as well have been in Norwich or Hartlepool. Some of the teachers, such as the kind-hearted, bashful Mr Llew Walters, were Welsh-speaking, but we didn't know that at the time. I can scarcely believe this sentence about the branch of the *Urdd* that appeared in the school magazine in 1950: 'After we had sung '*Calon Lân*', the headmaster stressed the importance of fostering a deeper and stronger interest in our country's history and language.' I didn't even know there was a branch of the *Urdd* in the school, let alone that it had 64 members, and I was astonished to read that Piggy could express such sentiments.

I learned more about Wales in the Scouts than in school. I joined the Cubs at the age of seven and remained a member of the movement until well into my undergraduate years. The 2nd Pontypridd Troop met in a large hut at the bottom of Meadow Street, which was convenient for me on winter evenings. I earned quite a few proficiency badges and enjoyed the sense of adventure and the open air which are essential aspects of Scouting. I don't recall ever having to salute the union flag and the quasi-military aspects like marching were easily avoided. As for organised sport, although I played the occasional game of rugby for the school – I was useful in the second row – I wasn't really sporty: my name doesn't appear even once in *The Pontypriddian*. Indeed, although I have a vague recollection of running *after* the ball from time to time, I can't recall ever running *with* it.

I am grateful to the Scouts for giving me a chance to enjoy physical exercise while exploring the district and contiguous places such as the Vale and, in due course, upland Glamorgan. This was one of the few opportunities that sons of the working class had to visit Dyfed and Powys and Gwynedd. I went to a jamboree in Abergele where I met boys from every part of the country and heard them singing songs in Welsh that weren't hymns, and that was a new experience for me. During one unforgettable trip I went with our leaders, Ron Giles and Pip Eyles, on their motor-bikes, as far afield as the Lake District, Scotland and Snowdonia; we went up Helvellyn, Ben Nevis and Snowdon in the same memorable week. Nearer home I discovered Darren Deusant, the prehistoric carvings on the wooded hill above Trefforest and slept in bivouacs in the grounds of the farm at Castellau.

All the Scout troops in East Glamorgan had a badge with a miner's lamp on it and a Red Dragon on their epaulettes, and I wore these as a first proof that I belonged to Wales.

One of the things we did almost every Saturday during the early 1950s was collect waste paper and cardboard from shops and offices in the centre of Pontypridd, piling it up on a huge two-wheeled bogey-cart which we lugged and pushed around the streets for hours on end. We then went back to the shed in Meadow Street for a supper of faggots and Vimto paid for by Pop Phillips, another of our leaders. I gave my Scout tunic, complete with white neckerchief, leather woggle, lanyard and two armfuls of badges, to the Folk Museum in Saint Fagans some while ago. I also have somewhere a certificate signed by one Elizabeth R, which expresses the wish that life for me will be 'a joyous adventure'. The Scout hut is no longer there: it was burnt to the ground by local kids a few years ago.

If neither chapel nor school nurtured my patriotic feelings, how come I grew to be a patriot? Strangely enough, it was mainly thanks to an Englishman, namely my grandfather, Charlie Symes. Now we all had Welsh accents at 50 Meadow Street, except for Gramp. My mother was brought up in Trefforest and never moved from Meadow Street. My father was brought up in Heolgerrig in Merthyr and in Dynea, near Rhydfelen. My grandmother hailed from the Rhymni Valley, a policeman's daughter, as his truncheon hanging on my wall still reminds me. Nan was the most Silurian of us all, although her people, by the name of MacDermott, had come over from County Roscommon in search of work at the beginning of the Industrial Revolution.

I have a vague recollection of my great-grandmother, Ellen Gray, in Cwm, near Ebbw Vale, when I was about nine or ten, and I remember my grandmother's sisters, Rose, Cissie and Eva, very clearly. Indeed, I used to go to Cwm for my holidays in the days when the steelworks dominated the place, a fact that always makes Vaughan Williams, the former Education Director of Monmouthshire and a native of the village, laugh heartily. By the way, I'd like to note here that I've been able to trace the MacDermotts back to a Bernard and Julia

36

MacDermott who lived in County Roscommon towards the end of the eighteenth century but further than that it's proved impossible to go because all the records have been destroyed. This hardly qualifies me for an Irish passport but I'm proud of my Irish ancestry nevertheless.

But Gramp was a Londoner and, unlike the rest of us, he spoke with a Cockney accent all his life. His way of speaking was enough to draw my attention to the fact that he was somehow different. He would use a bit of rhyming slang, or a snatch of song from the music hall, and his vocabulary was always colourful. This was how I pricked up my ears to the various registers of the English language, as I began to notice Gramp's way of speaking and to see the rest of the family, and myself, in a new light. It was a slow, imperceptible process, of course, and part of the complexity of adolescence, and I'm not sure I'm doing it justice by describing it now. But Gramp's Englishness was the grit in the oyster, as it were, as far as I was concerned. I've been sensitive to people's accents ever since.

How did Charlie Symes come to meet Lilian Gray? Well, my mother's parents met for the first time in Cardiff in 1907. The young man from Islington had a year's contract to work as an electrician laying cables for the busy city's new trams. One morning, while he was working in St Mary Street, it started raining pouring, and the trench began to fill up with water and the lightning to threaten the wires. So he jumped out and sought shelter from the weather in a nearby arcade. There, he fell into conversation with a young woman who was on an errand for her mistress. She fell, she once told me, for the rose in his muddy lapel and the jaunty bowler hat on the back of his head, and his ceaseless patter. *Oui, un coup de foudre!*

By the time the sun reappeared the pair had arranged to meet again. Before the year was out they'd married and had made their home in Meadow Street in Trefforest, since Charlie now had a job with the Pontypridd Urban District Council.

He never went back to London, except for brief visits, and in time he more or less lost contact with his people there. I don't know how many relatives I have in England but I must have scores, if only I knew where to look for them and what they're called. So it was a fateful moment, especially for me, that day in 1907, and it shows how random a man's genetic inheritance can sometimes be. I have tried to capture something of the romance of that morning in my poem 'Cawod', which is now in my book, *Wilia* (2014).

I spent quite a bit of time with my grandfather while I was growing up, much more than I did with my father, who used to work eight-hour shifts – mornings, afternoons, nights with monotonous regularity – in the power-station at Upper Boat. Often when I was at home my father was in work, and when he was at home, I was in school, and he worked Saturdays and Sundays, too. Because of the nature of his work, he didn't have much time to himself, and what he did have went on the most mundane things – his union, his dog Guto, and so on – the worker's lot is a hard one in every age and every country. Gramp, on the other hand, retired in 1945, and so he was always about the house – a proper Rodney, my grandmother called him, though I'm not sure whether she was referring to the fact that he'd been brought up in Rodney Street, Pentonville, or whether she was using the name to denote someone disreputable, which was the usual meaning in those days. Be that as it may, it was Gramp who told me bedtime stories, mostly about three little men named Volto, Ampam and Watty.

My grandfather was doubtless a 'character' and everyone in the village knew it. Every Thursday he would go up to Ponty for his pension and a pint or three in the Tumble pubs with his Council workmates. Sometimes, on my way home from school, he would be on the same bus as me and, to my great embarrassment, would get me to sit at his side, so that he could swank to the other passengers that his grandson was wearing the Grammar School cap and blazer. From time to time, when he was finding it difficult to walk in a straight line, I had to go up to the bus-stop at the top of Meadow Street and bring him home. Then, after his dinner and a quick nap, he would sit in our porch and entertain passers-by with his tin whistle, chatting the while with all and sundry. There's a portrait of him doing just that in my poem 'Miwsig'.

There was another difference between the personalities of my father and grandfather, and this was crucial as far as I was concerned. My father was quiet, thoughtful, phlegmatic, reserved, with a bashfulness more typical of country folk than of the hot-tempered, mercurial, garrulous proletariat; the reason for this will become clear in due course. While he was ultra-careful, conscientious, polite and teetotal, Gramp was talkative, devil-may-care and sociable. Indeed, I don't recall the two ever speaking to each other, and I think the coldness of their relationship stemmed from my father's disapproval of the older man's bibulous ways.

Ours was a happy home on the whole, full of love and laughter, but this tension cast a long shadow that the lad could sense without understanding it properly. Although I don't recall any open friction, the ill feeling on my father's part sprang from having to share a home with his parents-in-law, a less than satisfactory arrangement at the best of times. Even so, there was economic advantage to living under the same roof, especially after the birth of us boys, because living costs could now be shared. But my father didn't get on with my grandfather, that much was clear to me. I sometimes think, whenever I feel myself pulled in two directions, between the extrovert, mischievous, logopœic behaviour of the one and the more patient, orderly, inarticulate, introverted character of the other, that it's a clash between the two men failing to see eye to eye that's causing the tension in me. This turns the usual caricatures of the English and the Welsh on their heads, but there it is.

It was my grandfather who taught me the history of the square mile. Perhaps his interest had grown from the fact that he'd left London long ago and wanted to avoid depriving his grandson of knowledge of his locality. Or this may have been completely unintentional. Anyway, Gramp used to refer to Wales as 'John Jones's country'. I'm not sure what his politics were, although he looked a bit like Winston Churchill, having a passing resemblance which earned him the nickname Winnie among his workmates. But I can say with some certainty that he wasn't a Tory because he was a union man all his life. I still have his Electrical Trades Union badge with the words 'To Bro. Symes for services rendered' and the motto 'Light and Liberty' inscribed on it; it's one of my most cherished possessions.

I was puzzled sometimes, at election times, when Gramp put on his dark-blue suit and best boots, his white silk muffler, and, with a flower in his lapel, sat at our front door waiting for the Conservative car to take him to the polling booth. On his return, he would laugh heartily and announce that he'd cast his vote for the Labour Party, thus wasting the time and resources of the opposition. But I'm not absolutely sure this was true, because he was always very dismissive of Arthur Pearson, the long-serving, somnolent Labour M.P. for Pontypridd, referring to him as Rip Van Winkle. It may be that Charlie Symes was a Liberal at heart – he admired Lloyd George on account of his pension – but I'm only guessing.

Anyway, my grandfather managed to awaken in me an interest in local history. In his company, I walked for miles on the hills around Pontypridd, from Llanfabon to Llanwynno and across to the Meio on the other side of the valley, which stood between us and Abertridwr. Gramp was among those who claimed to have seen the Senghennydd explosion in 1913 (although the fire, in fact, was visible only underground); this was the first I heard of the district's mining history. He also spoke of the Merthyr Rising of 1831 and the Tonypandy Riots of 1910 as if they'd happened only the other week. On the vexed question of whether Churchill had sent troops to

Tonypandy, he was of the general view: 'Well, even if he didn't, he did!'

We also went to see the stone circle where the gates of the University stand today, and I read the words: *'Duw ni feddaf, Haf ni ofalaf, Gauaf ni theimlaf, Angau nid ofnaf'* (I have no God, I care not for Summer, I feel not Winter, I fear not Death'). These stones had been put up by Francis Crawshay and his brother Henry in memory of their family, and there was another much smaller memorial, shaped like Cleopatra's Needle, near the weir at Glyn-taf. The needle is still there but the stones were removed and broken up to make footings for what became the Glamorgan Polytechnic.

I remember accompanying Gramp on more than one occasion to see the remains of the tower, known as the Glass Tower, on the hill above Trefforest from where Francis Crawshay had looked north to check whether his furnaces in Hirwaun were in production; he had another tower up there which gave its name to Tower Colliery. We also went to see the words cut on one of the tinworks' walls: 'Perseverance. Who is not a fool? If this raise anger in the reader's thought, the pain of anger punishes the fault. W.C. 1836'. I've no idea how Gramp interpreted this last lapidary inscription – William Crawshay meant it to admonish his feckless son Francis – but I'm sure the boy didn't understand it. It's unfortunate that Gramp didn't know about the chamber I discovered under Tŷ Fforest while I was teaching at the University years later. His lively imagination would have come up with a colourful purpose for it, I'm sure.

I also recall, one fine summer's evening, walking, my grandfather and me, a boy of about fourteen, all the way through Ton-teg and Efail-isaf as far as the Garth, that whale-backed hill that marked the southern boundary of our small world when I was a lad. As we walked, Gramp taught me the names of flowers, butterflies, and birds. From the summit we saw the valleys of Glamorgan winding smokily to the north, the Brecon Beacons imperiously purple in the far distance, and under us shimmering in a heat-haze, Cardiff, and beyond, the Channel and the misty hills of Somerset. 'See over there?' he said, 'that's England!' I fancied I heard a note of longing or regret in his voice, but maybe I'm mistaken. Anyway, that was the day a map began to take shape in my head. On that spot I've always felt the primitive tug of belonging to a particular place that's at the heart of all true patriotism. This is the fifth point of my compass, and from here I can look out confidently to the four corners of the world. When the time comes, as come it will, I should like my ashes to be scattered from the summit of the Garth. I hope the weather will be fine so that my family and friends can enjoy the magnificent view. All will be welcome to a hot meal of faggots and Vimto afterwards, followed by beetroot sandwiches and chunks.

It wasn't long before my grandfather was talking to me about William Edwards, who built the Old Bridge in Pontypridd; Mabon the miners' leader; Freddie Welsh the boxer; Morfydd Llwyn Owen the composer who was born in Trefforest; Francis Crawshay, of course; and a host of other characters with connections to the district. Gramp was fond of leafing through *A History of Pontypridd and the Rhondda Valleys* (1903) by Morien who'd lived in Trefforest at one time. Although the book has been described by the historian R. T. Jenkins as a hotchpotch of neo-druidism, mythology, geography, local history and biography, it fascinated Gramp because it gave a colourful portrait of the industrial valleys of Glamorgan during the nineteenth century. I still have his copy.

The Rhondda held great appeal for me and, as I went into my late teens, I spent a little of my pocket money on visiting the famous valley as often as I could. I had seen a few colliers in Trefforest, usually squatting against a wall while waiting for a bus, with black faces and bundles of firewood under their arms. Those who lived in Meadow Street had free coal delivered to their front doors. But in the Rhondda there were colliers everywhere! And townships like Porth, Treherbert,

Tonypandy and Ferndale were places so busy, and the people so friendly and noisy, I was much taken with them. This was the true Wales, or so I thought, and I've never tired of visiting the valley and talking to its warm-hearted inhabitants.

After getting a bike for passing my 11+ exam, I had a certain freedom to roam wherever I wished. I visited the National Eisteddfod held in Caerffili in 1950, where I saw Aneurin Bevan in his pinstripe suit. I went up to Merthyr, where my Aunties Annie and Gwen lived, and to Cwm, near Ebbw Vale, to see my grandmother's sisters, but they had nothing on 'the valley narrow as a cockerel's strut' in the parish of Ystradyfodwg. I was glad of the opportunity to get to know a part of the Rhondda better when I taught for a term in Tonypandy during the 1990s.

But although my grandfather had introduced me to the geography and history of my square mile, the most important thing he did for me was awaken an interest in my country's English-language literature by giving me, on my seventeenth birthday in 1955, a copy of Idris Davies's *Selected Poems*. I still have the copy, with his copper-plate handwriting on the fly-leaf, and this too is one of my most treasured possessions. Reading this book was a revelation for me. Whenever I take it down from the shelf nowadays I feel again something of the excitement I felt when I read it for the first time. Here were places and people I could recognize as my own! Oh, I know how easy it is to fall under the spell of poetry that's full of familiar place-names and homely sentiment. But I responded to Idris Davies – the experience wasn't unlike falling in love for the first time – with so much delight that I don't feel one whit embarrassed all these years later. Indeed, I sometimes wish I could savour again something of that sweet experience that made my heart beat faster.

From Idris Davies I moved on to books by other Welsh writers that I found on the dusty shelves of the Pontypridd Public Library. In a little while I was devouring everything the Library had under 'Local Authors'. In this I had the help of Mairwen Jones, one of the young women who lived next door to us in Meadow Street. She worked in the Library and whenever she was on the counter she'd let me take out as many books as I wished, never mind how many tickets I had. Among the authors I discovered in this way were Jack Jones, Glyn Jones, Rhys Davies, Gwyn Thomas, Gwyn Jones, Dylan Thomas, Alun Lewis and many more. Copies of their books were among the first I ever bought. By happy chance, Mairwen's daughter, Luned, and her husband Howell, are among my daughter Heledd's best friends these days.

I have touched upon some of the main influences on me during the days of my youth. There were others, of course, such as going to Cardiff Arms Park to see Wales play rugby and reading the *Western Mail* every day – a habit I've been unable to shake off, despite the shortcomings of our 'national newspaper'. But my grandfather was the catalyst who sparked my growing awareness of becoming a Welshman, or at least at this stage, a local patriot. It was an Englishman by the name of Charlie Symes, an intelligent man with little education but a great heart, that I have to thank for that.

Gramp was among the people who came out to the eponymous hayfield at the back of our house to wave me off that day in September 1956 when I left home for the first time to go as a student to Aberystwyth. That's another picture that's remained vivid in my memory, a rite of passage as the first of his family to receive higher education went through a ceremony that was meant to cut him off from his roots, with no expectation he'd ever return. This experience usually leaves scars on a lad that take years to heal, as Richard Hoggart and others have shown, and it was to affect me for a long time afterwards. But as I saw my people sending me off like this, I was aware of standing on the threshold of a new world, and I decided there and then that I'd never forget the rock from which I'd been hewn, come what might.

3

Letters after my Name

'THERE'S SOMETHING IN the air of Aberystwyth,' complained the egregious George Thomas, Secretary of State for Wales, 'that turns young people into Welsh Nationalists.' Quite right, I'd say. I went up to the College by the Sea in 1956 without Welsh and with no experience of the rest of Wales, and five years later the boy from Trefforest had become a Welsh nationalist – of sorts.

My first intention had been to take a degree in English, but I soon realized I was having difficulty with Anglo-Saxon, in which Gwyn Jones, the Professor, was a specialist. It was necessary to pass this paper to be accepted for the Honours class in the English Department. At the end of my first year, I had quite good results in French and Education, and in two out of the three English papers, but I ploughed Old English. Unfortunately, this meant failing in English as a whole and, what's more, I wouldn't be allowed to take a degree in it, and worse still, it meant I'd failed my first year altogether. It's strange to think it's possible nowadays to take a degree in English without the slightest knowledge of Anglo-Saxon, but in Aberystwyth in those days it was the all-important paper and a student had to pass it if he wanted to remain in the Department. There was nothing for it but to repeat my first year.

This obstacle had the effect of adding an extra year to my

course but, fortunately, the Pantyfedwen Trust was prepared to give me a grant, for which I was extremely grateful. I confess that I didn't do a stroke of work during my repeat year, since the syllabus in English, French and Education remained unchanged, so there was no need for revision until the last moment. The only thing I did was make sure I knew my Old English: I learnt large passages of Sweet's *Anglo-Saxon Reader* off by heart and could conjugate the verbs in my sleep. I still remember how many deer Ohthere of Hålogoland had when he went to the court of King Alfred, and how Cædmon's hymn begins: '*Nu sculon herigean heofonrices weard, metodes meahte and his modgethanc...*' It may come in handy one day.

Having taken the Old English paper again, I was given a mark of 96 per cent, the highest in the class, but when I went to see Prof Gwyn to ask whether I could now do Honours English, he wagged his famous finger and said, in short, that I had transgressed in his view and that I'd never be allowed to take English as my degree subject. Gwyn later became a friend of mine – he was Chairman of the Arts Council when I was appointed Literature Director in 1967 – but he could be unbending and something of a tyrant at times; despite my admiration for him as a scholar and man of letters, I saw that side of him, too, when I was a student in his Department.

Even so, there was some advantage in it for me, as things turned out. As well as swotting up my Anglo-Saxon, I had a busy social life during my repeat year. I drank my share of beer and coffee, I went out with a few women, I read a good deal of contemporary English poetry, I bought books in Galloway's, I walked on Pumlumon almost every Saturday afternoon with the Rover Scouts, I began talking politics with my fellow-undergraduates, I got to know Welsh-speakers for the first time, and several English people too, I ate a lot of chips and peas (at ten pence a plateful), I contributed to the *Courier*, the college newspaper, I walked the prom late at night, I stayed up putting the world to rights, I read what Jimmy Porter called the posh Sunday papers, and so on.

I enjoyed meetings of the Debates Union, the singing and fun of it all, and admired characters like the rotund Norman Rea, one of the stars of these occasions, who bore an uncanny resemblance to Friar Tuck. My own contribution was quite small, but I remember speaking in favour of self-government for Wales. I was once ruled out of order for referring to the railings outside Alexandra Hall, where female students said good-night to their men-friends, as 'more sinned against than sinning'. I have never felt the need to join the old students' society, but the high jinks of those days are sweet to remember.

At the same time, one of my greatest pleasures was to browse among a collection of books by Welsh writers in English that I found in the college library. Unfortunately, not one of these was on the syllabus of the English Department because Gwyn Jones, one of the leading writers of his day and editor of *The Welsh Review*, wasn't willing to admit them. But I read most of them with great relish.

Another discovery I made during my repeat year was that 'the world is bigger than Wales but little old Wales is part of the wider world'. Politics was in the air, even in such a sleepy place as Aberystwyth. I read in the papers that Nasser had seized the Suez Canal and nationalized it. The Soviet Union invaded Hungary and the people came out into the streets to fight the tanks; several students from Budapest came to Aberystwyth and a fund was opened to pay their college fees. A band of students walked to Aldermaston to protest against nuclear weapons. Sudan, Ghana, Pakistan, Morocco and Tunisia all won their independence, the war was still dragging on in Algeria, and the sun was fast going down on the British Empire. The Soviet Union launched the Sputnik rocket. There was police violence against black people in Little Rock, Arkansas. Archbishop Makarios, one of the Greek leaders in Cyprus, was released from prison. Heady times, indeed.

Everyone I knew (well, just about everyone) was reading Colin Wilson's *The Outsider*, Jack Kerouac's *On the Road*, John

Osborne's *Look Back in Anger*, and Richard Hoggart's *The Uses of Literacy*, a book that became a sort of bible for me in its portrait of working-class culture. My favourite musicians at the time were Joan Baez, Bob Dylan, Woody Guthrie, Pete Seeger and Ewan MacColl. In the Film Club I saw *Battleship Potemkin*, *The Seventh Seal*, *Les Enfants du Paradis*, *La Grande Illusion*, *Ashes and Diamonds*, and *Le Salaire de la Peur*. Among the stars I admired most were Gérard Philipe and Simone Signoret, but oh! Grace Kelly married that bloke from Monaco, thus disappointing at least one of her fans in Wales.

The cause that attracted most students during my first year was the row over the sacking of the Principal, Goronwy Rees, who'd been associated with Guy Burgess, the spy who went over to the Soviet Union in 1956. Very foolishly, Rees had published a series of articles in one of the Sunday papers which had incurred the wrath of the college Sanhedrin, in particular David Hughes Parry. The journalist Keidrych Rhys had a finger in the pie, or so it was said at the time. The students showed their support for the Principal by holding a packed, noisy meeting in the Quad. We weren't aware of the details, of course, but the Principal was a popular figure among us students, who seemed to show a genuine interest in our welfare. His suede shoes, white socks and debonair manner were, moreover, things to wonder at.

I have only one personal anecdote about Goronwy Rees. I was standing at the bar of the Belle Vue Hotel early one Saturday evening on my way to meet a woman from one of the hostels on the prom before going on to a hop in the Parish Hall. There was only one other person in the place and, to my great surprise, he smiled, bought me a dry sherry and then, turning on his heel, left the premises. He didn't know me; this is what he did with every student, or so it was said, whenever he came across one in a pub. About an hour later I saw the Principal in the hop – yes, he sometimes turned up at hops – but he didn't acknowledge me.

The stories about Goronwy Rees were legion: some said he'd had a part, during the 1930s, in a Nazi propaganda film, in which he played the captain of a British submarine peering through his periscope and giving the order, 'Ah, a German hospital ship – fire all torpedoes!' Rees was doubtless an unreliable man, but I can't imagine the son of a Calvinistic Methodist minister making propaganda films for Hitler. Be that as it may, he took his secrets to the grave, leaving at least two volumes of autobiography that are among the very best of their kind, namely *A Bundle of Sensations* (1960) and *A Chapter of Accidents* (1972). The man who succeeded him as Principal in 1958, Thomas Parry, wasn't half as colourful: his socks were always dark grey and no one ever saw him jive.

I entered politics as a friend of D. Ben Rees, a staunch Socialist who'd launched a magazine called *Aneurin*, after his hero who had just been elected treasurer of the Labour Party. I was invited to become Chairman of the Political Club by Rodric Evans, the son of Lyn Evans, head of the Independent Television Authority in Wales, and in this capacity I was able to invite a number of well-known speakers, including some from the Labour Party and others from Plaid Cymru, to address us. The Club didn't achieve very much, if the truth be told, but we did discuss ideas and listened to guest speakers, and that was quite important work among impressionable young people who were forming their political ideas at the time. Even so, I was uncomfortable with all the talk and fanciful theories in the ranks of Plaid Cymru and I longed to do something more practical. It was, after all, silly to be arguing about Wales taking its place in the United Nations when it didn't have a single parliamentary seat. There was no sign yet that anyone was prepared to take 'direct action', for all the talk among those who were concerned about what was happening in Capel Celyn, the village in Cwm Tryweryn.

Only a few numbers of *Aneurin* were published, but enough to make me think seriously about politics in Wales. This magazine tried to reconcile Socialism with Nationalism, although the most substantial number was filled with articles about the second of these. Ben was very fond of debate and public speaking, despite the fact that, as a native of Llanddewi Brefi, he was more at home in Welsh than in English. He later became a minister with the Calvinistic Methodists in Liverpool and it's only at the National Eisteddfod that we bump into each other nowadays, alas. He's still a member of the Labour Party and has become an authority on the history of the Welsh community in Liverpool. He has just published a splendid biography of James Griffiths, the first Secretary of State for Wales.

The main problem exercising Welsh-speakers in those days was Cwm Tryweryn. It didn't touch me personally, although I found pictures of the Capel Celyn villagers walking the cold, inhospitable streets of Liverpool with their banners appealing for the city authorities not to drown their valley enough to tug at the heart. At the same time, I saw immediately how public opinion in Wales could easily be ignored and how the Welsh M.Ps. were powerless to stop the building of the reservoir that was going to supply water for Liverpool. The lesson was clear: there had to be a body that would defend the interests of Wales and take action on its behalf, politically and culturally. And there was only one party that would do that, as far as I could see.

I joined Plaid Cymru at the end of my repeat year, in the summer of 1958. I remember J. E. Jones, the Party's Secretary, coming to Meadow Street to check that I was a real person, because a Plaid member in a place like Trefforest was about as rare as a butterfly at the North Pole in those days. I admired some of the Party's leaders, such as D. J. Williams, Wynne Samuel, Trefor Morgan, Glyn James, Jennie Eirian Davies, Elystan Morgan and, of course, Gwynfor Evans. But I must admit that I couldn't take to J. E. Jones: he was, in my experience, a dour fanatic. I didn't know Elystan personally but I was very disappointed when he left Plaid Cymru and went over to Labour in 1965; turning one's coat like that, for whatever reason, was difficult to understand among idealistic young people of my generation.

Among other Welsh-speakers I'd got to know by the end of my repeat year were Cynog Dafis, who became a Plaid M.P. and later a member of the National Assembly; Gareth Price and Patrick Hannan, who held important jobs with the BBC; Emyr Llewelyn Jones, who went to prison for his act of sabotage in Cwm Tryweryn; Aneurin Rhys Hughes and Hywel Ceri Jones, who went on to have distinguished careers with the European Commission in Brussels; and Irfon Clarke and John Pryce Williams, both amiable lads with whom I've since lost contact. I also had several chats with Alan R. Thomas, a native of Crai in Breconshire, an authority on the dialects of Welsh and editor of a special number of *The Dragon / Y Ddraig* in 1958, the year of the Festival of Wales, where poems by one Michael Stephens appeared for the first time; reading them now, I can't avoid the feeling, 'Say, could that lad be I?' Two years later there were poems by Meic Stephens in the same magazine. I'd decided to use the Welsh form of my name at the suggestion of D. J. Williams, and I've used it for all purposes ever since. The only disadvantage has been that some people confuse me with the singer Meic Stevens!

There were also contributions by Byron Rogers, Teifion Griffiths and Norman Rea in that number of *The Dragon / Y Ddraig*. I had some small success at this time as a writer of short stories, winning a prize in a competition organised by the Alun Lewis Society, and some of my poems appeared in the annual anthology *Universities' Poetry* and in *The Anglo-Welsh Review* under the editorship of Roland Mathias. It was I who arranged for *The Courier*, the college newspaper, to take Gwyn Thomas, Kingsley Amis and Goronwy Rees to task for having fired broadsides about Wales in a 'Welsh' number of the *New Statesman*. I was especially critical of Gwyn Thomas, calling him 'the clown of the coalfield', which soured our relationship ever after. Anyway, the cub journalist had begun to get a taste for polemics.

By the time *The Dragon / Y Ddraig* appeared in 1961 under my editorship, I was in France; I was helped by Emyr Llewelyn Jones, the Welsh editor, to put it together just before I left Aberystwyth. This was the number in which an article by Graham Hughes, a lecturer in the Law Department, appeared; entitled 'A Plea for Wales', it was in my opinion the best synopsis of the case for self-government I'd ever read. It's disappointing that this brilliant and patriotic Welshman from Aberafan went to live in the United States, where he still is, as far as I know. Gwilym Prys Davies, another lawyer whom I admire, is very like Graham Hughes in his facial features and keen mind.

I lodged during my first and repeat year in Portland Road with Jeff Jones and Wayne Davies, both of whom were from Trefforest and whom I'd known since we were boys. I lost contact with them after leaving Aberystwyth, although I've heard that Jeff subsequently worked for the Coal Board and Wayne became Professor of Urban Geography in Seattle. But by my third year, I was living with about a dozen other students in the Sun Hotel on North Parade, the home of Mr and Mrs Williams and their daughter Dorothy. Like all the others, I doted on Dot, who was funny and good company, and looked a bit like Audrey Tautou, the French actress; she taught me a lot about the psychology of women. The 'swinging Sixties' hadn't yet reached Aberystwyth and sexual relations among the young were quite innocent, on the whole. The great feat among male students was to visit a woman in one of the hostels on the promenade of a Sunday afternoon and slip into her room, if possible, although she could be punished for receiving gentleman callers in this way. A man had to rely on the woman's friends to knock the pipes when the warden was on the prowl, circumstances that often put a curb on the call of the flesh.

One of our pleasures in the Sun was to go swimming naked with Dot on South Beach by the light of the moon, the most daring thing I'd ever done up to that time. In the same digs I got to know Ifor Owen from Pen-y-bont-fawr in Montgomeryshire, a Welsh-speaker who, after gaining a doctorate, went to serve the government and people of Borneo, where he still is. He was the only one to bathe with his swimming-suit on. He used to go to chapel twice every Sunday, which was why the other lads pulled his leg mercilessly, but I had many an interesting chat with him about Welsh hymnology. Ifor didn't approve of our decision to parade with the coffin of Henry Brooke, the Minister for Wales, in a Rag procession through the streets of the town, but a few of us, including Rodric Evans, Megan Kitchener Davies, Alan Wynne Jones and Eurion John, carried it anyway.

My best friend in the French Honours class was Michael Powney from Brynaman, but he was busy courting June Davies throughout our last year and, indeed, they married soon after graduating, so we didn't see much of each other except in the lecture-room in Laura Place. I learnt a few choice Welsh phrases from Powney, such as '*Paid â chwympo i lawr y twll*' (Don't fall down the hole) and '*Mae'r haul yn disgleirio yn y ffurfafen*' (The sun is shining in the firmament). When I went to spend a weekend with the Powneys in Brynaman I heard Welsh being spoken among family members for the first time. I saw more of my other friend, Glyn Evans from Aberdare, who lived with us in the Sun, although he too was courting Lynwen Leach, his childhood sweetheart whom he was later to marry. His sister married the broadcaster Roy Noble.

Not that I was without female company. I went out quite a few times with Beti Williams, an attractive woman from Burry Port, a Welsh-speaker and member of Plaid Cymru. I see her occasionally with the journalist Mario Basini, and it's a pleasure to chat with her in the language I couldn't speak in Aberystwyth. I remember, too, Isobel Evans from Hendy, near Pontarddulais, the daughter of Llanelli's Director of Education, who was Welsh but English-speaking. She married a man who later became Principal of Atlantic College.

The College by the Sea was a small place in those days. About 440 freshers had come up to Aberystwyth in October 1956 and there were only 1,258 students, including 448 women, in the College as a whole; so there was keen competition among the men students. I don't remember the names of any of the women in the Honours French class, except for the one who told me she'd never heard of Albert Camus; it turned out she was also the only one to get a first. I'd lost contact with the students who had come up to Aberystwyth with me in 1956, partly because they'd spent a year in France while I was in my second year. By the time it was my turn to go to France, they'd graduated and left Aberystwyth. And I don't remember the names of the other women who walked the prom with me, I'm sorry to say.

The most colourful and popular lecturer in the college by a long chalk was the historian Gwyn A. Williams, who'd been on the staff since 1954. Although I wasn't a student in the History Department, I went to some of his lectures from time to time for the sheer pleasure of listening to his rhetoric, usually delivered with an attractive stammer. Another privilege was going late at night to the flat he shared with his wife Maria, who was also from Merthyr, to drink coffee and talk politics. One of Gwyn's friends was Richard Cobb, an authority on the French Revolution, who lectured to us from time to time, in French that was full of Parisian slang. I learnt more about the institutions and politics of France from these two than ever I did in the French Department.

Indeed, the Honours French course was a disappointment on the whole. The Head of Department was Professor E. R. Briggs, a shy old codger with an atrocious French accent, who, without looking up from his notes, read his lectures on scientists and philosophers of the eighteenth and nineteenth centuries: people like Lavoisier, Descartes, Diderot, Ampère, Bergson, Pascal and Pasteur. Briggs was a very remote figure, and a poor speaker, and I don't recall ever having a conversation with him. Then there was J. Killa Williams who, military in manner, taught Old French, which gave me the same trouble as Old English; I didn't make the slightest effort to master the glosses on Latin texts that Killa seemed to delight in. The Scotsman David Hoggan was much more pleasant, but again pathologically shy and given to blushing; nevertheless, I read Denis de Rougement's book *L'Amour et l'Occident* (*Passion and Society*) as part of his course. I learnt a lot about phonetics from Yvonne Niort, who later married Hoggan; I heard recently from Michael Powney that after her husband's death she took her own life. The only classes I found of interest were those of Margaret Philips (Maggie Pip), a sedate old lady who taught the dramatists Racine and Corneille, and those of Dennis Fletcher and Stuart John, who were responsible for the modern period.

Stuart was my tutor and very *sympa*. It was he who supervised my dissertation. Its grandiloquent title was 'Mechanical, Industrial and Urban Themes in French Poetry from 1830 to 1870, with special reference to the later achievement of Émile Verhaeren'. A poet from Flanders in Belgium, Verhaeren was a leading figure in the Flemish Renaissance that took place towards the end of the nineteenth century. Although he was a Flemish patriot, he wrote in French, like most of the intelligentsia of his day, a fact that was of particular interest to me. His favourite theme was how industry had transformed the landscape of northern Europe in his day and how this was going to usher in a new era of peace and international brotherhood. He also saw new forms of beauty in industrial and urban scenes. Taken up the Swansea valley by his friend, Percy Mansell Jones, he was delighted by the flames and smoke of the chimney-stacks he saw from the train, exclaiming, '*Ah, que c'est beau! Que c'est beau!*' The train was for him a symbol of the new industrial age, and his verse is full of docks, machines, factories, busy roads and workers trudging home from furnace and mine. I found it easy to respond to his work. It was a terrible irony when, in 1916, the poet fell under the wheels of an express train at Rouen station; his last words were reported as *'Je meurs. Ma femme! Ma patrie!'*

The old Fascist Ezra Pound once referred to Verhaeren as 'the most boring man in Europe', but he's one of my literary heroes and I often read the poems in his books, *Les Villes Tentaculaires* and *Les Campagnes Hallucinées*. As I write this, I see a portrait of him on the shelf above my desk. The Welsh poet J. M. Edwards took a special interest in his work – the only Welsh writer ever to do so, as far as I know – but I'm sorry to say I never met Edwards. I had a chance to work on my dissertation during my year in France, the obligatory year for all students taking Honours French. And so another year was added to my course.

I'd been in France once before, in the summer of 1956, while I was awaiting my A level results. I stayed at the home of my pen pal Gilbert Legendre in Gacé in Normandy. On the boat from Dover, I took off the silk belt my grandmother had made to hold my French currency and consigned it to the waters of the Channel – as if to say, 'I'm a big boy now, Nan, and can look after myself.' But having reached Paris, I was taken by Gilbert and his mother to see a performance of *White Horse Inn* and I had to leave the theatre during the interval to vomit in the street outside: it was the sun on the Channel crossing that caused this upset, though the music was enough to turn the stomach, too. That evening I lost my francs to a pickpocket and had to rely on the generosity of Mme Legendre during the rest of my visit. Not an auspicious introduction to life in France!

Gacé was a sleepy little village not far from Alençon and Argentan in *la Normandie profonde*, about the size of Ffostrasol, say, but without the night-life; the village people used to get their entertainment by going to the next village to watch the bacon-slicing machines. There were a few shops, including the *boulangerie* owned by Gilbert's mother, as well as a church, convent, petrol pump, police station and elementary school. My friend worked in the bakery all night and slept most of the day, leaving me pretty much to my own devices. Every morning I used to walk along the quiet country roads that converged on the village square, where I saw almost nobody and where the only traffic was the occasional tractor, this being an agricultural area. I noticed people staring at me in the village and had the impression they took me for a German because they weren't even prepared to say 'Bonjour' or even smile at me. So I didn't have much contact with French people during my month in Gacé.

The Germans had been in Normandy during the war which had ended only eleven years before, and they hadn't left any good impressions among local people. Or perhaps they took me for one of the Americans who had bombed northern Normandy indiscriminately prior to the Allied landings. When I tried to speak to them in my schoolboy French, they would say, 'Ah, Monsieur est allemand!', to which I would respond, 'Non, non, je suis gallois!' only to get the response, 'Ah, danois!' Madame Legendre addressed me in that strange way some people reserve for speaking to foreigners, that is to say, in a loud voice, repeating everything at least twice and very fast. This was the first time I'd heard French being spoken outside the classroom and I understood very little of what this kind woman said. Every now and then, usually over breakfast, she would mention her late husband and this would cause tears to roll down her cheeks and her ample bosom to heave, though I never learnt what had happened to him and I didn't like to ask. I had a letter a few days ago from Gilbert's wife informing me my old friend has died.

Nevertheless, and it's strange how some trivial things stay in the memory for so long, I learnt the folksong 'Ma Normandie', the words of which I still remember: 'Quand tout renaît à l'espérance, et l'hirondelle est de retour, j'aime à revoir ma Normandie, c'est le pays qui m'a donné le jour.' I heard recently that the song has been adopted as the anthem of Jersey. The local patriotism of the song was what appealed to me, of course. And when Gilbert came to stay with us in Meadow Street, he was taken to the hearts of Trefforest people, so much so that he came back a few years later on honeymoon with his bride, Maryvonne.

But now, in September 1959, I was about to face a whole year in France. I remember being told off by my father the night before I left home. I'd been out all day helping John Howell, the Plaid Cymru candidate in Caerffili, and my mother was feeling emotional about seeing her son go overseas. Quite right, too: I should have stayed at home on that day of all days.

I'd asked to be sent to Brittany and went as *assistant de langue anglaise* to the *École Normale des Instituteurs* in Quimper (Kemper in Breton, not that the name was to be seen anywhere in that form in those days). This establishment was a college for training elementary school teachers, rather like the Normal College in Bangor, but for men only. My role was to help improve the English of students in their final year. But what a task! These unruly lads had no interest whatsoever in improving their English and I had quite a bit of trouble with them. Most were sons of farmers, with Breton surnames but essentially French in interests and outlook. About two months after the start of my year it became clear that I wasn't going to teach them anything. When I went to ask Monsieur Briand, the English teacher, for advice, he didn't show the slightest concern, except to say, '*Ah, ne vous inquiétez pas, Monsieur Stéphan, c'est un vieux problème!*' Fine, I said to myself, if it's an old problem, it's not my problem.

The *pions*, too, were students, that is to say young men of my own age who were trying to earn money to pay for their studies in Rennes, Nantes and Brest by helping the Bursar run the college. I remember their names still: Marcel Lefloc'h, Paul Madec, and Jean Lozac'h; but what has become of them I have no idea. We didn't see anything of the staff from one week to the next, because they left the premises immediately after their classes, and so the *pions* were the only company I had. This provided me with a splendid chance to improve my French and pick up some of the latest slang and learn the words of bawdy songs such as *'Les Filles de Camaret'* that were not to be found in *Barzaz Breizh*. I started going around with them, usually on the back of their Vespas. I also enrolled at the University of Rennes where I went once a week and where, without much effort on my part, I gained a diploma in French. Towards the end of the year, I spent many a sunny afternoon on the beach at Bénodet.

There wasn't much to do in Quimper after about eight o'clock in the evening except to sit on the terrace of the Café de Bretagne just across the road from the river Odet. For company we had Joël-Jim Sevellec, a Latin teacher at the Lycée and an accomplished artist, like his father Jim Sevellec before him, who displayed his Breton sympathies by wearing, rather flamboyantly it must be said, an embroidered waistcoat and broad-brimmed hat that created a theatrical impression wherever he went. He died a few years ago but six of his plates decorated with figures from Breton folklore stand on our dresser to this day.

I drank more than one glass of red wine with Neil Jenkins, who was an assistant in the Lycée in the same year as me. I soon learnt that he could put down more than me but that I could hold it far better; I learnt to give Neil a wide berth when he was the worse for wear, as he often was. I also saw quite a bit of Rhys Lewis and Nia Daniel, students of Welsh in Cardiff, who came to Quimper from nearby towns, and of Maurice Varney, an assistant in Rennes, an Englishman who became a forensic linguist and who has learned Welsh since then.

For female company I had a young woman called Odette de Broc whose father, one of the minor aristos in that neck of the woods, asked me to give her private English lessons. There really was no need because she'd learnt English while working as a stewardess with PanAm and spoke it fluently; all I had to do was encourage her to get rid of her American accent. The real reason we met in a flat belonging to one of her friends once a week was it gave her a chance to escape from her parents who kept an eye on her lest she had *aventures* with men. She was a very beautiful woman who dressed in the latest fashion and every time I saw her on her Vespa I was reminded, inevitably, of Brigitte Bardot. I heard recently from her niece, Nathalie de Broc, the popular Breton novelist, that Odette now lives in Los Angeles; *ça s'explique*.

In those days, the Breton language didn't receive much public attention. The national movement had gone under a cloud in the years after the war, during which a small number of separatists had sided with the Germans, and only the folkloric aspects of Breton culture – the costumes, the dances, and traditional music – were now tolerated by the French government. I remember the bagpipe band that paraded round and round the yard beneath my window, playing tunes such as '*Rhyfelgyrch Capten Morgan*' that I recognised. The ambience of the College was completely French and its attitude to the Catholic Church and everything Breton was strictly Jacobin, that is to say, deeply hostile.

Although most of the students had been brought up on farms in Breton-speaking districts, I never heard a word of their language, *brezhoneg*, and they were very reluctant to discuss their backgrounds. They were, they informed me, *ploucs* (from *plou*, Welsh *plwyf*, a parish), the derisory word for people from the backwoods or bumpkins. Although I explained more than once that I was a Welshman, they always referred to me as an *Anglais*. I soon gathered that Brittany and Breton were in dire straits and I couldn't see much hope for them. My attitude at the time was summed up as '*La Bretagne, c'est belle mais c'est triste*', although I've seen quite a bit of improvement since then. The Breton political movement remains as schismatic as ever, as far as I can see. I keep in touch with events in Brittany by exchanging emails with Pierrette Kermoal, editor of the magazine *Aber*, and with Riwanon Kervella, director of *Kuzul ar Brezhoneg*, who is Welsh-speaking, both splendid women.

I didn't meet Pêr-Jakez Hélias, author of the popular book *Le Cheval d'Orgueil* (*The Horse of Pride*, 1975), about growing up in a Breton-speaking district, who was on the staff of the *École* when I was there, because he was in hospital at the time. But I had the pleasure, about fifteen years later, of joining him in a rendition of '*Hen Wlad fy Nhadau*' and '*Bro Goz ma Zhadou*' at a poetry festival in Rotterdam. But I did meet Per Denez, one of the greatest of Breton writers and scholars, who remained a good friend until his death in July 2011; also Ronan Huon, editor and publisher of the influential periodical *Al Liamm*; Maodez Glanndour, the poet who translated the New Testament into Breton; and Marc Le Ber, who kept a Breton crafts shop on the banks of the Odet and was always ready to chat with me about Brittany, usually from his neo-druidical perspective. I had an opportunity to thank the first three of these by inviting them to the Taliesin Conference in Cardiff in 1969. I also met, by sheer chance, Louis Guilloux, author of the novel *La Maison du Peuple*, in a café in St Brieuc, where I'd gone to visit Glyn Evans. A few months ago I chatted about Guilloux with Heather Dohollau *née* Lloyd, a Welsh woman who writes verse in French, but heard recently that she has since died.

In Brittany I had an opportunity to improve my spoken French and came to speak it quite fluently, since I was living through the medium of the language on a daily basis. What's more, I learnt a lot about living independently and how to enjoy things like the cinema, the theatre, wines, the fine arts and contemporary literature. I found a stack of copies of *La Nouvelle Revue* in a cupboard which provided me with reading material for months on end. By the time I came back to Wales I'd earned enough to pay for the rest of my course at Aberystwyth, but more importantly, I'd gained a certain *savoir-faire*, at least in my own estimation. The gawky lad in his blazer and college scarf had disappeared. I now dressed in the style of the Left Bank, in a black roll-neck sweater, corduroy trousers, suede shoes and yellow socks, like Sartre and Camus, although I didn't smoke Gitanes. I'd also put on weight, thanks to the *pommes frites, crêpes* and *brioche* that appeared on the table at the College twice a day.

I could sing the songs of Yves Montand, Georges Brassens and Edith Piaf, and I'd learnt poems by Apollinaire, André Breton, Paul Eluard, Louis Aragon and Jacques Prévert off by heart. Among the novelists I'd read were Raymond Queneau, Alain Fournier, François Mauriac, Marcel Pagnol, J-K. Huysmans and Maurice Barrès. The last of these, a French nationalist of extremely conservative views, influenced the young Saunders Lewis and Charles Maurras and the *Action Française*, and that's why, having learned to read Welsh I was dubious about the political and literary convictions of the hero of Penyberth. I'd acquired a certain amount of French culture, at least what was available in a provincial, middle-class town like Quimper. Even so, I knew I would never make a Frenchman any more than an Englishman, because Wales was now on my mind night and day. I had to make an effort to get to know my country better.

During my year in Quimper, I saw Wales in a wider context, and also began to think about Brittany and other national communities, which was the germ of the interest that led me to write my book *Linguistic Minorities in Western Europe* in due course. By the time I graduated I was describing myself as a nationalist, although the word is somewhat inappropriate to denote the phenomenon of patriotic fervour that is sometimes to be seen in Wales. Let's put it like this: Wales was my country, I knew that much now, and I'd fallen in love with the *idea* of Wales with its own government and institutions. From now on I resolved to work for Wales at every opportunity, come what may, and to see everything from a Welsh perspective and, even more importantly, try to change the political and cultural life of the country. That had to be in the ranks of Plaid Cymru rather than the Labour Party for the latter, it seemed to me, was indifferent to the claims of Wales as a country and nation. The Liberal Party held no appeal for me whatsoever and I've remained scornful of it ever since.

I wasn't able to speak Welsh at this time, mind you; indeed, I was proud to be a nationalist without being able to speak the language. I was of the opinion that Wales should govern itself as a matter of principle, and my view didn't depend on land and language, which in my understanding usually belonged to the right wing. I was more concerned about the industrial valleys than about rural Wales, although I also tried to see Wales in the round. More than anything, I wanted to encourage English-speaking Welsh people to play a fuller part in the nation's life and to make opportunities for them to do so. I must admit that I tended to look down my nose at many of the Welsh-speakers I met in Aberystwyth, especially those from rural and small-town backgrounds, who struck me as conservative and narrow in their chapel culture. Above all, I had no interest in harps, clog-dancing and singing *penillion*, and I never went near the Celtic Society.

But I still knew next to nothing about literature in the Welsh language, nor was I aware of the presence in Aberystwyth of such writers as D. Gwenallt Jones, T. H. Parry-Williams and T. E. Nicholas. The few words of Welsh poetry I'd picked up were those to be heard in the macaronic college song: *'O Coleg ger y Lli, what may your motto be, nid byd byd heb wybodaeth, answer we. Rage ye gales, ye surges seethe, Aberystwyth fu a fydd!'* Not the best introduction to the national muse and it's no loss to the Land of Song that nobody sings those embarrassing words any more.

None of this had anything to do with my college work, of course. I knuckled down fairly hard in my last year in the hope I'd do well enough to get a good degree. But it was not to be. As I began my final exams the girl from Cadoxton suddenly brought our relationship to a close. I didn't blame her too much for my doing badly in my exams – that would have been an excuse; but her timing was thoughtless, to say the least. I was glad in a way, because my feelings towards her had cooled off and there'd been long gaps in our relationship over the previous year. I knew we'd been growing apart. We'd spent a week together in Paris at Eastertime when I'd been a bit miserable and she hadn't been happy either. It was a good, sensible thing to break it off, and that's what happened. Even so, this wasn't the kindest moment to do it and I expressed my contempt by not replying to her letter.

If I'd had a better Honours classification than a lower second or 2:2 (what students nowadays call a Desmond) I should have done research on the work of Émile Verhaeren, but I did badly in the translation paper, like just about everyone else in the class, and so couldn't have a final grade more than one higher than what I was given in that paper. My dissertation, according to my tutor Stuart John, was good enough to put me in the first division, but that made no difference to the final grade. Years later, in 2008 to be precise, Ruth and I visited Verhaeren's grave at Sant Amand / Sint Amands on the bank of the Escaut / Scheldt in Flanders, and I sent a photo of the spot to Stuart John. This was my way of showing my gratitude for his strenuous attempts to help a second-class student like me. Stuart died in 2010.

At the graduation ceremony in the King's Hall in July 1961 I had a chance to show I was a bit of a rebel by remaining in my seat while the English anthem was being played, together with a few other members of the College branch of Plaid Cymru. Even so, I was acutely aware that I was a nationalist who could express himself in English and French without difficulty but who was unable to speak the language of his own country. I could read French novels and poetry, but I couldn't read a line of poetry in Welsh. I felt this lack very keenly. And so, while God was saving the Queen, I decided there and then that I would start learning the language as soon as possible. Welsh would be my third language.

It took me five years to get a degree. There was one advantage to the fact that I'd taken so long to get letters after

Charlie Symes,
my mother's father

Lilian and Charlie Symes,
my mother's parents

Annie Sophia Lloyd, the girl from Glascwm, my father's mother

Herbert Arthur Lloyd, my father, before arriving in Heolgerrig, December 1910

Alma Symes, my mother, on her 21st birthday, 1931

Alma and Arthur Lloyd Stephens, my parents, on their wedding day, 1935

My father in the Upper Boat power-station, c.1955

Me at five years old

With my brother, Lloyd, in 1944

Trefforest with Meadow Street bottom right

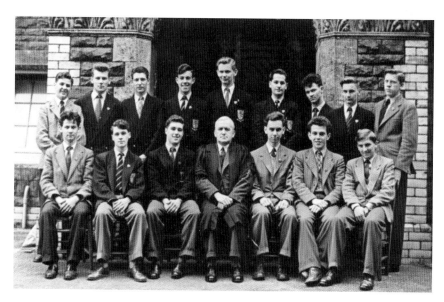

Prefects at Pontypridd Boys' Grammar School, 1955–6

Be prepared, 1956

French Department, UCW Aberystwyth, 1961

A slogan I painted on the wall of Laura Place, Aberystwyth, 1961

Graduation day, Aberystwyth, 1961

Plaid Cymru Summer School,
Pontarddulais, 1962

With Harri Webb outside Garth
Newydd, Merthyr Tydfil, 1963

Trefechan Bridge, Aberystwyth, February 1963

Trefechan Bridge, Aberystwyth, February 1963

The famous slogan I painted near Llanrhystud

Ruth and me on our wedding day, 1965

The Plaid Cymru candidate, Merthyr Tydfil, 1966

Ruth, 1966

Victory for Plaid Cymru and
Gwynfor Evans, July 1966

Literature Director, Welsh Arts
Council, September 1967

Playing the fool in the office with Fay Williams and Elan Closs Roberts

The bureaucrat at his desk

With our children,
Brengain, Huw,
Lowri and Heledd

My friend Glyn Jones
Photograph:
Julian Sheppard

My friend Harri Webb
Photograph: Julian Sheppard

My friend
Leslie Norris
Photograph:
Julian Sheppard

Ruth, 1990

Brigham Young
University, Provo, Utah

Visiting Professor, BYU, 1991
Photograph: Ben Hussain

Our son, Huw

With our daughters, Heledd,
Lowri and Brengain, 2010

With our
grandchildren, 2011

Our home,
Blaen-bedw, in
Whitchurch

my name, which was that, in the mean while, military service had been abolished, fortunately for me, since I wouldn't have made a very good soldier. Three years previously I'd filled in some forms to the effect that I intended registering as a conscientious objector on political grounds, but it wasn't necessary to go before a tribunal after all. I heard nothing further from the authorities. I'd had a narrow escape, and now I was free.

So I had to decide what exactly I was going to do next. *'Dysgais yr eang Ffrangeg,'* said Ieuan ap Rhydderch, *'doeth yw ei dysg, da iaith deg'* (I learned the widely-spoken French, its learning is wise, it's a good, beautiful language). But the truth was that there wasn't much a man could do with a degree in French in those days, except teach it to others. Of the dozen students in my Honours class, I think every one became a teacher, most of them in England. Diplomatic language or not, Her Majesty wasn't likely to accept someone like me who hadn't been to a public school and Oxbridge. And who wanted to serve the Queen and her imperial interests, anyway? There was far more important work to do nearer home. So teaching was my only real option and that's what I decided to do, happily enough.

4

Fire in my Belly

BEFORE RECEIVING THE letter from the Cadoxton girl, I'd intended going to Exeter to train as a teacher, to be near Rolle College in Exmouth, where she was a student. But now I was able to consider other options.

During the summer of 1961, while working as a gravedigger at Glyn-taf, I'd contributed an article to *Y Wawr*, the short-lived magazine published by the youth branch of Plaid Cymru, and presently I received an invitation from Douglas Vaughan Williams, a native of Llanelltyd, near Dolgellau, to become its editor. I jumped at the chance and after a fast-track interview at the University Registry in Cathays Park with D. W. T. Jenkins, the Professor of Education at Bangor, I decided to go to the University College of North Wales, where Douglas was a student, rather than Exeter. I'm not sure to this day whether this was a wise move because I knew nobody in Bangor, but there it is: a university education is supposed to broaden your horizons, or at least change the scenery; a pity I didn't go to Edinburgh or Dublin or even Rennes or Paris, where I would have been more than happy, but it was too late to apply to any of them.

Be that as it may, I was warmly congratulated on my choice by the kindly Professor, and learned from him that a magazine with the same title as *Y Wawr* had played a lively part in the history of Welsh nationalism at the time of the First World War. But the periodical had folded after the young D. J. Williams, in 1918, had published an article in it which, in the opinion of the Home Secretary of the day, contained 'treasonable elements'. D. J., of Penyberth fame, was to become a hero of mine and I had many a memorable chat with him over the years, the last in the Bristol Trader in Fishguard where he lived with his lovely wife Siân.

The Professor didn't ask me a single question about my wish to become a teacher, and within a week or two I was on my way to the College on the Hill. Things began promisingly enough between Douglas Vaughan Williams and me. In the number of *Y Wawr* that appeared in the spring of 1962 there were articles by him, H. W. J. Edwards, Anthony Conran and Peter Hourahane, and one of mine entitled 'The Status of the Anglo-Welsh' that was meant as a riposte to the dramatist John Gwilym Jones, a lecturer in Bangor's Welsh Department at the time, who had cast a slur in the College newspaper on the validity of an 'Anglo-Welsh' literature. Even so, relations between Douglas and me didn't flourish and I never got to sit in the editor's chair because, I soon realized, he was intent on occupying it himself. For some reason that's unclear to me, my name appears as business manager on the magazine's first page. We argued ferociously on this score and Douglas used colourful language that he hadn't learned in Sunday school to accuse me of trying to dislodge him as editor. His fury was beyond all reason and it nearly came to blows between us. I lost contact with this able but eccentric lad before the end of my year in Bangor and I haven't seen him since.

I knew just about nobody in the College to begin with, not even my fellow-students because there were no lectures as such, only an occasional seminar attended by about five or six of us. There were many more English people around the place than in Aberystwyth and a lot fewer English-speaking Welsh. Almost everyone belonged either to the English crowd or to the Welsh-speaking one, and only a handful to both. A very few Welsh-speakers went out of their way to speak to me, despite my reputation as a Plaid activist having preceded me from Aberystwyth. Among the students I remember Dafydd

Glyn Jones in a cowboy hat and firing off his toy-revolvers as he ran down the corridors, and the fresher Derek Lloyd Morgan (as he then was) speaking brilliantly in the Debates Union in favour of the motion 'Good fences make good neighbours'. I later came to admire both Dafydd and Derec but we exchanged not a word, in either Welsh or English, during 1961/62.

The only Welsh-speakers I got to know were Robert Griffiths (Robat Gruffudd later), Gruffydd Aled Williams and John Clifford Jones, all three freshers and members of Plaid Cymru. I gave them a few tips on how to use a brush and pot of Dulux paint and soon slogans began appearing on walls around Upper Bangor. I remember one in particular, daubed on the garden wall of Professor Brambell: 'Home Rule will come,' it proclaimed in large white letters. A few days later an unknown hand had added the words 'to Puffin Island'.

But I was looking for a chance to leave a more permanent mark, and this is how it happened. One evening in Debates Union, Robert tried to address the meeting in Welsh, only to be ruled out of order by the chairman, an Englishman, on the grounds that Welsh was not 'a parliamentary language'. This was in the days before instantaneous translation. I immediately drafted a letter to the editor of the college's English-language newspaper in protest against this paltry excuse and to demand fair play for the language. Among those who signed it were John Clifford Jones, Robert Griffiths, Janie Guy, Martin Eckley, a Scot by the name of Inis Clear and Anthony Brereton, the last-named an Irishman and native Irish-speaker with whom I shared a flat in Princes Road.

John Clifford Jones went on to become an officer of the North Wales Arts Association, Janie Guy a Plaid Cymru member of the Vale of Glamorgan Council, Gruffydd Aled Williams Professor of Welsh at Aberystwyth, and Robert a distinguished publisher. Three years later, on graduation day 1964, Robert stood before the congregation and refused his degree. 'I won't accept a degree from the University of

Wales,' he announced, 'for as long as it denies the Welsh language – the language of the nation it's supposed to serve. For nearly two years we students have repeatedly asked for Welsh to be given its rightful place in the life of this college. The authorities have consistently refused every request. The campaign will continue, but this is my last chance. I refuse this degree and shall continue to do so for as long as the University is hostile to the Welsh language.' All praise to him for his brave stand and his unyielding commitment to the cause of the language since then. The campaign to win official status for Welsh in Bangor went on until 1984 and the appointment of Eric Sunderland as Principal and successor to the autocratic Charles Evans, but I like to think it had begun back in 1961.

Since I've mentioned his name I must say something about Anthony Brereton, or Antoine Ó Breartuin to give him the Irish form of his name. Anthony was a handsome but diffident young man living away from home for the first time, and chronically lacking in experience of the opposite sex. But I soon learned on which evenings it was tactful of me to be out of the flat while he was entertaining a woman there and, in due course, he grew a lot more confident. He was from Dublin and he and his four brothers had been educated through the medium of Irish, a language they all used in their work in the city; one was a Christian Brother and another worked for an Irish-language newspaper. Da Brereton was a cobbler, very fond of his Guinness, and his wife a character straight out of Sean O'Casey. The whole family were Sinn Féiners and very critical of the other parties which, in their estimation, had betrayed their Republican principles. We went across to Dublin several times during my year in Bangor, Anthony and I, and I learned a great deal about the politics and history of Ireland, enough to correct some of the false impressions of the Emerald Isle that I, and most of my contemporaries, had.

It's a fact that many young Welsh Nationalists in those

days were under the influence of Irish history, the sacrifice and heroism of it all, with little or no regard for the bloody reality of the situation. Like so many, I'd been intoxicated by the Fenians, the Easter Rising of 1916 and the civil war that followed. Even so, I still admire the Irish for their efforts to free themselves from English rule. I'm glad, too, that some of my ancestors were from County Roscommon and that's why I keep a bust of Michael Collins on the shelf above my desk. I'm also fond of declaiming the words of the Proclamation that Patrick Pearse read from the steps of the Post Office in 1916: 'In the name of God and of the dead generations from which she receives her old tradition of nationhood, Ireland, through us, summons her children to her flag and strikes for her freedom...' Heady stuff for idealistic youth, most definitely. Even so, mixing with Irish Republicans was not quite the same as working for Wales.

Unfortunately, it wasn't possible to avoid the English in Bangor. They were in the majority and many were mature students, and it was with them I tended to socialize. Scientists like Anthony, who was doing a doctorate in Botany, made up the Humanist Society, and with them I discussed politics, literature and religion. There wasn't a single Welsh student among them, apart from Jim Davies, a genial Monmouthshire man who now lives in Merthyr.

About this time I began keeping a diary, on and off, a habit I've had ever since. I have a cupboard full of them and they help me to remember some of the people and events I mention in this book. The main spur to start me off as a diarist was reading a copy of Kilvert's *Diary* which I happened to pick up one day from a wet pavement in Upper Bangor. I didn't know at the time that I would soon have a keener interest in this enchanting book.

It was through them, the Humanists, that I first came into contact with Tony Conran. I'd heard of him in 1960 when he won a prize from the Welsh Committee of the Arts Council for his book *Formal Poems*, and I'd read his ground-breaking articles in *The Anglo-Welsh Review*. But this was the first time I'd seen the poet and had a chance to talk to him. And what talk! Although Tony had great difficulty in speaking on account of his cerebral palsy, and patience was needed before he could be understood, once you were on his wavelength, as it were, he was well worth listening to. Here was a keen mind, richly informed, full of original ideas and vivid expressions that were the fruit of his wide reading. That said, I couldn't accept all his theories about the Muse and the influence so many women had exerted on him (this was before his marriage to the charming Lesley Bowen), but I learned a good deal from him over countless cups of coffee at his flat in Upper Bangor. I am particularly grateful for the conversations we had about the need for a poetry magazine in Wales, which bore fruit about three years later when I launched *Poetry Wales*. I also recall that Tony was the adjudicator who awarded me a small shield for a sequence of poems I'd sent, anonymously, to the Inter-College Eisteddfod of 1962. The prize was presented to me by J. Eirian Davies, another poet whom I greatly admired.

I didn't have much of a social life during my time in Bangor, because I had to take a train to Rhyl every day for practical teaching experience. But I remember travelling with Joan Phillips, who would patiently answer my questions about Welsh grammar, although the names of our companions have gone from me. I wrote a dissertation entitled 'The Teaching of English Verse Appreciation' based on my experience of teaching English at Rhyl Grammar School, but strangely enough, I wasn't asked to give a single French lesson there. As a special project I made a series of proverbs in the six Celtic languages, thus demonstrating my interest (if not my skill) in calligraphy and uncial letter-forms. But that was all: a very undemanding course, to say the least of it, and I was surprised at year's end to receive an Education Diploma as proof, perhaps, that I was a qualified teacher. They must have been desperately short of teachers!

At the same time I decided to do something about my lack of Welsh by taking lessons with Islwyn Ffowc Elis. It was a privilege and pleasure to get to know this gentle, cultured man as he took me slowly through *Cartrefi Cymru* by O. M. Edwards, a text that gave a firm foundation to my knowledge of the written language later on. I appreciated Islwyn's method of teaching because he was able to explain the grammatical rules and draw comparisons with French and Italian, and so I made good progress under his tutelage. I got to know Islwyn even better during the bye-election campaign in Carmarthenshire in July 1966, when Gwynfor Evans was elected, and when, later on, I was translating his two Lleifior novels. The first Welsh book I read without help was his *Wythnos yng Nghymru Fydd*.

There's one more person I must mention at this point, namely Jennifer Salmon. I went out with two or three women during my year in Bangor, among whom was a blonde hockey-player called Christine Riley, all of them English. So was Jenny. Her home was in one of the leafier suburbs of London. She'd been brought up in India and could speak Urdu – well, enough to communicate with her ayah. She was a fine-looking young woman, or so I thought, and I fell for her in a big way. I remember one night in particular when we went up Snowdon to see the sun rising over Eryri, after which we breakfasted on bacon and eggs that had an otherworldly taste to them. Things came to an end during the following summer, after I'd visited her in Cornwall, where she had a holiday job near Padstow. I never saw Jenny again but I heard recently that she married an Indian doctor; I hope she's happy with a house full of children and grandchildren.

Jenny Salmon played another part in my life, albeit indirectly. On my way to visit her, I stayed a few nights with Monica Jones, the daughter of my Auntie Gwen, who lived nearby. One evening over supper Monica referred to my father, saying, 'Of course, your father and my mother weren't really brother and sister, were they?' This was news to me.

'Oh?' I replied, as Monica went on to say my father had been born 'up in the hills of mid-Wales' and had been brought up by William Stephens, a policeman in Heolgerrig, and his wife. The child's father had been killed in the First World War, she said. 'I didn't know that,' I said. 'Oh dear, have I let the cat out of the bag?' said Monica before quickly changing the subject.

Yes, she had indeed let the cat out of the bag. This information was going to take up a lot of my energy (and a chapter in this book) but I didn't think much about it at the time. Only Jenny was on my mind during the summer of 1962 and, besides, I was going to have to find a job soon, in Wales. I wasn't prepared to work in England. In fact, that was the bone of contention between Jenny and me: she didn't want to live in my country and I didn't want to live in hers. What's more, I think the fire in my belly was too much for a young woman from a middle-class English family. Heigh-ho.

Luckily, I got a job that suited me at my very first attempt. In September 1962 I joined the staff of the Grammar School in Ebbw Vale as a French teacher at a salary of about a thousand pounds a year. The councillor who chaired the panel that interviewed me shook my hand afterwards and said, 'We wish you hevery 'appiness, Mr Stephens,' fair play to him. In those days Ebbw Vale was a prosperous industrial town with about 15,000 of its people employed in the steel industry. When asked the names of the three men who were thrown into the fiery furnace a schoolboy is reputed to have replied, 'Richard, Thomas and Baldwin, sir' – the name of one of the major steel companies in the area.

I soon discovered that, at the age of 24, I was the youngest member of staff. The headmaster was R. C. Smith, a dour Welsh-speaker from Rhosllannerchrugog with whom I had only the most vatic of conversations. The only colleagues I can remember with any clarity or warmth are Olwen and Dewi Samuel, who taught Welsh and Latin and had edited the magazine *Y Crynhoad*; Tom Davies, the Art master, who had known the painters Cedric Morris, Heinz Koppel and Arthur Giardelli when they worked in Dowlais during the Depression; Idwal Davies, who taught Biology and gave me a lift to work every morning; Wynne Roberts, the English master, a Rhondda man who'd been at Oxford with Gwyn Thomas; Lynette Harries, the Physical Education teacher who later became Chair of the Sports Council, a Welsh-speaker and Plaid member; Marsden Evans, who also taught Physical Education, a genial man who'd lost his wife, a native of the Hebrides, as a result of the pollution in the air of Ebbw Vale; Edwin Jones, the History teacher and gifted historian, who later became headmaster of a Catholic school in Port Talbot; and Aleksandr Moncibowić, who taught Mathematics.

Monty was the most exotic of all these. He'd had a most calamitous military career: he'd fought with the Ukrainian army against the Poles, and lost; he'd fought with the Polish army against the Germans, and lost; he'd fought with the German army against the Russians, and lost again. He didn't have a very firm grasp of English, especially English idiom, and would say things like 'You are a spanner in the grass' and 'One swallow does not make a silver lining'. Once, during a heated lunch-time debate in the staff room, someone said, 'Monty, you know bugger all about politics.' 'Yes,' he replied in high dudgeon, 'I know bugger all and you know bugger nothing!' When I had a fortnight off to stand as the Plaid Cymru candidate in Merthyr in March 1966, Monty, Lynette Harries, Eddie Jones and the Samuels were the only ones among my colleagues to wish me well. The rest were all Labour, probably.

When I joined the staff of the Grammar School in Ebbw Vale I was single and living in Garth Newydd, a ramshackle old house in Merthyr that no one actually owned. I'd met Harri Webb in August in the Old Arcade, one of the last of Cardiff's pubs to preserve some of its Edwardian charm. The meeting nearly ended disastrously. Leaning on the counter, I'd been chatting with Harri when an old man came over to us and, ever so politely, said to him, 'Excuse me, sir, your friend's on fire.' And indeed I was: the leather patch on my jacket was smouldering, having come into contact with a small flame used to light cigars. At this, Harri didn't quite spring to my rescue (he wasn't as nimble as that), but instead he held up my arm and poured a pint of Guinness down my sleeve, extinguishing what might have become a conflagration.

I don't remember what we talked about that incendiary evening, but that was the moment our friendship began. Harri and I had a lot in common. For one thing, both our fathers had worked in electric power stations and so our backgrounds were quite similar. We had both taken degrees in Romance languages, and our conversation in the Old Arcade that evening was of the macaronic kind. Among our favourite poets were Lorca, Prévert, Éluard and Laforgue, and even more importantly, we had similar ideas about literature and society. I am glad that I've avoided the English view that literature and politics don't mix. Although we were members of Plaid Cymru we both belonged to the Left and wanted to work for the Party in the south-east of Wales, the part that was going to be instrumental in winning self-government, or so we thought then. The chat with Harri proved more intoxicating than anything on offer in the Old Arcade that evening and by stop-tap I'd accepted his invitation to join him in Garth Newydd.

I must admit that the idea of living in Merthyr held great appeal for me. As a boy, I'd visited my Aunties Annie and Gwen, and knew the town centre and Cefn quite well. The place, moreover, had connections with people like Dic Penderyn, Charlotte Guest, Thomas Stephens (no relation, alas), Henry Richard, Keir Hardie, Glyn Jones and Jack Jones. Furthermore, I liked the egalitarian spirit of the townspeople and I was interested in the industrial archaeology that was to be seen everywhere until the council started knocking down the old town. One of the virtues of Merthyr people is that they're always friendly enough to give you directions, even when it's quite clear they haven't the foggiest idea where the place you want is situated.

Garth Newydd, at the bottom of the Brecon Road opposite the Glamorgan Arms, was one of the oldest houses in Merthyr. It had been owned by an ironmaster before becoming the home of Dr Joseph Biddle, the town clerk in the 1920s. There were about a dozen large rooms on three floors and two others in the attic. Since all the original trustees had died, the house was deemed to belong to no one. Branches of the Women's Voluntary Organization and Red Cross met downstairs and there was a small hall at the rear where public meetings were held from time to time. The only other occupants were a small group of pacifists who were trying to live according to Gandhi's teaching by doing good works in the community. Harri was no pacifist but from these idealistic, middle-class, English people, he acquired his fondness for the hot curries that he scoffed with such obvious relish, spattering his beard and chest with rice and sauce as he did so. By 1962 the Fellowship of the Friends of Truth, as the group called themselves, had fallen out with one another (What, after all, is Truth?) and Harri was living in the house on his own.

Within a week or two others had joined us, including Judy Gurney and her son Goulven / Dyfrig; Paol Keineg the young Breton poet who was the child's father; Rodric Evans whom I'd known since Aberystwyth days; Tony Lewis (the accountant not the silversmith); Peter Meazey, owner of Siop y Triban in Cardiff; the genial Englishman Dave Buckel; and, for a while, Neil Jenkins, who was teaching Welsh in the town. Neil could raise the hackles of even his fellow-Nationalists, especially when he was the worse for wear, and he nursed a pathological hatred of Gwynfor Evans. In the end, after he'd painted 'Gwynfor is a bastard' on the newly-painted chimney-breast of Garth Newydd shortly before the Party's President was to address the local branch, it was decided to ask him to leave the house; no, to be more precise, his belongings were put out on the pavement and the lock on his door changed. He was also expelled by the Party a bit later. As Neil ap Siencyn he continued to muddy the waters of political debate in Wales with his negative, *ad hominem* bile.

We were all Plaid members and Garth Newydd became a centre for political activity, a sort of mecca for Nationalists young and old. The local branch of Plaid Cymru met there and an open door was kept for activists, and hangers-on, from all over Wales. I still have the visitors' book and it's interesting to see the names of a broad spectrum of Nationalists from Gwynfor Evans and Phil Williams to Geraint (Twm) Jones and Cayo Evans, and a number of others who were leaders of the Party and Cymdeithas yr Iaith, the Welsh Language Society, during the 1960s. We also saw a lot of John Uzzell Edwards, the young painter from Deri, whose funeral in Swansea I attended the other day, and Paul Riley, whose painting of ponies on the Whitey, as the Dowlais tip was known, Harri gave Ruth and me as a wedding present.

We also had other visitors who weren't willing to write their names in our book for reasons that must remain confidential. But I can name Padraig ar Gouarnig, a young Breton who was on the run from the French police, and Dai Pritchard and Dai Walters, 'the boys from Gwent', who in September 1962 damaged machinery at the site of the reservoir that was being built in Cwm Tryweryn. Years later Dai Pritchard married Judy Gurney but he died suddenly while they were on holiday in Brittany. We also had the company of Yann-Ber Piriou, a Breton who was an assistant in Aberdare at the time and who went on to become an important poet and one of the founders of the political party known as *Union Démocratique Bretonne (UDB).*

Difficult though it is to imagine, Plaid Cymru was denied the right to broadcast on the radio and television in those days. I had a small part in the protests against this injustice: with Councillor Bill Williams, I painted the words 'Lift the TV ban on Plaid Cymru' on the front wall of Cyfarthfa Castle and was fined £12 by the Merthyr magistrates after a Labour member who happened to be passing spotted us and we were caught white-handed, as it were: the fines were paid by someone who remains anonymous to this day. At about the same time an unknown hand painted anti-Welsh words on the wall and window of 50 Meadow Street, my parents' home in Trefforest. I'd been wondering how they would respond to my political activities, but there was no need to worry on that score. Although my father had always voted Labour, he was very supportive of his rebellious son.

Soon afterwards I received a visit from two strangers wishing, they said, to discuss starting a Welsh Scout movement which would teach boys how to use rifles and dynamite. Although I was in bed with 'flu at the time, I twigged immediately that these men were *agents provocateurs*. One asked me for the names of people who might be interested in such an idea and I mentioned Miss Ethel Williams, a genteel old lady who had taught History at Cyfarthfa School, and Mr Dai Jones, the highly respectable treasurer of the local branch of Plaid Cymru who, in his younger days, had worked for Keir Hardie, both now in their eighties and the most eirenic, law-abiding of all our members. Dai Jones had been a member of the I.L.P. before being attracted to Plaid Cymru by Saunders Lewis who had lectured in Dowlais during the 1930s. His favourite story about the old Merthyr was one in which his great-great-great-grandfather had been given a ride on the step of Richard Trevithick's steam engine by the man himself in 1804.

I heard nothing more from the two sinister visitors. But in 1963, at the time of the direct action carried out by Emyr Llewelyn Jones and others in Cwm Tryweryn, I had to go down to the police station in Merthyr to give my fingerprints and answer a few questions. When asked whether I knew anyone whose initials were E.R., I replied 'Elizabeth Regina', at which one of the cops had to restrain the other from grabbing me by the throat; I used this incident in my short story 'Damage'. In the same year, on the 22nd of November 1963 to be precise, I was speaking with Emrys Roberts against Neil Kinnock in a debate about self-government in the Students' Union in Cardiff when the news came that John F. Kennedy had been shot in Dallas.

The Merthyr branch of Plaid Cymru had only a handful of active members. We had a few councillors, such as Penri Williams and Gwyn Griffiths, Troed-y-rhiw, but no real power. Even so, the prospects weren't altogether bleak. When I led a procession through the town at the head of a brass band on Owain Glyndŵr Day in 1963, I was followed by about three hundred people all the way up to Dowlais Top. Plaid came near to winning the seat in a bye-election in 1972 when Emrys received 11,852 votes against Labour's 15,562. And when Plaid won a majority on the council under Emrys's leadership a few years later, I sent him a telegram with the words: 'Proud to have helped wind the clock. Delighted to hear it strike.'

From Garth Newydd I launched the magazine *The Nationalist*, in which my lecture 'The Matter with Wales' appeared alongside an article by Dai Walters and Dai Pritchard about what they'd done in Cwm Tryweryn. This was my attempt to start a magazine for the youth of Plaid Cymru, but only one number appeared, unfortunately, so it's a collector's item. I wince at the apocalyptic note struck in the article by John Legonna, in which he proclaimed 'We, Plaid Cymru, are the nation of the Welsh. Without us there is no Nation,' and nonsense of that sort. The Party has attracted its fair share of cranks and misfits over the years. Legonna was a right-wing Englishman whose real name was Brooks. I didn't like him and never understood why Harri Webb was a friend of his. Among his co-conspirators were Roger Boore, Meic Tucker and Emrys Roberts. I steered clear of their group, New Nation, and its magazine *Cilmeri* that was the mouthpiece of the campaign to get rid of Gwynfor as the Party's President. But I had a lot of sympathy for Emrys Roberts when he was dismissed from his post as the Party's Secretary, a shabby episode described by Rhys Evans in his biography of Gwynfor. As for Roger Boore and Meic Tucker, they seem to have withdrawn from Plaid activities altogether.

Looking back like this, I see that the national struggle filled my life in those days, and that I was glad to be doing something practical for the Party, instead of talking about it. I spent four whole years in active politics in Merthyr. I stood as Plaid candidate at local elections. I took part in broadcasts by Radio Free Wales from my rooms in the attic of Garth Newydd. I sat on the Party's Executive Committee for a while. I wrote ballads and topical songs with Harri, notably 'The Exile's Song' which was meant to get up the noses of the London Welsh such as Hafina Clwyd and Tudor David, which it duly did.

I gave Harri a helping hand in editing *Welsh Nation*, the Party's monthly paper, and I learned from him how to put a paper together with scissors and paste. I was the first to read his column about Cwmgrafft, a fictitious township in the Valleys that was run by a corrupt Labour Party. Harri gave me an opportunity to write book-reviews such as those of Hugh MacDiarmid's *Collected Poems* and R. S. Thomas's *The Bread of Truth* in the December 1963 number. The Scot had long been a hero of Harri's and I too came to appreciate his verse and polemics, and his example in editing periodicals like *The Voice of Scotland* was certainly in my mind at this time. I had the pleasure of introducing the two poets at Lampeter in 1974 and taking them to see the grave of Dafydd ap Gwilym in Strata Florida.

I looked on Harri as a mentor, comrade and friend. Yet I found it hard to put up with him at times. If something annoyed him – and he was easily upset – he would stuff his fingers into his mouth, go red in the face and shudder for several minutes before regaining his composure. I and other Garth Newydd residents had learned to ignore this display but others were horrified. I then had to explain that Harri's nerves had been affected by the big guns of the ships on which he served during the war. It was more difficult to explain his behaviour at the supper table and his lack of personal hygiene. Despite all this, we remained good friends all down the years.

I've been asked several times whether Harri was homosexual. My answer is always, no, he was definitely not. I've read his voluminous diaries, which span about forty years of his life, in which he lists the women with whom he had sex, about ninety in all, although I suspect most were prostitutes and one-night stands. He was especially fond of young actresses. What people don't know is that Harri had a common-law wife in Cardiff during the 1950s, in the days when he was active with the Welsh Republicans, before he tried to shake her off by fleeing to Cheltenham, and that they had a daughter named Heather who must be in her sixties now.

In 1963 a group of us, including John Davies (Bwlch-llan), Rodric Evans and Peter and Shelagh Hourahane, travelled round the west of Ireland, visiting just about every site associated with the civil war; we also spent a week in Dublin. When a woman came up to me on O'Connell Street and asked for my signature on a petition to save some Georgian building or other from demolition, I wrote 'Leopold Bloom, 7 Eccles Street'; 'Thanks for your support, Mr Bloom,' she said. I wonder how she would have reacted if I'd signed as Humphrey Chimpden Earwicker. 'Loud, heap miseries upon us, yet entwine our arts with laughters low.' Not everyone, it seems, even in Dublin, has read *Ulysses* and *Finnegans Wake*.

One evening, sitting in a pub, we saw, to our great surprise, a number for the President of the Republic listed in a telephone directory and the following day Bwlch-llan arranged for us to visit him. By now De Valera was almost blind but we had a lively conversation about Wales and Welsh, subjects about which he was very knowledgeable. Then, as our time was nearly up, he leaned across his desk and said, very quietly, 'In my position they won't let me talk politics, you know. But I'd just like to say this: I hope something of what you want for your country will come true during your lifetime, as it has for my country during mine.' Wow! This was a benediction from the hero of Boland's Mills and his words have remained clear in my memory to this day.

I didn't hear the lecture by Saunders Lewis, *Tynged yr Iaith*, in February 1962; I was in Bangor at the time and didn't have enough Welsh anyway, but I remember the excitement among Nationalists of my generation, people like Harri Pritchard Jones, Dafydd Orwig, Owen Owen and Gareth Miles. I took part in the first demonstration by the *Cymdeithas* on Trefechan Bridge on the 2nd of February 1963 when several Garth Newydd residents travelled up through the snow to Aberystwyth, and I wrote a ballad to mark the event. I saw a number of familiar faces on that famous occasion: Gwyneth Wiliam, Anna Daniel, Gareth Roberts (Treffynnon), Robat Gruffudd, Gruffydd Aled Williams, John Clifford Jones, Gwilym Tudur, Peter Meazey, Rodric Evans, Megan Kitchener Davies, Aled Gwyn, Neil Jenkins, Eurion John, Gwyneth Rhys, Llinos Jones, Dyfrig Thomas, Geraint Jones, and Rhiannon Silyn Roberts.

Having recently made enquiries as to who exactly was on the Bridge – a full list has never been published – I can now name the following: Huw Carrod, Eric Jones, Joy Harries, Penri Jones, Edgar Humphreys, Tegwyn Jones, Guto ap Gwent, Peter Cross, Menna Dafydd, Enid Davies, Tomos Prys Jones, Ruth Meredith, Giovanni Miseroti, Mair Owen, Rhiannon Price, Dennis Roberts, Hafwen John, Angharad Jones, Menna Williams, Morwen John, Gwyneth Jones, Gareth Roberts, Catrin Gapper, Tegwen Roberts, Ann Eleri Jones, Elenid Williams, Rachel James, Gareth Gregory, Anne Morris Jones, Beti Jones, Ann Eirwen Gruffydd, Joy Harries, and Geraint Eckley. Quite honestly, I don't remember each and every one of these actually sitting on the Bridge but I accept their word for it that they were in Aberystwyth that day. Although the protest was unsuccessful – no one was arrested for impeding the traffic for about half an hour and so no bilingual summonses were issued as we'd hoped – it was clear to some of us that a new day had dawned in Wales, and I was glad to be there to help it on its way. Among my treasures is a poster published by the National Library publicising an exhibition, *Protest*, on which I can be seen sitting with others in front of a Post Office van. As another souvenir of the event, I have a small scar on my leg which I'm prepared to show to serious students of the period.

Over the next two years I was active in favour of the language in several ways. With John Daniel and John Davies (Bwlch-llan) I went to Pembrokeshire one dark night and removed the road-sign outside a village that read 'Trevine' and put up another with the correct spelling on it: Tre-fin. The offending signs were then displayed on the Eisteddfod field until a plain-clothes policeman came to fetch them. With John Davies, the Cymdeithas Secretary, I went to Dinas Mawddwy and persuaded the woman who kept the Post Office there to put up a bilingual sign that I'd made in my best calligraphy. These were among the first tentative moves to win official status for the language.

The death of John Davies last February, as I was reading the proofs of this book, has reminded me that the language activists of the early 1960s will soon be shades; a man could not wish for a better comrade than Bwlch-llan.

From Garth Newydd in 1962 and 1963 we went out into the night to paint slogans on public buildings. I painted the words '*Cofiwch Tryweryn*' on a wall near Llanrhystud which has become something of a national ikon, so I'm told. This was done in the company of Rodric Evans, the only one of the Garth Newydd crowd who owned a car. I didn't note the details in my diary that night – for obvious reasons. But the slogan, which has been touched up and repainted over the years by other hands, has gladdened the hearts of patriots and kept the name of the drowned valley in view of the Welsh people ever since. It's a pity the campaign to buy and repair the wall hasn't raised enough money to preserve it; where are the Nationalists, I wonder?

I was present at the demonstrations in the post offices in Dolgellau and Lampeter in 1965 and in Machynlleth in January 1966, and I spent a fortnight in Carmarthen during the bye-election in which Gwynfor Evans was elected in July 1966. I recall the tears bowling down my cheeks that night. The picture of me and Dai Bonner carrying Gwynfor on our shoulders across the square in Llangadog the day after his election is often shown on television and in the papers. I worked hard in the Rhondda when Vic Davies came near to winning the seat at a bye-election in March 1967, and when Phil Williams nearly won Caerffili in June of the year following I was among the hundreds of canvassers.

All the same, I didn't want to spend all my energy working for the language while the political battle remained to be fought. I didn't agree with the analysis by Saunders Lewis which claimed that self-government would follow once the fortunes of the language had been secured, although I still believed in direct action on its behalf. Official status was a legitimate aim in my opinion, but it wasn't really my business to fight for it if others, particularly Welsh-speakers, were prepared to bestir themselves. It was more appropriate for Welsh-speakers, especially those living in the language's heartlands, to wake up from their long sleep and make more strenuous efforts on behalf of their own culture. I preferred to challenge the hegemony of the Labour Party in the industrial areas. It may be this argument will be rejected by many of this book's readers but there's a limit to what one person can do and it's prudent to share the work rather than try to fight on several fronts. I had challenged the law on several occasions, throwing myself in front of policemen and vehicles and causing damage to the property of the authorities such as the county councils and central government. I'd also acted unconstitutionally, sometimes in the dark and behind the scenes. It was now time for my Welsh-speaking countrymen to play a more active part.

My personal circumstances changed for the better when Ioan Bowen Rees stood as the Plaid Cymru candidate in Merthyr at the General Election of October 1964; I was his agent. Ioan polled 2,878 votes against 23,275 cast for the Labour candidate, the venerable S. O. Davies, and the Tory got 4,767. The election was memorable for me because this was when I met Ruth Wynn Meredith, Ioan's sister-in-law, who'd come to Merthyr from her home in Aberystwyth to help his campaign. I couldn't drive in those days, so Ruth took me over the mountain to Pentre in the Rhondda to collect boxes of electoral leaflets. Although I found myself attracted to her during that short trip – indeed, I was to be smitten within a few short weeks – I didn't know at the time that Ruth would be my wife before the next election, but so it turned out. Having got engaged the following Easter, and gone to Dublin to buy a ring, I suffered a bout of glandular fever and had to stay in bed at Ruth's parents' home for a fortnight. As a result, I missed a chance to be interviewed for the post of French master at Cyfarthfa School in Merthyr. The weakness used to recur from time to time, especially when I'd been overworking, but it hasn't for a long time now. We married at Tabernacl chapel in Aberystwyth on the 14th of August 1965. Ruth's father, the Reverend J. E. Meredith, and the Reverend Ifor Enoch took the service and John Davies (Bwlch-llan), in his Sunday suit and with his hair newly cut, was Best Man.

At the General Election held on the 31st of March 1966 I was the Plaid Cymru candidate in Merthyr and the slogan was 'Step ahead with Stephens!' In my campaign leaflet I called for a Coal Board for Wales, more heavy industry in the valleys, the teaching of new skills for our young people, better roads and shopping facilities, improved conditions for small businesses, a halt to depopulation, more cultural facilities such as theatres and galleries, and above all, an

Elected Council for Wales as a first step towards the creation of a Parliament. One afternoon, while canvassing high on the Gurnos estate, a woman asked me why Wales needed a Parliament, and I replied, 'To look after its own affairs.' The response came quick enough: 'Oh, we don't 'ave affairs up 'ere, love... It's too cold. We do all go down to Ponty for that.' And an old man told me, 'The thing you 'ave to remember about the people up 'ere is to yewer face they're all be'ind you and be'ind yewer back they're at yewer throat.' I received 3,361 votes and old S. O., as he always referred to himself, 21,737; the Tory got 4,082. On the night of the count I refused to shake hands with the Tory and when S. O. came out on to the balcony of the town hall I shouted defiantly 'Remember the Parliament for Wales, S. O!' But if I'm truthful, I was disappointed by this result – I'd hoped to keep my deposit, at least. And I decided there and then that I would never again seek a political career.

But I was ready to fight on another front. I had set up a publishing imprint called the Triskel Press in 1963 with the aim of publishing material that would appeal to Nationalists. Among the first titles had been the booklet *Caneuon Rhyddid Cymru / Songs of Welsh Freedom*, a collection of patriotic ballads that sold 300 copies in two months. It contained Harri's 'The Cross Foxes' which celebrated the night when, in Rhosllannerchrugog, a pub was drunk dry, and my own 'The Boys from Gwent' which became a favourite among the less abstemious of our compatriots. I also brought out Harri's pamphlet *Our National Anthem* and Peter Hourahane's *Names for the Welsh* which sold more than a thousand copies; I have met many people over the years who claim their parents found their names in this booklet and its successor, *Welsh Names for your Children*, collected by Ruth and revised by me; it's still in print.

But the most substantial publication was Gerald Morgan's book, *The Dragon's Tongue* (1966), a masterly study of the fortunes of the Welsh language in the public life of Wales.

Three thousand copies were printed and it sold at seven shillings and sixpence. About two hundred copies were sold before publication (I still have the list of subscribers). D. J. Williams bought a dozen and Jac L. Williams half a dozen. The only person to refuse to support my initiative was Sir Ifan ab Owen Edwards, founder of *Urdd Gobaith Cymru*, who wrote me quite a pompous letter that ended, *'Torchwch eich llewys, ddyn ifanc!'* (Roll your sleeve up, young man!) The sentence became a bit of a catchphrase in our family: David Meredith and I use it whenever we wish to josh each other into making greater efforts.

My main interest by 1965 was to find ways of promoting the culture of the English-speaking Welsh, especially their literature, by strengthening their awareness of belonging to the Welsh nation, and so my attention began to focus on the poets and prose-writers. The English-language literary scene in Wales was a stony desert in the early 1960s and it had to be developed so that English-speakers could begin to express themselves as Welsh people. Quite frankly, this was always my only ambition as an animateur. I began by bringing out a selection of my own poems together with a few by Peter Gruffydd and Harri Webb under the title *Triad* (1963). Some 500 copies sold within three months and it was followed by small selections of poems by Leslie Norris, John Tripp and Herbert Williams, three of the most prominent English-language poets in Wales in those days.

But the most important publication of the Triskel Press was undoubtedly the magazine *Poetry Wales*. I got the idea for the title from *Poetry Ireland*, edited by John Jordan, whom I'd met in a Dublin pub in 1962. The first number appeared in the spring of 1965, just before I married Ruth. The print-run consisted of 500 copies and it was printed by H. G. Walters in Narberth, for £47, and each copy sold at three shillings. Among the contributors were Roland Mathias, Harri Webb, Gwyn Jones, Peter Gruffydd, Herbert Williams and Alun Rees. The magazine was given a warm welcome by a number of Welsh-speakers, including Aneirin Talfan Davies, Jac L. Williams and Gerald Morgan. By the time the second number appeared in the autumn of 1965 the names of Dannie Abse, Anthony Conran, Leslie Norris, and Sally Roberts had been added to the list of contributors. In this number I published 'Ponies, Twynyrodyn', the poem of mine which has been reprinted more than any other of my poems. Gwilym Rees Hughes was the magazine's Welsh-language editor. I had Ruth's help from the second number on. Although she worked long hours in the laboratory at St Tydfil's Hospital, not far from our home in Courtland Terrace, she was always ready to use her administrative skills in dispatching copies to subscribers and shops in all parts of Wales and beyond. We managed to do this with the help of a very small grant from the Welsh Committee of the Arts Council of Great Britain (as it then was) that was barely enough to pay for the stamps.

But my commitment to living in Merthyr was starting to wane and I was looking for some other way of earning a livelihood. By the time the fifth number of *Poetry Wales* appeared in the winter of 1966 I'd left Ebbw Vale and Merthyr, and was living in Rhiwbina, one of the suburbs of north Cardiff. May I explain how this came about? The Head of French at Ebbw Vale was a man called Milwyn Jenkins, a native of Ynys-y-bŵl and, like me, a former pupil of the Boys' Grammar School in Pontypridd. He'd probably had a large say in my appointment because he knew I'd been taught by Jack Reynolds, who had a reputation as an excellent teacher. Although I got on well with Milwyn, he was not willing for me to take the sixth form because, in his view, that was his perogative. I therefore decided to leave Ebbw Vale and take a job with the *Western Mail* in Cardiff. *'Tenet insanabile multos scribendi cacoethes,'* said Juvenal: 'The itch to write affects many.' Quite right, too.

I was not sad to be leaving the school though I'd enjoyed getting to know some of the older pupils with whom I had more in common than with my middle-aged colleagues. On the last day of the summer term I was chatting with some of the sixth-formers, among whom were Patrick Harrington, now a successful barrister with chambers in Cardiff, Robat Powel, who won the Chair at the National Eisteddfod in 1985, and Greg Lynn Taylor, another barrister who sings with the Hwntws, and I learned from them the nicknames by which some of my colleagues were known. I got on well with these lads because we used to play records (mainly Irish rebel songs) behind the stage in the assembly hall during the lunch-hour and they'd come over to Merthyr to help when I stood in the General Election. I ventured to ask what my nickname was, expecting to get the answer Spike, the name by which I'd been known as a schoolboy, but no, they'd called me Noddy. When I asked why, they explained that I was in the habit, at four in the afternoon, of clearing the classrooms by clapping my hands and saying, 'Time to go home! Time to go home!' – exactly like the puppet on television. Strange what image a teacher projects unconsciously to his pupils.

During my last year at Ebbw Vale I'd made good progress in my efforts to acquire more of the Welsh language. I had great help from Ruth, who comes from a patriotic and liberal-minded family. She's a sensible, capable, patient and determined woman, loth to say an unkind word about anyone and ever true to her religious and political principles. It's quite ironic to think that she and I had to wait until 1964 before meeting, but while I was in Aberystwyth Ruth was in Bangor, and while I was in Bangor, she was in Aberystwyth working in the college's Zoology Department. From the time I first knew her, her parents never spoke to me in English because they knew I wanted to get a better grip on Welsh. I received a warm welcome in their cultured home in Llanbadarn Road, which helped my vocabulary to grow quickly. If today I speak a mixture of Glamorgan and Merioneth Welsh, I have Ruth and her family to thank for that. Even so, the process of achieving complete fluency was a very slow one. Years after we married, Ruth's mother told me she'd thought at first I was a quiet young man who suited her daughter well, but that she'd later realized I wasn't quiet, just short of Welsh vocabulary!

The same thing is true of Ruth's brothers and sister. I've never spoken English with John Wynn Meredith, a solicitor and until recently a Plaid Cymru member of Gwynedd County Council, nor with David Wynn Meredith, the former Head of Public Relations with HTV and S4C, nor Margaret, who was married to Ioan Bowen Rees. It was a heavy blow to us as a family when Ioan died in May 1999, two days before the first elections to the National Assembly. He'd been Chief Executive of Gwynedd County Council and had worked indefatigably as a thinker and writer about Devolution and local government in Wales for most of his life. Belonging through marriage to the Merediths and their extended family, who included Auntie Nannon, the wife of Gwynfor Evans, has been a great privilege and I'm grateful for their patience and friendship. It's a delight, too, to see members of the next generation, such as Gruff Rhys, Margaret's son, lead-singer with the Super Furry Animals, making their mark in the cultural life of Wales, and the other Gruff, David's son, the rapper, who goes by the name M. C. Mabon.

By the time Ruth and I had moved to Cardiff in August 1966 so that I could work in Thomson House, she was expecting our first child. Lowri Angharad was born on the 27th of October, a few days after the tragedy of Aber-fan. Indeed, I was mooching about the village when I received a message from another reporter that Ruth had gone into labour. I shall never forget what I saw in the chapel where the little bodies were being kept and I find it difficult to write about it or see it on television without tears welling up in my eyes; I shall move on now without going into detail. There was no way of phoning home (this was before the days of mobile phones) and there were no buses or trains running in the valley. There was nothing for it but to hitch a lift to

Cardiff in a Gas Board van and, not without difficulty, reach the maternity hospital about twenty minutes before Lowri was born.

I didn't have another day half as distressing as those I spent in Aber-fan while working for the *Western Mail*. The paper's policy was to give the dullest stories to its junior staff. Among those who joined the same day as me were Tom Davies, who later went to the *Sunday Times* and became a novelist; Geraint Talfan Davies, who worked in the media in England before returning to Wales as Controller of BBC Wales; Ian Edwards, who had a career in public relations in Wimbledon; and Alun Michael, who became a Labour politician in the National Assembly and at Westminster, joined the *South Wales Echo* at about the same time. In those days the paper sold about 100,000 copies daily – compared with 25,000 or fewer today – and it was generally regarded as a quality and authoritative newspaper, believe it or not.

The only other person I can recall, apart from Beata Lipman, who used to come into the newsroom every day and wipe down her desk, chair and typewriter, as though they were infected, and Michael Lloyd Williams, a Rhondda man who was kind to me, is John Humphries – not the John Humphrys who asks the questions on *Mastermind* but a Newport man who was the paper's news editor at the time. John had a very sharp tongue for anyone who'd been to university or who spoke Welsh or came from 'North Wales' which, in his view, was the *terra incognita* to the north of Brecon.

For a few weeks in the winter of 1966/67 I was put in charge of the paper's office in Newport. One evening, about nine o'clock, I was told to go to Cwmbrân to speak to a woman who'd phoned Thomson House to say the fire brigade was trying to rescue her cat, which was stuck in the upper branches of a tree in her garden. By the time I reached her home by taxi this exciting event had ended, but I managed to have a word with the woman and write the story before phoning my copy over and catching the last train from

Newport to Cardiff. Then, around midnight, as I was about to go to bed, the phone rang and it was John asking me for the name of the cat. On hearing that I hadn't got this vital detail, he ordered me to go up to Cwmbrân again, despite the late hour, and get it. About an hour and a half later I rang the news desk and said, wearily, 'Tibby'. John's reaction was typical: 'I don't believe you. You Welsh graduates make things up'; then he slammed the phone down. The story appeared in the paper next day in the News in Brief column – but neither the reporter nor the cat was mentioned by name!

It was a great surprise for me to learn, in his book *Freedom Fighters* (2008), that John Humphries, who went on to become the *Western Mail's* editor, was a Nationalist of the most extreme kind, an admirer of groups such as the Free Wales Army and Mudiad Amddiffyn Cymru. I never saw any sign of his patriotic fervour while on the paper's staff, I must say. Indeed, his contemptuous attitude to things Welsh was one of the reasons why I made up my mind to leave Lord Thomson's employ at the first opportunity.

The chance came sooner than I expected. In April 1967 I happened to call at the offices of the Welsh Committee of the Arts Council in Museum Place, on the scout for news, when I heard from the Director, Aneurin M. Thomas, that the Council was intending to create a new post, that of Assistant Director with responsibility for Drama and Poetry.

Now this sounded like a job much more to my liking, and that evening I began to draft an application for it. Islwyn Ffowc Elis, Roland Mathias and John Stuart Williams agreed to write references for me and I also had the support of Glyn Jones, Gwilym R. Jones, Vernon Watkins, D. J. Williams, Tudor David, D. Gwenallt Jones, Gerald Morgan, Alun Talfan Davies, and Dewi-Prys Thomas; it's a sobering thought that all of these, with the happy exception of Gerald Morgan, are no longer in the land of the living. In due course I submitted my application and, in July, went for an interview in Museum Place. The panel consisted of Gwyn Jones, my old English Professor; T. J. Morgan, Professor of Welsh in Swansea and Chairman of the panel with responsibility for Drama and Poetry; Iorwerth Howells, Director of Education in Carmarthenshire; and Miss Evelyn Ward, a former English teacher who had nurtured the talents of the young actor Kenneth Griffith. In the evening after the panel's meeting, to my great joy, I heard from Aneurin Thomas that I'd been successful. Here was a splendid chance to serve Wales and its literature, in both languages. After a week at the National Eisteddfod in Bala, and a trip to Galway with Ruth and Lowri, I took up my post on the 4th of September 1967.

5

The View from Museum Place

I WAS WITH the Welsh Arts Council from September 1967 to July 1990. As I had special responsibility for Literature, I shall deal here only with the work of the Literature Committee. If it happens that my memory, or my desk-diaries, prove to be faulty, the reader is referred to the Council's Annual Reports and the Committee's minutes, all of which are kept in the National Library.

While I was at the Arts Council I had the help of a number of Literature Officers, administrative personnel and secretaries who were of great assistance in implementing the Literature Committee's schemes, particularly as the workload grew from year to year. I remember especially Fay Williams, Gwenith Morgan, Fiona Lloyd Lewis, Rhiannon Watkiss, Elan Closs Roberts (who married Roy Stephens), Siân Edwards, Gwerfyl Pierce Jones, Peter Finch, Gwyneth Evans, Roger Jones Williams, Sue Harries, Nan Griffiths, and Tony Bianchi. I was really fortunate to have such excellent colleagues. We had our tribulations but on the whole the Literature Department was a happy and busy one all the time I was its Head. I kept my secretaries with plenty to do on account of my writing letters and memoranda at home and asking for them to be typed up next morning.

1967–1972

The Literature Committee's Chairman during these pioneer years was T. J. Morgan, Professor of Welsh at University College, Swansea. From the start he gave me a free hand to devise and develop policies and administrative procedures for expenditure of the Council's funds. As part of the Welsh Committee of the Arts Council of Great Britain, the Drama and Poetry Panel had had very little to spend. But after a change was made in the Royal Charter early in 1967, Literature had joined 'the fine arts' that were eligible for subsidy and the Panel became the Literature Committee.

At the Committee's first meeting on the 5th of October 1967 it was recommended that small grants be offered to *Y Genhinen* and *The Anglo-Welsh Review*, and a guarantee against loss was offered to John Idris Jones for a poetry reading he was organizing in the Reardon Smith Lecture Theatre in Cardiff. Consideration of a number of applications for grant-in-aid to publishers was postponed pending a clarification of the Council's purview. It came as something of a disappointment when the Council refused to accept the Literature Committee's suggestion that prizes and bursaries should be offered to writers. This was at the insistence of the Council's Chairman, Gwyn Jones, who, wagging that famous finger I'd seen before, took the view that such 'largesse' had not existed when he was a young writer and to spend money in this way, he thought, would be a waste of public funds. It thus became evident that we should have to wait for a more enlightened attitude on the Chairman's part and this came about when Sir William Crawshay succeeded Gwyn Jones later in the year.

One of the factors that prevented the Literature Committee from taking a clear view of what its function might be was that the Arts Council wasn't the only patron in the Wales of 1967. I saw at once that it would have to discover how best to spend its funds without duplicating the work of other bodies such as the University of Wales Press Board (which administered the Government grant to Welsh books for adults), the Welsh Joint Education Committee (subsidy to Welsh books for children), and the Welsh Books Council which was already offering publishers grants for books of a popular nature.

I immediately set about writing a long memorandum with the title 'The Literature of Wales: a Preliminary Survey', and it was this hefty document that served as a framework for the Literature Committee's work over the next few years. The Council's aim would be: 'to lay the foundations for a new environment in which writers in Welsh and English would be able to enjoy the financial acknowledgement that is their due as creative artists; in which publishers would be helped to raise their standards; and in which the public would be provided with a better service from the publishers and booksellers of Wales.' This was the document in which I sketched a number of projects that, in my opinion, the Council could launch in addition to those already administered by the National Eisteddfod, the University of Wales Press, the National Library, the literary societies, the Union of Welsh Publishers and Booksellers, and the literary magazines. In short, we had to define what the Council could and couldn't do that would give it a unique place in the system of patronage already in existence.

By the time the Committee met in the new financial year, 1968/69, the Council had earmarked the sum of £20,000 for Literature. It was fairly easy to reach agreement on the following: £3,000 for magazines, £3,000 as production grants for books, £3,000 as prizes and bursaries, £2,500 for book design, £2,000 for translations, £2,500 for Yr Academi Gymreig, £1,600 for records, £1,000 for the purchase of manuscripts, £1,000 for commemorative plaques, and £400 for poetry readings. In the event, we managed to spend about £18,000.

I'd mentioned the creation of an English-language section of Yr Academi Gymreig, the national association of writers in Wales, at my interview. One of the first things I did after getting my feet under the desk was write to sixty English-language writers asking for their approval of the Welsh Rule at the National Eisteddfod, under which all activity had to be in the Welsh language and which was in jeopardy from a few Welsh-speaking individuals who were calling for a bilingual festival. The letter went out in the name of Harri Webb but it was I who wrote it. This move helped to build bridges between Welsh-language writers and their compatriots writing in English and to dispel the suspicion that had existed on both sides of the language divide since the days of Caradoc Evans. It wasn't long before I was able to discuss with members of the Academi, among whom Bobi Jones was prominent, my proposal for the creation of an English-language section. As a result, I wrote to the same writers again, this time inviting them to attend a meeting in Swansea on the 10th of April 1968. Among those present at the meeting was D. J. Williams, who had done time for his action in Penyberth and who was enthusiastic about welcoming English-language writers to the Academi's ranks. He began addressing the meeting with the words, 'Please excuse my English – I learnt it in Wormwood Scrubs!', after which the ice quickly melted and everyone got on famously.

The first meeting of the section was held in the Park Hotel, Cardiff, on the 9th of November 1968. Glyn Jones spoke about his book *The Dragon Has Two Tongues*, Gerald Morgan read from his anthology *This World of Wales* and the veteran Jack Jones sang us a song he'd learned as a schoolboy in Merthyr. Almost all English-language writers had agreed to become members of the Academi. There was only one discordant voice, that of a tipsy Menna Gallie, who walked out of the room for some reason that remains obscure to this day. She was never seen at the Academi's meetings again.

Although the sums earmarked for Literature seem small now, we had made a good start: the literary culture of Wales had begun to benefit from the resources of the British state.

We were criticized in some quarters for receiving money from this source, especially in the satirical magazine *Lol*, which could be funny though wide of the mark at times, but slowly criticism from this quarter began to subside. I personally looked upon the money that came our way, which was really money paid by the people of Wales in taxes, as reparations for some of the damage done to our country's culture over the centuries.

My main problem was to get the publishers to understand what their responsibilities were as recipients of the funds. More particularly, Alun Talfan Davies, the owner of Llyfrau'r Dryw/Christopher Davies, one of the major publishers in those days, gave the impression that he expected favours in return for having supported my application for the post of Literature Director; asking him to do so had been a serious mistake on my part. We also had difficulties almost immediately with Gwasg y Sir, publishers of the weekly magazine *Y Faner*, which they claimed sold 7,000 copies a week. I know, too, that certain writers who'd been awarded bursaries, especially those who hadn't written or published books, took advantage of the Council's scheme. But there we are: patronage from the public purse was something new in the cultural life of Wales and we all had to learn how to handle it. I remember Caradog Prichard, for example, asking me at the National Eisteddfod to write him a cheque for £300 on the spot, so that he and his wife Mattie (not to mention the poodle) could go on holiday to Cornwall, and being most put out when I explained things didn't work like that.

Fortunately, I wasn't required to attend meetings of the Arts Council of Great Britain's Literature Panel, because it had a very different role in the literary life of England; nevertheless, I went up to London from time to time. I remember one meeting in particular at which I met Richard Hoggart, author of *The Uses of Literacy*, and the poet Robert Graves. I shared a taxi with Graves and, a few days later, received a letter in which he complained that his famous book

The White Goddess had been shunned by scholars in Wales. He was also anxious to let me know that he was familiar with Welsh literature: among the things he told me was 'I know all the rules of Senghenydd'. On another occasion I received an apology from Robert Mugabe. I was killing time in Poets' Corner in Westminster Abbey when I saw a posse of large men in black suits and sunglasses coming towards me, so I stepped aside to let them pass. As they went by, the chap in the middle smiled at me and said, 'I beg your pardon'. Another reason for not attending meetings of the Literature Panel in London was the presence of Charles Osborne, the Literature Director, a supercilious little fellow. When I suggested Euros Bowen as a representative of Wales in his annual show Poetry International, he turned my suggestion down because, in his opinion, Euros, a most sophisticated poet, was 'one of the country bumpkins from Wales'.

Support for magazines, one of the Literature Committee's priorities, increased: *Poetry Wales*, *The Anglo-Welsh Review*, *Y Traethodydd*, *Taliesin* and *Barn* all received grant-aid. A series of annual anthologies was launched as well as *Writers of Wales*, with R. Brinley Jones and me as co-editors. I worked happily with Brinley, Director of the University of Wales Press, for many years and several books were published that were the fruit of our close co-operation. The Young Poets competition was won by Nesta Wyn Jones and an Englishman named Glyn Hughes, whom we mistakenly took to be Welsh. A grant of £750 was given to Gregynog, the University of Wales centre in Powys, for the purpose of appointing a Fellow and the English writer B. S. Johnson, whom I knew from *Universities' Poetry* days, became the first recipient of the award. The Books Council held a Books Fair for the first time, paid for by the Arts Council. More than 600 people listened to Dial-a-Poem / Clywch-y-Beirdd every week. This scheme was devised after I visited Friesland in the Netherlands, where I picked up a number of ideas that I was able to implement in Wales; the Oriel Bookshop was another. The Literature Committee began to show an interest in book design at this time, too, a badly needed intervention because the standard of book-design in Wales at the time was pretty lamentable. A number of other ideas ran into the sand, such as the attempt to purchase manuscripts, but at least the Committee was prepared to experiment, and I was glad about that.

The main event of 1969 was the Taliesin Conference when writers from Ireland, Scotland and Brittany came to Wales: Austin Clarke, Máirtin Ó Cadhain, Ronan Huon, Per Denez, Maodez Glanndour, Somhairlie MacGill-eain (Sorley MacLean), Hugh MacDiarmid, and Ruaraidh MacThòmais (Derick Thomson). The lectures were published by the University of Wales Press as *Literature in Celtic Countries* under the editorship of J. E. Caerwyn Williams, a splendid scholar who knew all six Celtic languages.

The Academi now began receiving grants towards its administrative costs and the Writers in Schools project began. The photographer Julian Sheppard was commissioned to take photographs of some of the most distinguished writers of Wales; many of his pictures (the negatives are now housed in the National Library) are to be seen in the press and on television nowadays. I shall never forget visiting David Jones in his room at Harrow-on-the-Hill. During an hour-long conversation, while Julian was taking photos of him, I spotted a copy of *Welsh Nation*, Plaid Cymru's newspaper, on a table piled high with books and papers, and said, 'I'd have thought that would have been a bit extreme for you, Mr Jones,' to which he replied, 'Oh no, not extreme enough!' – the influence of his friend Saunders Lewis, more than likely. Then there was the poet Waldo Williams, in the schoolyard at Goodwick, with little boys all around him so obviously fond of their teacher. A substantial grant was given to the Books Council for setting up Editorial, Design and Publicity Departments, and to the BBC for a series of long poems for radio. The first number of the magazine *Planet* appeared in

August 1970 with the financial support of the Arts Council, and almost immediately some of the Welsh Members of Parliament began complaining about the magazine's 'political content'. Prominent among them were Wil Edwards, Leo Abse, Goronwy Roberts, Gwynoro Jones and the Tory Wyn Roberts. They gave the impression that what was rattling them was the fact that criticism of the Government was being published in English and so was available for all to read. Mind you, the cartoon of George Thomas on the cover of the first number of *Planet* did nothing to dispel the claim that the Council's subsidy could be construed as 'political'. At about this time the Secretary of State for Wales, Peter Thomas, received a complaint from Keidrych Rhys that the Literature Committee was a front for the Free Wales Army and I was its Commandant!

One evening in January 1971 I happened to meet a group of writers from the Soviet Union in the lounge of the Park Hotel in Cardiff, among whom were Sergei Narovchatov, editor of the influential literary magazine *Novy Mir* and member of the Supreme Soviet; Giorgi Gulia, the editor of *Literaturnaya Gazeta*, the country's main literary periodical; Mikhail Dudin, a poet who had taken part in the siege of Leningrad; and another poet who went by the splendid name, or pseudonym, of Maxim Tank. Their 'minder' was Anatoly Melnikov, a notorious free-loader who was more interested in shopping than in literature. After chatting to these men for about an hour, I offered to take them up the Rhondda Valley next day, since Narachatov wanted to see whether he could find the Rhondda miner who had sat with him around a bonfire during the war. We had a lovely day on the Valley's streets and in the cafés, and people invited us into their homes and treated the visitors with their usual warmth, curiosity and enthusiasm.

The four visitors also wanted to meet the novelist Gwyn Thomas because they were great admirers of his novel *All Things Betray Thee*, which is set in Wales at the time of the

Merthyr Riots of 1831. We invited Gwyn and his wife to have supper with our new friends that evening, and it turned into a lively literary session. Around midnight, our three-year-old daughter Heledd came downstairs in her pyjamas and plaits and sat next to Gwyn, who was drinking a pint of beer. 'What is that?' she asked in her best English. 'Pop,' answered Gwyn. 'Are you liking pop?' she asked. 'Yes,' said Gwyn. 'A lot?' asked Heledd. 'Yes, a lot,' said Gwyn. 'Too much?' asked Heledd. 'Yes,' said Gwyn, with tears bowling down his cheeks, 'too much.' The child's innocent observation was too near the mark.

A few months later I received an invitation to visit the Soviet Union and from then on, usually with Welsh writers such as Brian Morris, Harri Pritchard Jones, R. Gerallt Jones, Roland Mathias, Peter Finch, Wynn Thomas, Michael Parnell and Gillian Clarke, I became a regular visitor. We were taken almost every time to Georgia, and to Abkhazia, where Giorgi Gulia was revered as the son of the man who'd edited the first newspaper in the Abkhazian language soon after the Bolshevik Revolution of October 1917. I spent weeks in the Caucasus and began to understand something of the myriad languages that are spoken there. I remember on one occasion we were met at the airport by a young woman who greeted us with the words, 'I your translator am. My name is Titsianna, my friends are calling me Anna,' to which the incorrigible Brian Morris responded, 'Well, they would, wouldn't they?' It was from Brian, a leading Anglican and Principal of St David's University College, Lampeter, I heard the observation that Eternity is a pretty boring prospect – 'so long and so little to do'. Ionesco, whom I took to Lampeter during his visit to Wales, used to refer to Lampeter as *le village universitaire*.

On another visit I went with Ruth to Svaneti, a community of about 25,000 people speaking their own language, high up in the mountains, where until 1945 they had worshiped the sun and had no wheels in their culture. We saw ibex on the road outside the hotel and eagles circling above Mestia, the only sizeable village. Elbruz, a mountain of about 18,000 feet, was shining in the distance. I learned a bit of Georgian, phrases such as *Sakartvelo mudam!* (Georgia forever!) and *Karchima jós!* (Forward!) which I haven't forgotten. I wonder how much Georgian the Newport M.P. Roy Hughes picked up during his visit? One morning, as we came down for breakfast from the eighteenth floor, Ruth and I were chatting in the lift in the hearing of a group of M.Ps. from Britain and, as we reached the ground floor, I heard Roy Hughes say to one of his colleagues, 'You know, this Georgian language sounds a bit like the Welsh we have back home.'

I felt very close to quite a few individuals I met in Georgia, and despite the obvious differences between us, saw enough resemblances to suggest we are essentially all brothers and sisters. Among the poets I remember Josef Nonashvili and Grigor Abashidze. I've followed the difficult relationship between Georgia and Russia ever since, always siding with the smaller nation, of course. It became more difficult when the conflict was between Georgia and Abkhazia, with Russia intervening for its own advantage.

On another visit to Tbilisi, in the company of Gerallt Jones and Gillian Clarke, I caught the sun on the roof of the Iveria Hotel and, as a consequence, I don't remember much about the next stage of our journey, in a ramshackle plane, to Samarkand, where I spent three days lying in a bath of yogurt. On the other hand, I had the unforgettable experience of hearing Gillian, at the pool's side, declaiming over and over again the famous line by James Elroy Flecker, 'We take the Golden Road to Samarkand.' Come to think of it, not everyone has seen the National Poet of Wales in a bathing suit.

I also went to Finland with a group of writers who included Sam Adams, Gwyn Williams, Pennar Davies (and wife) and John Rowlands; Sue Harries, the Academi's English-language officer, was with us. I had the great privilege of spending several hours during the conference chatting to the French poet Eugène Guillevic. We went to the Åland Islands which belong to Finland but where Swedish is spoken. There, on a lonely beach, we built a huge bonfire on the shortest day of the year, and saw the sun go down low in the sky but not below the horizon, and aurora borealis flashing overhead, one of the most stunning sights to be seen on earth. The Welsh contribution to the entertainment around the bonfire was dancing the hokey-cokey and convincing our Finnish hosts that this was an ancient Celtic custom, and fair play, Pennar joined in the fun in his usual lofty manner.

But to return to the grants. It was about this time that the Literature Committee's budget began to increase by about ten per cent every year. An essential part of my work was to prepare memoranda and estimates; drawing up the final budget, showing the precise sums for all our projects, usually took a whole weekend to prepare. By now I'd learned how to write the minutes of the Literature Committee and its Panels, as well as for numerous working-parties and meetings with clients. I enjoyed this aspect of the work and discovered, to my surprise, that I was something of a bureaucrat. But it meant spending more time working at home than was good for my health, and the old glandular fever returned almost every winter. The favourite game of Lowri and her two sisters, Heledd and Brengain, who were born in 1968 and 1969 respectively, was 'Daddy in the office', to my great embarrassment. From time to time one of them would ask, 'What are you doing, Dad?' and I would answer, 'Writing a memorandum.' For this reason the study became known in our house as the 'memorandroom'.

I don't want to give the impression here that meetings of the Literature Committee always went entirely smoothly. There were very heated discussions from time to time and voices were raised. I remember D. Tecwyn Lloyd reacting most ferociously to an application from Alexander Cordell for a novel competition of which, he proposed, he would be the sole adjudicator. There was a long discussion before the Committee recommended grant-aid to Gwasg Gregynog in which some members expressed the view that the production of finely printed books in limited editions was a rather elitist way of spending public money. I struggled hard to persuade members to offer grant-aid to *Y Faner*, only to find that the publishers were unable to submit an application that was comprehensive and credible, particularly as to how many copies of the newspaper they sold: the answer was different each time we asked the question, depending on whether they wanted to show a loss or profit. We failed to find a way of helping the National Eisteddfod supplement its main literary prizes such as the Chair, Crown and Prose Medal; there was enough money in the festival's coffers to do this without subsidies, according to Tom Parry, who was presumed to have insider knowledge.

Some of the members were suspicious of the suggestion that the Literature Committee should co-operate with the Art Committee in establishing the Oriel bookshop-gallery. But eventually the Committee decided to give serious attention to a memorandum by Raymond Garlick, 'The Final Link', that is to say the link between author and reader, the bookshop. The Committee spent hours discussing the Council's definition of 'creative literature' and whether the Arts Council should support magazines like *Barn*, which was not wholly literary in the strict sense. The famous question was: 'When Kate Roberts writes about jam-making, is it Literature?' Nor was there unanimity about the Regional Arts Associations and their policies for Literature.

Because it had to disappoint a large number of applicants, the Committee began to attract a swarm of critics; this was a sign of good health as far as I was concerned, but on the other hand, it was a waste of time while the complaints were so groundless and the criticism so wide of the mark. The Chairman's attitude was not to answer our critics back: in the words of Kipling, 'The answer is that we have got / The Gatling gun and they have not.' Alun Richards said something similar on one of HTV's programmes: 'Unless you are prepared and able to be at least as well informed as the Welsh Arts Council itself, you will never be able to land anything more than glancing blows.' The words that came to my mind more often than not were *Aquila non captat muscas* (The eagle does not catch flies), the motto of A. E. Housman's family, but I could hardly quote them to our critics.

And so the Literature Committee's work went on at full pelt, with me learning how to stay in the saddle from year to year, while at the same time (changing the metaphor) trying to lay foundations on which the Arts Council could build. The view from Museum Place began to grow clearer.

1973–1976

The Chairman of the Literature Committee during this phase was Dr Glyn Tegai Hughes, the Warden of Gregynog in Powys. Glyn, as Vice-Chairman under T. J. Morgan, had made keen contributions to our discussions up to now, but tended to be more hands-on than his predecessor, who'd been content to let me get on with it for weeks on end. The new Chairman was a lot more determined to have his own way.

What's more, Glyn had been suspicious of me, especially after I wrote a memorandum, 'The Publishing of Books in Wales Today: towards a National Publishing House', in June 1970. The idea of creating a well-funded and fully-staffed publishing house, to replace a motley band of small publishers who failed to maintain professional standards, held great appeal for me but was anathema to the Liberal in Glyn because he believed the creation of a national publishing house would be tantamount to 'nationalizing' the publishing industry in Wales. Anyway, Glyn succeeded in arguing against the idea and, in the end, it was knocked on its head. But out of this discussion came the decision to fund the four departments of the Books Council – a sort of *de facto* nationalization, I suppose, since the Council depended wholly on subsidy – so my efforts were not in vain after all. Glyn and I became more friendly thereafter, particularly during the attempt to revive the Gregynog Press when we had to work together.

By 1973 the Literature Committee's budget had increased to £89,500 but the pioneer days were over. Even so, there was plenty of work still to do. The Committee asked several times for its allocation of the Council's funds to be increased to about ten per cent, so that its schemes could be adequately financed, but this never happened. The Council's attitude seemed to be summed up in the words of Sidney Smith, 'We cultivate literature on a little oatmeal'. No wonder there were Oliver Twists asking for more!

Let me give some more statistics. The Welsh Arts Council's grant from the Arts Council of Great Britain in 1973/74 was £1,152,430. Opera was given £316,000, Drama £275,150, Music £148,480, the Regional Arts Associations £109,000, Literature 89,500, Art £63,420 and music festivals £34,020. The Literature Committees in Scotland and Northern Ireland were envious of their Welsh counterpart and several meetings took place at which we discussed the situation with Trevor Royle and Michael Longley, my counterparts in those countries; over the years I became friendly with Trevor and Michael. Trevor is now a distinguished military historian and Michael one of Ireland's most important poets.

It was in Trevor's company that I first met Hugh MacDiarmid in November 1972 and again in June 1973 when we went to his cottage near Biggar in Lanarkshire. Then, in 1974, the poet and his wife came to stay with us while on a visit to Wales. One evening I asked whether he'd like to meet Glyn Jones. Now this was a bit imprudent of me because the Scot had taken a section of a short story by Glyn and published it as one of his own poems. There had been a long correspondence in the *Times Literary Supplement* as to whether this was plagiarism. But there was no need to worry. When MacDiarmid came into the room, Chris (his real name was Christopher Murray Grieve) shook hands with Glyn and said, 'My wife thinks a meeting between you and me might prove an embarrassment. But I'm not embarrassed. Are you?' Glyn, grinning broadly, replied, 'No, I'm not embarrassed, why should I be?' The two poets then sat down, one with a glass of his favourite Glenfiddich and the other with an orange juice, and there took place one of the most lively discussions ever to be held in our house.

The Literature Committee's work went on as before. I took a break in April 1973 when I went to Yugoslavia for ten days as a guest of the Government there, although it turned out to be a bit of a busman's holiday as I was taken around the offices of various cultural organizations, publishers, newspapers, writers' organizations, and libraries in Belgrade, Zagreb, Macedonia, Vojvodina and Kosovo. During this trip I had the strange experience of seeing a performance of *Jesus Christ, Superstar!* in Serbo-Croat. I heard nothing to suggest that Yugoslavia had any of the ethnic problems that in due course would tear it apart, because visitors were kept in a sort of corridor, far from anyone or anything that might suggest otherwise. In the year following a delegation of Yugoslav writers came to the Academi conference and Gwyn Thomas went to represent Wales at the International Poetry Festival in Struga, Macedonia. Among the poets I met in Sarajevo was Izet Sarajlić, the greatest poet of Bosnia Hercegovina since the Second World War. He would be in the city during the terrible siege by the Serbs between 1992 and 1996; he lost his wife and sister and died in 2002 at the age of 72. As I write this chapter I see Ratko Mladić has been captured and will soon be joining Radovan Karadžic in The Hague. Men like that get nationalism a bad name.

I also went to Quebec in 1975 and Stockholm in 1975 with the intention of gathering information about patronage for writers in Canada and Sweden. In the same year a number of publishers were sent to the International Books Fair in Frankfurt. Among the poets I got to know was Ivan Malinovski, a Danish poet living near Reftele in the south of Sweden (not far from Ystad where Kurt Wallander catches criminals). We went to stay with him and his wife Ruth, a carpet designer and weaver whose work was in great demand. Ivan, one of Denmark's most famous poets, was a very taciturn man. He told me he wrote his poems while sitting on a huge boulder in the forest. He and Ruth were Communists and had been members of the Resistance in Denmark. When I asked Ruth what she had done during the war, she grabbed me by my nape, put two fingers to my temple and replied with a snarl, 'I kill very much Germans!'. But in truth they were both very gentle, kind, hospitable people. Their daughter, Nina Malinovski, is a poet, dramatist and film-maker.

During my vist to Stockholm I met Liv Ullmann, the Norwegian actress whom I admire a lot. Indeed, I had the pleasure of dancing with her – for about three minutes. 'Where are you from?' she asked me, her blue eyes smiling at me. 'From Wales,' I replied. Then it was someone else's turn. Next day, in a bookshop where she was signing copies of her book *Forandringen* (later published as *Changing*), I joined the queue and eventually stood before her waiting for my copy to be signed. 'Where are you from?' she asked. 'From Wales,' I said again. And then it was someone else's turn. Heigh-ho!

In November 1973 we organized an exhibition to commemorate Dylan Thomas, twenty years after his death, and Peter Finch was appointed manager of the Oriel Bookshop. Peter was already well-known as a poet and editor of the magazine *Second Aeon* but from now on he was to become a leading bookseller, too. Oriel kept in stock every Welsh book currently in print, as well as magazines, records and posters. His responsibility was not only the selling of books but organizing a programme of literary activities, including poetry readings and a series of poster-poems, and he did this with commitment and enthusiasm, growing all the while into an exceptionally able arts administrator. Peter retired from his post as Chief Executive of the Academi and its successor Literature Wales in June 2011.

'Literature flourishes best when it is half a trade and half an art,' said William Ralph Inge, and the Committee saw some truth in the Dean of St Paul's observation. If the books of Wales were going to reach readers then bookshops would have to be supported: we needed better shops and more of them. To this end the Committee began offering grants to shops in various parts of the country, although this scheme was not really successful. Patronage from a public source and the requirements of small private businesses didn't always lie comfortably together and so the scheme was discontinued after a year or two.

The French dramatist Eugène Ionesco came to Wales in October 1974 to receive the International Writer's Prize and we organized a full programme of events in the University Colleges. Alexander Cordell immediately attacked the Council because, he said, we shouldn't be giving money to UNESCO! I had to go on television to explain in words of one syllable that he'd misheard, and as a consequence Ruth and I were invited to dine at Llanfair Court, near Abergavenny, the home of Sir William Crawshay. He strongly disapproved of Cordell on account of his portrait of William Crawshay, the ironmaster of Cyfarthfa, in his novel *Rape of the Fair Country*. His opinion of my part in the television programme was 'Capital! Capital!' – the first time I'd ever heard that expression. It was from Ionesco that I heard *le zizi pan-pan*, a slang expression used to describe the sexual act.

Mairwen Gwynn Jones was commissioned to prepare a report on how the Literature Committee could extend its support for children's literature. The Council was already giving bursaries to the authors of children's books, grants towards the cost of publishing them, and prizes to their authors. Her typically long, thorough and inclusive memorandum led, in due course, to the establishment of the Children's Literature Panel under her enthusiastic chairmanship. This was the beginning of a new phase in the patronage offered by Council to a vital sector of our country's literature.

110

Although the Committee strove hard to keep a balance in its expenditure on the two literatures of Wales, it wasn't always possible. In the Young Poets Competition, for example, which was won by Tony Curtis, Duncan Bush and Nigel Jenkins, the adjudicators were unable to choose Welsh-language poets because the standard was so low. Even so, the Committee's hope was that the two languages would get equal sums spent on them. I had two Literature Officers now, namely Pamela Parry-Jones (English) and Gwerfyl Pierce Jones (Welsh); Pamela was soon followed by Sue Harries. After leaving the Arts Council in due course, Gwerfyl had a successful career as Director of the Welsh Books Council and Sue as head of the English-language section of the Academi. The Literature Committee's budget had now increased to £187,500.

The question of what to do about *Y Faner* dragged on from meeting to meeting, an albatross around our necks. The Council rejected a recommendation from the Committee that it be offered grant-aid because it believed subsidy from public funds should not be given to newspapers. But in order to help the paper in some small way a grant was given to a booklet of excerpts from its pages. The publishers made little or no attempt to publicize the booklet and it sold pitifully few copies. It seemed as if the newspaper's days were drawing to a close as a consequence of a lack of initiative on the part of the publishers and lack of support on the public's.

It was then decided to start afresh by asking Council to reconsider whether it could offer subsidy to newspapers. At the same time, Glyn Tegai Hughes drew attention to the considerable difficulties encountered by the Committee in dealing with the publishers of *Y Faner*, an old radical Liberal paper that had an honourable place in the history of Welsh literature. Among the matters he highlighted were the weekly's poor quality, which was very unsatisfactory in the opinion of many; a lack of precise information about its production costs and circulation, since it was both printed and published by Gwasg y Sir in Bala and there were no credible sales figures; the abilities of its editors, Gwilym R. Jones and Mathonwy Hughes, both of whom were now well beyond pensionable age; and its political slant which was more and more in sympathy with one party, Plaid Cymru. Bedwyr Lewis Jones and Glyn Tegai Hughes, both of whom had played prominent parts in discussions about funding *Y Faner*, took the view that the paper's standards left a good deal to be desired, and the matter was left on the table. At the same time a grant of £5,600 was offered to the editor of *Y Cymro*, another weekly paper, for an arts supplement, but this was refused because, in the view of the owners, it would not have been proper for a newspaper to receive financial support from a public body. Why ask, then?

Ruth had an accident at Gregynog in 1974. We'd been staying the night there on our way north and, while I was at a late-night meeting of the Press Board, she tripped on a piece of old carpet and fell headlong down a flight of stairs, dislocating her shoulder. There was no doctor in the vicinity and so I had to drive her across country to hospital in Shrewsbury. We came back to Gregynog just as dawn was breaking. After resting for about an hour, Ruth was still in pain and so we decided to make for home before breakfast. But as we passed the refectory there awaiting us was a bill for a night's accommodation and breakfast. I was advised by friends and colleagues to take Gregynog to court on account of the lamentable state of its carpet, but Ruth was against it.

The Gregynog Press Board was the most miserable committee I ever had to attend. I'd been enthusiastic about resurrecting the Press and had defended it against those on the Literature Committee who were not in favour of giving it grant-aid. The Board's Chairman was Lord Kenyon, an old toff so deaf and short-sighted that there was no point trying to draw his attention to anything because he ignored everyone except Glyn Tegai. His main delight was swanking about the fine editions in his library and we all had to listen while he went on and on about them. At one meeting he began laying into Ioan Bowen Rees, the Chief Executive of Gwynedd County Council, Ruth's sister's husband, on account of his support for devolution. The other members knew full well that I was related to Ioan but nothing was said until I interrupted the Chairman with: 'I think you're being scurrilous, Chairman. I suggest we move on to the next item on the agenda.' It's sad how the Welsh can be so servile in the presence of old Tories like Kenyon. *Ça ira, ça ira, ça ira...*

There was friction sometimes not only between the Literature Committee and those in receipt of the Council's funds, or those who were applicants, but also between Committee members themselves. I knew Sir Thomas Parry was against sending Welsh writers to countries under Communist rule and just as adamant about not welcoming writers from those countries to Wales. There was a lively debate about this: Tom Parry's proposition was lost six votes to ten, with one abstention, and so it was agreed to continue with what I considered an important scheme. Sir Thomas left the Committee shortly afterwards. It was quite consistent and honourable of him to refuse one of the Council's main Prizes in 1976: his contribution to scholarship had already been acknowledged by the University of Wales, he said, and what was more, he wanted to avoid the inconsistency of accepting a Prize after arguing in Committee against the award of Prizes to writers. The main awards that year went to T. J. Morgan, who was no longer the Committee's Chairman, and Gwyn Thomas the novelist.

Our chief critic at this time was Vivian Griffiths, a cousin of the poet Bryn Griffiths. His applications for a bursary had been turned down several times for lack of merit. He'd begun writing unpleasant letters to me and to members of the Committee, and although I didn't mention this to members at the time, had been ringing me at home late at night. Glyn Tegai offered to meet him in the company of Roland Mathias but he failed to turn up, another reason for our not taking him seriously. The Chairman continued to write to him but he couldn't be convinced that the Committee had given proper consideration to his applications. Thereafter I was instructed not to respond to any attempt by this disappointed applicant to contact me, but his vile letters and late-night phonecalls kept coming for years afterwards. Another one of the same breed was Evan Gwyn Williams, who signed his ridiculous letters Ebenezer Chapel and The Hawk of Kuwait, before he too fell silent. I think both these operated on the basis of: great writers are neglected; I'm neglected therefore I'm a great writer.

1976–1979

The Literature Committee's next Chairman was Roland Mathias, a former headmaster and a distinguished writer. This was the first time an English-speaking Welshman had chaired the Committee. Roland was patriotic and well-informed and he supported the use of Welsh at every opportunity. He was, moreover, a fluent speaker who could charm people with his cultured voice and genial manner. When I asked him what changes he wanted to see in the Committee's policies, he replied that as a historian he believed in continuity not revolution and that he wanted to build on what had already been put in place. And that's what happened during his chairmanship.

But I soon heard from Aneurin Thomas, the Council's Director, that the Marchioness of Anglesey, the Council's Chair, thought I misled Roland by pressing my political views on him. This was not the first time I'd heard this insinuation and yet it startled me. Lady Anglesey was unaware that Roland, a lifelong Liberal, had been a keen patriot many years before he met me. When he was Headmaster of Pembroke Dock Grammar School in the 1950s he'd been in hot water with the governors for raising the Red Dragon flag on school premises one St David's Day. But with my hand on my heart I assured the Director that I wasn't aware of a single instance of the Committee's being influenced in a political way – with the exception of when Sir Thomas Parry was thundering against Communism. It irritated me that some people, especially politicians, thought I was too 'political'; after all, they didn't complain about Aneurin Thomas, who had been a Labour councillor, or Roy Bohana, who was said to be a true-blue Tory.

The Council's allocation to Literature in 1976/7 was £220,000. One of the first things the Committee did in the new financial year was recommend a subsidy to *Barddas*, the society's magazine edited by Alan Llwyd. This happened after Roy Stephens charmed members into supporting the society's application. The grant to the Academi Gymreig was increased so that it could employ two full-time Secretaries, and with this support it became a power in the land. The Tir na n-Og Prize (it was I who suggested an Irish title with which literate Welsh-speakers would be familiar because T. Gwynn Jones had used it) was awarded to the American writer Susan Cooper for her children's novel *The Grey King* and to T. Llew Jones for *Tân ar y Comin*. The Swiss writer Friedrich Dürrenmatt came to Wales in November 1976 to receive the International Writer's Prize. I had the task of taking him and his wife around the Colleges. He drank a dozen bottles of the most expensive wines in every hotel and restaurant and by the time of the ceremony in the Angel Hotel in Cardiff he had drunk so much he was unable to get out of bed, so the evening proceeded without him. In 1976, too, we published on the Oriel label an LP record of R. S. Thomas reading his poems and a selection from the Hengerdd, the earliest Welsh poetry, on the Sain label.

The work of compiling the *Welsh Academy English-Welsh Dictionary*, under the editorship of Bruce Griffiths and Dafydd Glyn Jones, began at about this time. This, in my view, was one of the most important projects ever to receive the Committee's support. At the start, some members were unwilling to fund it and even some Academi members on the Committee were lukewarm, too. But I saw the value of such a reference book from the start and with the support of Richard Griffiths, Professor of French in Cardiff, the Committee was able to find money every year until the book was almost ready for publication. It's a great shame, by the way, that the University of Wales hasn't been able, or willing, to recognize the achievement of Bruce and Dafydd, both of whom were teaching at Bangor, and I can only think it has something to do with Dafydd's long-standing criticism of the University which continues to this day. At the same time, the Committee refused to approve an application from Roy Stephens for a bursary which would have helped him prepare the *Odliadur*, a rhyming dictionary which has since proved a very useful tool for Welsh-language poets, and that was because Gwyn Erfyl couldn't see the point of such a book and said so. Fortunately, the Committee went back on this decision at its next meeting, in Gwyn Erfyl's absence, and awarded Roy a six-month bursary for the compilation of his rhyming dictionary. The two dictionaries are among the most important books ever to receive the Committee's support.

Shortly afterwards the Chairman had to remind members that everything discussed in Committee was to be treated as completely confidential. There was reason to believe the HTV newsroom knew about the recommendation of a bursary for Roy Stephens just after the Panel had considered it and before it came before the Committee and Council. This wasn't the only instance, either. Members believed that Gwyn Erfyl, who worked for HTV, was leaking information to his colleagues: on one occasion, he left the meeting to phone the newsroom and the owners of *Y Faner* to let them know the newspaper's grant was in jeopardy. The meeting ended at 5:30 and by the time I got home the news about *Y Faner* was on the six o'clock bulletin.

At about this time the difficulty with Gwynn ap Gwilym began. He'd been appointed by the Arts Council to an administrative post with the Welsh-language section of the Academi Gymreig. He turned out to be a most unsatisfactory officer who didn't take his responsibilities at all seriously. In the opinion of some members he'd taken to the social life of Cardiff with too much enthusiasm, especially during the lunch-hour. This was a pity, but he was unwilling to accept any word of advice and things went from bad to worse. After a few months I had to inform Bobi Jones, Chairman of the Welsh-language section, about what had been going on, but still the officer wouldn't come to his senses. Bobi wrote a long and detailed memorandum in readiness for putting the matter in the hands of a solicitor. In the end, Gwynn ap Gwilym was dismissed by Council but, unfortunately, not quite within the trial period as defined in his contract. The matter then went to court and, in the end, he received a small amount of compensation which was well worth paying just to be shot of him. Everyone in the Council and the Academi was glad to see him go.

In 1978 we had an opportunity of taking stock of the Literature Committee's policies. There had been 78 Prizes and 41 travel-grants enabling writers to visit 18 countries. Of the 82 writers who received the Council's support in this way, and of whom 38 wrote in Welsh, we were disappointed by only about a dozen who didn't manage to publish anything. Ned Thomas chose to write his influential book *The Welsh Extremist* rather than the novel described in his application, but there was nothing wrong with that, and Islwyn Ffowc Elis didn't complete his long-awaited novel about Llywelyn ap Gruffydd, the Last Prince of an independent Wales. When Roger Jones Williams, the Welsh-language Literature Officer, wrote Islwyn a very polite letter enquiring about the progress of his novel, he complained that the officer was hassling him!

The most unlikely excuse for not publishing a book came from Keidrych Rhys: he'd written his memoirs, he said, but the poet Bryn Griffiths had broken into his flat in Hampstead and stolen the typescript. But on the whole the scheme had produced a number of significant books and was thought to have been worthwhile. At least a number of writers, including Ned Thomas, John Tripp, and Roland Mathias, had come back to live in Wales. Our aim was to create a nucleus of professional writers by casting our bread upon the waters. This has eluded every public body in Wales up to the present, except for the media, and despite the substantial subsidies now available.

In June 1978 the Literature Committee used instantaneous translation facilities for the first time. The Committee asked Council to provide the same for all its Committees and Panels, and it did so, but none took advantage of them, and not a word of Welsh was ever heard at meetings of Council, despite there being several fluent Welsh-speakers among its members. Indeed, I found it tiresome having to listen to the accents of metropolitan and provincial England at meetings of the Council, especially when Opera was under discussion. What irked me was that while the Literature Committee had to justify every request for a financial increase, however small, the Welsh National Opera company would receive hundreds of thousands of pounds in extra funding with no more than five minutes discussion, often among people like Alun Hoddinott and William Mathias who were associated with the Company and therefore stood to benefit.

Astrid Lindgren, the Swedish children's writer and author of the Pippi Longstocking books, came to Wales in October 1978. Roger Jones Williams had the pleasure of taking her around Wales. She was very sweet and showed interest in everything and everyone. She was taken to a number of places where she met hundreds of children who had read her books in Welsh and English. Even in the Museum at St Fagans her courtesy never failed her: 'He was a very nice man,' she said about an over-zealous officer who'd shown her around, 'but oh, he wanted to tell me everything!' The Arts Council gave grant-aid to the College of Librarianship for the establishment of a Children's Book Centre, which grew into a Department of the Books Council. By 1978 the Literature Committee's budget was £333,500.

Never a year passed without friction in the relationship between the Committee and Christopher Davies / Llyfrau'r Dryw, publisher of the monthly magazine *Barn*. While other clients got on with their work as best they could, this company only snarled and complained. John Phillips, the manager, had made wild claims in the press and now he asked, in a threatening way, for the names and home addresses of Literature Committee members. This was his way of retaliating against the Committee which had asked for an assurance that Christopher Davies had contracts with its authors and paid them royalties. We received many letters from authors who had not been paid what was their due, among whom was Marion Eames, author of several novels which had sold well. The company's working methods, including its estimates and sales figures, inspired this squib from Harri Webb, who was a member of the Committee at this time:

> Behold the books of Mammon Press
>   Which show a big deficit,
> The arts in Wales are in a mess,
>   Not worth the taxman's visit;
>
> But no, let apprehension cease
>   And fears and doubt stop biting,
> For this is just another piece
>   Of good creative writing.

What's more, John Phillips and Gwyn Erfyl, now the editor of *Barn*, claimed that the Council interfered with the running of the magazine by not increasing its grant as they would wish. This was sheer nonsense, and Gwyn should have known better, but the complaints continued from year to year. In the end, in April 1979, the matter was put before a meeting chaired by Prys Morgan, when John Phillips accepted that the Council had no intention of interfering with the editorial freedom of the magazine and did not wish to penalize the publisher for having complained about the Council's grant, but that it was concerned about the way the Council's money was being used by the publisher. Many members thought these groundless complaints were a brazen way of putting pressure on the Committee to increase its subsidy.

Even so, the Committee decided not to renew the grant to Christopher Davies with which it employed Lynn Hughes, the company's English-language editor, and the consequence was the post was abolished. Soon afterwards John Phillips turned his water pistol on the Books Council with similar complaints about its staff and policies. There was no satisfying Christopher Davies in its insatiable demands for subsidy from public sources. They were particularly jealous of the grants that went to Gwasg Gomer, suggesting more than once that I was taking back-handers from Llandysul. Talk about Bacon and Bungay! On the other hand, I found Gomer to be honest and professional in their attitude towards the Council and John and Huw Lewis were always gentlemanly and constructive in our discussions.

This was a troublesome time for the Committee on the whole. Peter Meazey, the owner of Siop y Triban in Cardiff, raised his voice against the Council for running the Oriel Bookshop, although Peter's problems – I'd known him since our days in Garth Newydd – stemmed as much from his domestic circumstances as from his business interests, and there was nothing the Council could do about that. Some members believed the Committee had expanded its work too quickly and had tried to help too many organizations out of inadequate coffers. There was indeed a grain of truth in that, and I should have curbed the members' ambitions and my own wish to help almost everyone who asked for help. But at least the foundations had been laid for a system of patronage the elements of which have lasted *mutatis mutandis* to the present day.

In an attempt to test public opinion, a forum was held at the University College of North Wales, Bangor, on the 17th of October 1979. It was attended by 14 members of the Literature Committee, six of the Literature Department's staff, the Council's Director, the Finance Director, the Chairman of Council and representatives of the bodies in receipt of grant-aid from the Council such as the Academi and Books Council, about 60 people in all. Only 18 members of the public turned up. The main speaker from the floor was Meirion Pennar, a young academic who made a rambling speech with few facts and not a single practical proposal. The Committee's conclusion was that the forum had been an expensive exercise and that it had not served as a useful exchange between Council and its critics.

Even so, I shouldn't give the impression that the years of Roland Mathias's stewardship were a complete failure. Maintaining the core programme was the aim and that much was achieved. Roland had been a member of the Committee since 1969 and he was a very popular Chairman. At his last meeting in November 1979 the staff and members paid tribute to him for the expert, affable way he'd carried out his duties and he was presented with a gift on the occasion of his leaving, something that had no precedent in the Committee's history.

A full list of the members who had sat on the Council's Committees appeared in *The Arts in Wales 1950–1975*, and its Welsh counterpart, towards the end of 1979. It would be useful if someone would edit a similar book covering the period 1975–2000, but it doesn't seem likely anyone will. I appreciated the fact that I was allowed to compile and write books during my time at the Council – the only member of staff so to do. These books included *The Lilting House* (1969), *Artists in Wales* (three volumes, 1971, 1973, 1977), *The Welsh Language Today* (1973), *Linguistic Minorities in Western*

Europe (1976) and *Green Horse* (1978). Even so, I felt obliged to give up my editorship of *Poetry Wales* in 1973. Gerald Morgan succeeded me for two numbers and was followed by Sam Adams. I'd made the mistake of selling the magazine to Christopher Davies and I was now anxious to escape the clutches of Alun Talfan.

In January 1979, together with 61 writers, I signed a letter supporting the principle of devolution. In the referendum held on the 1st of March, 243,048 voted in favour and 956,330 against. This was not a reason to give up hope, as far as I was concerned, but a stimulus to begin again. Even so, the referendum had one serious consequence for the Literature Committee: Ned Thomas announced his intention of discontinuing publication of his magazine *Planet*. Fortunately, members still wished to see another magazine that would discuss the affairs of Wales through the medium of English. It was suggested that the Council should fund *The New Rebecca*, Paddy French's crusading magazine, but this was too much for some Council members to swallow, especially those who remembered the broadsides he'd fired against the Welsh Establishment a few years before. The real reason was that the contents of the periodical he was now proposing were not, in the opinion of Committee members, sufficiently literary or to do with the arts, to justify support from the Arts Council.

In November 1979 I went with John Lewis (Gwasg Gomer) and John Dudley Davies (Books Council) to Husum in Schleswig-Holstein for the launch of a German translation of my book *Linguistic Minorities in Western Europe*. I'd begun writing it in 1974 after seeing a slogan on a wall in Biarritz: 3+4=1. I asked my friend Txillardegi (Jóse Luis Alvarez), one of the founders of the revolutiuonary group ETA, who was living in exile in Hendaye at the time, what this signified and was told it meant the three provinces in France and four in Spain made one country, Euzkadi. In Husum I read a Welsh translation of the famous poem by Theodor Storm about 'the grey city', which seemed to please the sobersided burghers present. One or two nearly smiled when I referred to the book as being hefty enough to keep a window open on a warm summer's evening. But strangely enough, I didn't receive a *pfennig* for *Minderheiten in Westeuropa* from the publishers in Husum and never heard from them again.

I made an effort to keep up my interest in minority languages. Among the bodies of which I was a member was the UK Committee for Lesser Languages, which had been set up by the European Commission, and the Centre International Escarré per a les Minories Ètniques i les Nacions (CIEMEN), an organization with offices in Barcelona. I gave a talk on the Welsh language in the abbey of St Michel de Cuixa in August 1980 where my friend Aureli Argemì, the organization's secretary, was in holy orders. I was also a member of the British Council's Literature Panel in London, although there was little point in my attending its meetings because it discussed only books by English authors. It seems to me scandalous that the British Council hasn't accepted responsibility for promoting the books of Wales except in a half-hearted manner.

1980–1983

By the time Prys Morgan, the distinguished historian (and one of T. J. Morgan's sons), became Chairman in February 1980 I'd been working on *The Oxford Companion to the Literature of Wales* for two years. This project was part of my responsibilities as Literature Director and I had permission to work on it during office hours. But, in practice, that wasn't always possible because the Department was so busy from day to day and I, in Reithian phrase, was fully stretched. A good deal of the work had to be carried out at home almost every evening and every weekend, even during holidays. It's no exaggeration to say that I looked forward to Christmas when I could take a break from the *Companion*.

The project became part of my way of life. When I started on it my eldest daughter, Lowri, was in her first year at Ysgol Gyfun Glantaf and by the time it was published she was a fresher in Bangor. The girls used to refer to it as 'the monster in the attic' and I once heard Heledd tell one of her little friends, 'Dad's favourite book is Dad's book.' I received no financial remuneration for compiling the *Companion* because, in July 1981, after the Academi, without warning, had announced its intention of seeking grant-aid from the Council towards production costs, the original contract was scrapped at my request and I agreed to work without a fee or royalty. I had the editorial and administrative assistance of Nan Griffiths, Christine James, Anne Howells and Ruth Dennis-Jones.

I learned a great deal about compiling and editing information while working on the *Companion,* and was grateful to Dorothy Eagle, who represented Oxford University Press on the management board, for teaching me 'the reference aesthetic'. She'd been editor of the reprints of the magisterial *Oxford Companion to English Literature* which had first been edited by Sir Paul Harvey in 1932, and several other reference books. We were sent very clean proofs by the Press. Even so, there were a few howlers at proof stage, such as 'Duns Scotus, the medieval photographer' and 'Celtic millionaires crossing between Wales and Ireland', but I soon developed the knack of spotting these lacunae, even while beavering away late in the attic. Someone once said, 'Working for Oxford University Press is rather like making love to a duchess: one is more conscious of the privilege than the pleasure.' But in my experience of working for the Press it was both. We finished reading the final proofs in December 1985 and copies of the *Companion* and its counterpart in Welsh, *Cydymaith i Lenyddiaeth Cymru,* arrived soon afterwards.

Gwyn Jones was the first Chairman of the *Companion's* management board and R. Brinley Jones followed him in 1985. Among members of the board were R. Geraint Gruffydd,

Pennar Davies, Harri Webb (whose idea it had been in the first place) and Ceri W. Lewis representing the University of Wales Press Board. The English typescipt was read by Roland Mathias and the Welsh by Tom Parry. Once again Tom Parry raised an objection: he disagreed with my intention of including entries on people such as Aneurin Bevan, Dic Aberdaron, Sarah Jacob, Keir Hardie, St Melangell, Adelina Patti, Gwladus Ddu and Dic Penderyn; on the other hand he was in favour of the North Wales Quarrymen's Union. In vain did I try to convince him that the *Companion* was meant to be a reference book, to be kept at the reader's elbow while reading *both* the literatures of Wales and so we had to include information about all sorts of people, not just literary figures, as matters of reference. He also complained about some of the entries written by members of the University's Welsh Departments in which he found mistakes. He left the board before the work was published in 1986. As a mark of my appreciation and admiration for him as a scholar, even in contrarian mode, I took a copy of the *Cydymaith* to his widow.

The Council's allocation to Literature in 1979/80 was £385,400. After *Planet* discontinued publication the Council advertised its intention of subsidizing another magazine in English. One of the first things the Committee did under the chairmanship of Prys Morgan was recommend subsidy to the periodical *Arcade*, which first saw light of day in October 1980. John Osmond was the editor and Ned Thomas, Dai Smith, Robin Reeves and Nigel Jenkins were among members of the editorial board. With so many talented people associated with the magazine, the Committee hoped it would flourish. But unfortunately, it didn't achieve its target of 5,000 copies and for this reason the Council withdrew its support and the magazine folded in March 1982. Members thought it was too expensive (the application was for £60,000) and there were no credible signs that it was likely to increase its circulation. Once again we had failed to show that there was a market for a quality/popular magazine in English and the Committee was keenly disappointed.

The *Companion* caused tension between the Council and the Academi during 1980. With a deficit of £10,000 in its budget, the Academi asked for a supplemetary grant and threatened to discontinue work on the *Companion* and lay off the editorial assistant, Christine James, for twelve months. The Committee considered the way the supplementary grant had been requested was below the belt: the Academi was threatening to put into mothballs a project it knew the Council was keen to maintain and of which I was editor. What's more, the Committee considered it unacceptable that the Academi had put its officers on university salary scales without consulting the Council, which funded the society's programme of work. In the end, it was decided to give £8,800 to the Academi as a supplentary grant towards meeting the deficiency. The Chairman of the English-language section at the time was G. O. Jones, Director of the National Museum, not one of my favourite characters, I have to say.

At the meeting held in April 1981, for the sake of several new members who included Meredydd Evans, R. Brinley Jones and Ann Saer, and in the presence of Sir Hywel Evans, who had just been appointed Chairman of the Council, Prys Morgan spoke eloquently about the Literature Committee's work. He conveyed the members' view that the sums allocated to the Committee were inadequate, that a number of schemes had already been wound up, and expressed the hope that Council would increase its allocation in a year or two. In reviewing the Committee's work Prys pointed out that a lack of money was at the heart of most of its difficulties and that it didn't have sufficient funds to carry out its responsibilities in a worthy and professional manner. The Committee accepted a suggestion by Brian Morris that a working party should investigate the way the Council funded Literature. The Council's allocation to Literature in 1980/81 was £439,500.

The working party considered a number of relevant facts.

It was a disadvantage, it reported, that Literature was not considered a performing art; Wales had two literatures, each with its own strengths and weaknesses; the Regional Arts Associations spent comparatively little on literary schemes; the culture of Wales was primarily literary; the literature of the past had to be taken into account as well as that of the present; there was a close relationship between Welsh literature and the Welsh language on the one hand and, on the other, between Welsh literature and Welsh society as a whole that was relevant to Council as a patron; most of the schemes funded by the Committee were seriously short of funds; the payments made to writers were much less than those paid to practitioners in the other arts. The members of the working party were Walford Davies, who was Vice-Chairman of the Committee at the time, Richard Griffiths, Brian Morris, D. Geraint Lewis and R. Brinley Jones. But nothing came of the request to increase the Committee's funds. The only increase was a grant that came out of the blue from the Arts Council of Great Britain towards the cost of printing the *Companion*.

It was not my place to complain about any of this: my responsibility was to put the facts before the Committee and leave the Chairman and those Committee members who sat on Council to argue the case for more adequate funding. My role was to do my best to administer what was on offer in the most effective, professional way. On the other hand, I couldn't bear the inconsistencies and lack of clarity that arose from time to time in the Committee's decisions, especially when it changed its mind from one meeting to the next, and I lost my moss more than once, I must confess.

Hywel Evans was a Welsh-speaker and former head of the Welsh Office, and it was hoped he would be more sympathetic to the work of the Literature Committee. But it was not to be: his chief delight was Music. I never had a chance to speak to this mandarin and he would pretend not to have seen me when our paths crossed outside the office: in the tradition of the Civil Service, he spoke only to the Director. But once, at a reception, I happened to quote Francis Bacon in his hearing: 'Money is like muck, not good except it be spread,' and his face went a bright red. What's more, perhaps he remembered me from the visit of a deputation from Cymdeithas yr Iaith to the Welsh Office during the early 1960s when we delivered a petition calling for bilingual traffic signs. Even so, this much must be said of him: he played a key role in getting Willie Whitelaw to change his mind about a Welsh-language television channel when Gwynfor Evans was threatening to go on hunger strike.

He complained regularly to the Director that I was 'political', despite the fact that I was no longer active with Plaid Cymru – not openly anyway. There's a tendency in some people to think that any activity in favour of the culture of Wales is 'political'. Hywel Evans knew, perhaps, somehow or other, that I'd taken part in a ceremony organized by Gorsedd y Beirdd at Cilmeri on the occasion of the seventh centenary of Llywelyn ap Gruffydd's death in 1982 and had been present when a memorial to the Last Prince was unveiled at Caernarfon on the 11th of December in the same year. But Aneurin Thomas did nothing about the complaints, fair play; he was good like that.

The Literature Committee tried hard and long to save *Y Faner*. The grant to Gwasg y Sir increased from year to year and there was an improvement in the paper under the editorship of Jennie Eirian Davies. She worked in primitive conditions without even a phone in her office and had to ask permission from the Evans brothers, the paper's owners, for just about everything. The death of this able, charismatic woman in 1982 was exceedingly sad. I feared for a while that the strain of keeping the paper going against the tide had had a fatal effect on her health. But I was glad to receive an assurance from her husband, Eirian Davies, that her death had nothing to do with the Council's policies. Emyr Price was appointed editor and

Marged Dafydd his Deputy soon afterwards. The Council then accepted a recommendation from the Committee that responsibility for funding the paper should be transferred to the Government Grant to Periodicals administered by the Books Council. However, the Books Council wasn't prepared to accept the responsibility, because there were other calls on the Government grant. So the matter of *Y Faner* dragged on and on.

Ruth's father died on the 16th of April 1981. She was unable to be with us and the rest of the family in the memorial service at Tabernacl in Aberystwyth because she was expecting our fourth child. Huw Meredydd was born in May and great was the joy of his parents and three sisters. As for me, I've had deep satisfaction from our children and family life, especially when in Ruth's company, and without them the pressures of work would have been all the harder to bear. On the other hand, I was in good health and my shoulders were broad and backside tough enough to take almost anything in those days.

The Committee's work wasn't entirely disastrous. Derek Walcott, the poet from the Caribbean, came to Wales in 1980 to receive the International Writer's Prize, and Margaret Atwood, the Canadian writer, in 1982. Tony Bianchi, the English-language Literature Officer, was responsible for the events organized as part of their visits. Among the writers who came to Dyffryn to honour Margaret Atwood were Beryl Bainbridge, Ruth Fainlight, Angela Carter, Fay Weldon and Eigra Lewis Roberts. But I missed the weekend owing to a bout of the old enemy, glandular fever.

It was my responsibility to keep things moving forward. In October 1982 I wrote a memorandum about the need for a new English-language magazine. There was quite a bit of doubt on this score to begin with, not only on account of our experience with *Arcade* but because the Welsh Writers' Union had announced its intention of publishing its own magazine. But when the Committee saw an over-confident, half-sloshed

John Morgan presenting the Union's application, it decided to support the proposal described in my paper.

A number of other publications began at this time, among which was *Bro a Bywyd / Writer's World*, an idea I'd brought back from Friesland. It was also decided to develop Poetry Wales Press as a publisher of books in English, an imprint which grew in time into Seren Books under Mick Felton's management. A number of nicely designed books were published under the aegis of the Children's Literature Panel, which was chaired by D. Geraint Lewis, and two volumes of the Mabinogi stories attractively illustrated by Margaret Jones.

The chairmanship of Prys Morgan came to an end in February 1983. At the same time the Council decided not to increase the Literature Committee's allocation. The Council had refused to acknowledge the Committee's argument that a lack of funds was having a detrimental effect on its programme. Walford Davies, the Committee's Deputy Chairman, and Richard Griffiths, who were in the meeting when the decision was taken, were of the opinion that the real reason for not giving Literature enough funds to do its work properly was a lack of understanding on the part of Council members of the need to serve and operate in two languages.

Nor did Tom Ellis M.P. succeed in persuading Council at a meeting in Cardiff in April 1977 when he wrote: 'The function of the Welsh Arts Council is to foster the arts in Wales in so far as they play a part in moulding our national cultural life. Welsh culture is overwhelmingly literary. If we lose our native literary tradition extending over fourteen centuries, all will be lost and there will be no such thing as Welsh culture. The very *raison d'être* of the Council will have ceased to exist... The heart and soul of the Welsh Arts Council must be literary.' His words fell on deaf ears as far as members were concerned – after all, they were there to protect their own interests in Opera, Music, Art and Drama.

A welter of letters from the public, including about fifty from eminent writers, all had the same effect. It was from about this time my disillusion with the way the Council operated can be dated and the view from Museum Place began to lose some of its appeal.

Prys Morgan had been an extremely able Chairman, in the view of members and officers alike. He's still a very amiable chap, of broad culture and excellent company on every occasion. At his last meeting he was presented with gifts for having served the Committee and Council so well since 1975. I recall how he took his leave – by referring to the warning on the old Western Welsh buses: 'Lower your head when leaving.' This was typical of him but Prys had good cause to hold his head high for having represented the interests of the Literature Committee from first to last in such splendid fashion.

1983–1986

Walford Davies, Director of the Extra-Mural Department at the University College of Wales, Aberystwyth, and editor of Everyman's Library, was Chairman of the Literature Committee during this period. The nucleus of the Committee's work continued as before – support for the Books Council, the Academi, the magazines, bursaries, prizes, book production grants, and so on – so from now on I shall describe only new projects.

My work in the Literature Department was interrupted for a while after I had an accident on the M4 while on my way to Llandysul on the 27th of October 1984. Early that morning, before sunrise, I drove into a runaway herd of shire horses, killing one of them and going off the road and down an embankment. This happened during the miners' strike and I was rescued by police who were parked under almost every bridge along the motorway. I spent a week in hospital while the glass shards in my face were being removed and then a month at home while I recuperated fully. I received quite a few cards wishing me a speedy recovery and yet not a word from John and Huw Lewis, the owners of Gwasg Gomer, who'd asked me to attend interviews for the post of editor that morning. They appointed Cathryn Gwynn, the daughter of Mairwen and Gwynn Jones, who later became the wife of Peter Jones, the Council's Art Director.

Among the first things the Literature Committee did in 1983 was sponsor a reading by R. S. Thomas at the Sherman Theatre on the occasion of the poet's seventieth birthday. He read a number of poems in that sepulchral voice of his without a word of explanation or comment except to say, 'They all seem the same to me.' No, we didn't sing 'Happy birthday, Mr Thomas,' afterwards. Among the other readers were Raymond Garlick and Gerallt Jones, and John Ormond's film about the poet was shown. I got on well with Gerallt and liked him very much and losing him in 1999 was a great blow.

In 1983 Alan Llwyd was appointed chief executive of Cymdeithas Gerdd Dafod, the society for poets in the Welsh language. Over the next few years I had several conversations about his feeling that his compatriots didn't fully appreciate him. I failed to convince him this wasn't true and his paranoia grew apace. I didn't let this difficulty impinge on the Council's support for the society and Alan, as poet and officer, however. He was still complaining that his people didn't appreciate him when he resigned from his post in June 2011. The Council's allocation to Literature in 1983/4 was £510,900.

Ned Thomas presented an excellent paper on a new English-language magazine for Wales in November 1983. The Committee approved of it, noting its confidence in Ned's ability as editor-publisher, and recognizing in the application his commitment and technical expertise that augured well for the project's success. The new *Planet* appeared in 1985. I made sure it received sufficient funding this time and the magazine has gone from strength to strength since then, especially when it was under the editorship of John Barnie and his wife Helle Michelsen.

I had to share a very sad duty with Ned Thomas in July 1983 when our friend Paolo Pistoi, a young academic from Milan, fell from Constitution Hill, the cliff that stands at the far end of the prom in Aberystwyth. Paolo was an expert on small nations and minority languages in Europe, and had come to Wales with a view to writing a book about our country. There were no witnesses to this dreadful accident, but the sun going down on Cardigan Bay must have dazzled the young Italian and he was found on the beach next morning, as if asleep. I had the task of driving his parents from Cardiff to Aberystwyth and Ned dealt with the police, hospital and undertaker. Ned and I started a fund in Paolo's memory and with the money we've been able to send young Welsh people overseas and pay for people from other countries to study in Wales.

The Council's Director, Aneurin Thomas, retired in March 1984. I'd always got on well with him but was sometimes amused by his circuitous way of discussing things, usually by analogy. He had a knack of putting his foot in it, too: on one occasion he raised the hackles of a group of artists petitioning the Council for grants when he said on television, 'If you organize a conference of seals you can be sure they will ask for more fish.' Witty enough, but an unfortunate thing for the chief executive officer of an Arts Council to say. On another occasion, while we were receiving the Nigerian Cultural Attaché, he asked what his son, a most sophisticated young man dressed in a Savile Row suit, was doing in London. He was in his fifth year at Guy's Hospital, came the reply. 'Oh, very good,' said Aneurin, 'so you're a medicine man.' Whether this was deliberate, or just a slip of the tongue, we weren't sure; we gulped down our sherry, but Aneurin beamed at one and all. He was from the village of Cilybebyll in the Swansea Valley but I never heard him speak more than a few words of Welsh; he was, nevertheless, always supportive of projects having to do with the language. I heard recently from his daughter, Jo Jarman, that he wrote verse and I attended an exhibition of his watercolours held in Penarth last summer. There was more to Aneurin than he was willing to reveal to his colleagues.

He was a kind-hearted, sympathetic, friendly man who had had a distinguished career in arts education, quite unlike his successor, Thomas Arfon Owen, the former Registrar of the University College of Wales, Aberystwyth, who was appointed Director in April 1984. Tom Owen, in my experience, was selfish, pushy and a very cold fish who once told me he expected to get a knighthood for his work. I had no respect for him and couldn't get along with him, unfortunately, and soon there was growing tension between us. I agreed with Peter Jones, the Art Director, in wishing the Council had appointed Roy Bohana, the Music Director and Deputy Director, but it wasn't up to us.

When Walford Davies retired from the chairmanship of the Literature Committee at the end of 1985/6 he was thanked for his work on the Committee's behalf since 1976. He was presented with a copy of the poems of Dafydd ap Gwilym in a fine edition from Gwasg Gregynog. The year 1986 came to a pleasant close for me when I was awarded a Fellowship at St David's University College, Lampeter. This was the first time someone had seen fit to acknowledge my contribution to the literary life of Wales since I'd been given the White Robe of the Gorsedd in 1976 and I accepted the honour humbly and gratefully. The only thing I now remember about the ceremony was sitting next to Euros Bowen, another Fellow-elect, and having to listen to him disagreeing in a loud voice with what was being said about him from the stage. Euros, an Anglican clergyman, was famous for his one-liners. Someone once asked him his opinion of Kate Roberts, whom he'd brought to an Academi meeting in his car, and he replied, 'Dr Kate gets on my bloody tits!'

1986–1990

The next Chairman, and the last under whom I was to serve, was M. Wynn Thomas, a Lecturer in the English Department at the University College, Swansea and later Professor there. Wynn was a fluent Welsh-speaker and unique among Committee chairmen in being knowledgeable and enthusiastic about both our country's literatures. His view from the start was that we shouldn't allow a lack of money to have a negative effect on the Committee's work, although at the same time he wanted to keep every aspect of it under review. The Council's allocation to Literature in 1986/7 was £566,500.

At the start of 1986 the *Oxford Companion to the Literature of Wales* and *Cydymaith i Lenyddiaeth Cymru* were published. Both versions were launched at receptions in Caernarfon, Aberystwyth and Cardiff. The books' appearance was a huge relief to me. I'd spent eight years compiling and editing the entries and had grown tired of working ten hours a day, seven days a week.

The Council's new Chairman, Mathew Prichard, came to a meeting of the Committee in November 1986 at which Wynn Thomas and other members spoke plainly once again about the need to fund Literature adequately. Mathew Prichard, who was a visual and plastic arts man despite his family connection with the estate of Agatha Christie and the Booker Prize, was of the opinion that such a move wouldn't be acceptable to Council but he didn't say why. Even so, this wealthy and generous man gave nearly £2,000 of his own money towards the cost of the *Companion,* without the Committee's asking for it.

The main topic under discussion by the Literature Committee in 1986/7 was the Council's support for periodicals. A preliminary report by Rhodri Williams was received in November 1986. The Committee was informed that there'd been a disappointing response from the public to the invitation to express an opinion of the magazines published under the Council's aegis and that the information received from the publishers and editors was also inadequate. Only the magazines published by groups of enthusiasts such as Cymdeithas Gerdd Dafod, the publisher of *Barddas*, had submitted full details. Astonishingly, some of the editors had little idea of how many copies of their magazines were being sold. Worse still, it was clear that some publishers were in receipt of subsidy from year to year without any intention of using it to improve the quality of their magazines or increase their circulation. It was time to clean the Augean stables!

Things came to a head in April 1987. Before turning to Rhodri Williams's memorandum, Wynn Thomas reminded the Committee that this was its hundredth meeting and it was a moment for quiet satisfaction, he said, that it had played a key role in transforming the literary life of Wales over the last twenty years. It was a coincidence, he went on, that a hundred members had served on the Committee since 1967, and he wished to put on record the Council's appreciation of their contribution too. He also congratulated the Literature Director, who'd been at every one of the hundred meetings, on the part he'd played. This was kind of Wynn but there was no need to refer to me since it was my professional duty to serve the Committee and Council.

The memorandum by Rhodri Williams made for startling reading. Here are some of its salient points. The public had complained about *The Anglo-Welsh Review*'s drab design and the views of the editor, Greg Hill, had been blocked by a lack of co-operation and ambition on the part of the publisher, Five Arches Press of Narberth. The response of the poets had been very favourable to *Barddas*, which had increased its circulation substantially. After years of stagnation, *Barn* had begun to show signs it was improving its circulation. *Y Casglwr*, the magazine mainly for bibliophiles, which had doubled its circulation in five years, was a model of how a periodical should use the Council's subsidy. A full response had been received from *Planet* in which the editor made a commendable commitment to professional standards. The editor and publisher of *Poetry Wales* displayed a dismal apathy: Mike Jenkins, the editor, could only complain that he hadn't been given enough time to complete the task of responding to Rhodri Williams's questionnaire, and the magazine nearly lost its grant for that reason. It was recommended that the grant to *The Powys Review* should be withdrawn because, in the Committee's view, the contents had little enough to do with the literary life of Wales, concentrating as they did on the work of the Powys brothers. Bearing in mind that *Taliesin* was the main medium for creative writing in Welsh, many had found it of little interest and members of the Academi were asked to think of ways of improving it. Despite its drab appearance and a dwindling number of readers, the contents of *Y Traethodydd*, a journal dealing mainly with philosophical and theological subjects, were thought to maintain very high standards.

As expected, the most controversial recommendation was the one Rhodri Williams made about *Y Faner*. This was the most difficult periodical to assess, he reported, owing to the reluctance of the owners, Gwasg y Sir, to co-operate with him. The only observation made by the Evans brothers, the owners, had been that the newspaper didn't receive enough subsidy and was losing £20,000 a year. By now Emyr Price had resigned as editor and Hafina Clwyd had taken his place. Meg Dafydd, an acting editor, had complained about the working methods of the publisher / printer, in particular the antiquated printing machinery, the lack of basic facilities for staff, poor communication between owners and editor, and constant interference with the editor's work. Sympathy was expressed for Hafina Clwyd who had to work in such poor conditions. It had been suggested that the only way of ensuring a future for *Y Faner* would be to transfer ownership to a trust, an idea that appealed to Robat Gruffudd of Gwasg y Lolfa, but nothing had come of it.

Rhodri Williams had reached the conclusion that the figures provided by Gwasg y Sir were wholly unreliable and it was recommended that the Council should withdraw its support at the first opportunity. At the same time, he was of the view that there was need for a weekly periodical in Welsh. Despite two policy statements and grants on an increasing scale since 1979, the Council had not adopted a comprehensive policy, in Rhodri's opinion. Nevertheless, the allocation for periodicals in 1987/8 was £156,030.

As a consequence of Rhodri Williams's memorandum, and after a long and heated debate, it was agreed to inform Gwasg y Sir that the Council's grant to *Y Faner* would be discontinued at the end of the financial year 1987/8. The Committee was unable to support a periodical that was not essentially literary and it was more appropriate that *Y Faner* should be funded from some other source. John Roberts Williams, an experienced editor who played an important part in this discussion, was firmly of the opinion that the grant should be stopped. But the main reason why *Y Faner* lost its subsidy was that its publisher, Gwasg y Sir, was not willing to make a full and credible statement about its financial situation. I think the Evans brothers were more interested in budgerigars than writers, for they printed a quite attractive magazine about breeding the birds.

The Council held a public meeting to discuss *Y Faner* at the College of Librarianship in Aberystwyth on the 27th of June 1987, when Mathew Prichard, Wynn Thomas, Ned Thomas and Rhodri Williams spoke from the stage. The debate generated more heat than light, especially when Ithel Davies and hotheads like Neil Jenkins and W. J. Edwards spoke against the decision to withhold the grant but without a modicum of understanding of the Committee's difficulties and the shortcomings of Gwasg y Sir. A number of letters were received from members of the public, almost every one critical of the Council but, significantly, nothing was heard from Gwasg y Sir, who couldn't be bothered to bestir themselves. Some time later the title was bought by my brother-in-law David Meredith and his wife Luned who'd been the paper's Deputy Editor. Hafina Clwyd, a capable journalist, was kept on as Editor but the paper's life came to an end in 1992. The publishers had kept it going for five years without subsidy, which confirmed some people's view that there was no real need for subsidy after all. Be that as it may, the Committee vowed never again to give subsidy to a periodical that was printed by its publisher because no credence could be given to statements of costs and circulation when that was the case.

Alun Creunant Davies retired from his post as Director of the Welsh Books Council in September 1987 and Gwerfyl Pierce Jones, his Deputy, was appointed to succeed him. The Committee agreed that I should write to Alun to thank him for his contribution to its work and for the close co-operation that had existed between the Books Council and the Arts Council over some twenty years. Alun Creunant was more than a colleague to me: he was a friend in whom I had complete confidence. This was attributable, perhaps, to the fact that he, like J. E. Caerwyn Williams, was a good friend of my father-in-law, J. E. Meredith, and a member of his congregation. Even so, I had to smile sometimes at his way of working and he regretted that I didn't share his ability to suffer fools gladly.

Alun was a man for whom the local was the real. He had a connection with the village of Llangeitho in Cardiganshire. Every Friday he'd send one of the office staff home early to buy enough stamps in Llangeitho to last the following week as a contribution to keeping the village sub-post office open. Another anecdote about him: when I was in Stockholm visiting the Swedish Academy with a view to preparing the ground for the Welsh Academi's nomination of Saunders Lewis for the Nobel Prize, I was astonished to hear a very ornate telephone ringing shrilly on the Secretary's desk and to be told Alun was on the line: he wanted to know whether

I was free on a certain date to attend a meeting of one of the Books Council's Panels. As soon as I said I was he put the phone down without further ado. The Nobel Prize went that year to Pablo Neruda. The explanation was that Saunders Lewis was not eligible for nomination because Wales was not a state with its own government, as the writer himself had foreseen.

Only one application was received for a new Welsh-language weekly and that was from a group led by Dylan Iorwerth. The excellence of the application was revealed when the Periodicals Panel met in December 1987. But once again there was an over-optimistic estimate that the proposed periodical was going to sell 5,000 copies within three years. Even so, the Committee welcomed the group's intention of producing a magazine dealing with a wide range of subjects in a lively fashion. The fluency and expertise of Dylan Iorwerth made a favourable impression on members of the Panel. The Committee were convinced that *Golwg* would make a substantial contribution to Welsh-language journalism and to publicity for the arts in Wales, and so, with enthusiasm, a recommendation was made in its favour. At the same time, it was decided to give subsidy to a new magazine in English, *The New Welsh Review*. The Committee's allocation in 1988/89 was £747, 600.

The Committee took steps towards establishing a writers' centre like the two in England that were administered by the Arvon Foundation. Emyr Humphreys, a member of the Committee and Council at the time, was not entirely in favour of the idea and Ann Ffrancon was anxious not to co-operate with an English organization. Nevertheless, in the spring of 1989, having visited the Arvon centre in Devon, I began searching for a suitable house in Wales. The first one I found was Cae'r Saer, on the Garthgwynion estate, which I visited at the invitation of Ruth Lambert, a splendid woman and founder of the Museum of Modern Art in Machynlleth. Having visited it once, I went again with Gillian Clarke, who'd been very supportive of the proposal from the very start. After a few months of deliberations, however, the estate decided it didn't wish to lease the house to the Taliesin Trust, the charity set up to run the proposed centre, and so I had to resume my search elsewhere.

Then, out of the blue, I received a phonecall from a woman called Sally Baker who'd heard the Council was looking for a house that could be used as a writers' centre: she wanted to know whether I thought Tŷ Newydd, Lloyd George's old home near Llanystumdwy, might be suitable. I went there like a shot and went back for a second look with Gillian. In short, we agreed the place would be ideal for our purpose. By November 1989 I could report to the Literature Committee that I'd found a house and that its owners, Sally Baker and Elis Gwyn Jones, were willing to co-operate with the Trust.

I therefore began collecting money for the project and raised £15,000 as a starting fund within a few weeks. Among the first individuals who contributed were Sally Burton, the late actor's wife, and the writers Elaine Morgan, Glyn Jones, Raymond Garlick and Gerard Casey. The Arts Council of Great Britain gave £3,000 and the Welsh Arts Council earmarked the sum of £25,000. I spent several days painting walls and bookshelves in one of the main rooms. I also managed to find furniture, thanks mainly to the generosity of Robert Maskrey who gave us a dozen brandnew sofas and easy chairs. Having worked so hard to establish the centre, and looking back now, it's strange to think I haven't received a single invitation to take a course at Tŷ Newydd or even to be present at the tenth anniversary celebrations.

I went to the Soviet Union in December 1989 with Wynn Thomas and Michael Parnell as guests of the Writers' Union. Things weren't too bad in Tallinn, the capital of Estonia, but in Kiev, the capital of Ukraine, the system was fast breaking down. There was no food in the hotel, the shops were empty and on every street-corner and in the Metro, there were crowds waving flags and banners with anti-Communist slogans on them. Things weren't a lot better in Moscow, although we didn't leave the hotel much because the temperature had dropped to minus twenty. This was my seventh visit to the Soviet Union, and I witnessed a deterioration in the standard of living and more public discord than ever before. The Soviet empire was on the point of breaking up, as every empire does sooner or later, and we'd found ourselves in the middle of it.

Welsh writing in English had a stroke of good luck in 1990. One day I took a phonecall from a man called Lewis Davies, brother of the writer Rhys Davies, who wanted to give me £100,000 as a contribution towards the cost of promoting the work of Welsh writers in English. I drove like Jehu down to Lewes, near Brighton, to meet this gentleman. He was a retired librarian who'd inherited his brother's literary estate as well as the money left by his three sisters. When I asked him why he wished to give money away like this, he replied, 'I'd turn in my grave to think that awful woman might get her hands on it'; he was referring, of course, to Margaret Thatcher. Although Lewis wished to give the money to me personally, I explained it would be better to set up a charity, and to this he readily agreed. After getting over my astonishment, I set about, in my own time and with the Council's approval, creating the Rhys Davies Trust. In due course I became Secretary and still act in that capacity, work which I enjoy to this day.

I left the Arts Council in July 1990, having spent a week in Prague with Vlad'ka and Leoš Šatava, lecturers at Charles University and old friends of mine. The Council had been a good employer over the years and gave me generous terms which made an early retirement possible. I received good wishes from the Literature Committee and a gift of money that I used to buy a painting by Ernest Zobole, one of my favourite Welsh painters. I also received kind letters from Glyn Tegai Hughes, Prys Morgan, Roland Mathias, Walford Davies and Wynn Thomas, former Chairmen of the Literature Committee, and from Gwyn Jones, the former Chairman of the Council, who had appointed me back in 1967. What's more, a host of writers and the officers of public bodies wrote to me, and that too was heart-warming. Every one referred to my work with the Arts Council and said kind things about the part I'd played in promoting our country's literature.

But this was no time to be looking back. A new chapter in my life was about to begin.

6

The Black Book of Blaen-bedw

ONE OF THE things weighing on my mind throughout the 1980s, while I was with the Arts Council, was what Monica Jones, Auntie Gwen's daughter, had told me during my stay at her home in London in July 1962: my father was illegitimate. I was to spend a lot of my free time over the next two decades trying to find out about his mother and, in due course, his father. It was comparatively easy finding his mother but it took until 2002 to ascertain who his father was. Fortunately, even the most humble life leaves traces, however feint. It was a matter of knocking on doors, making discreet enquiries, reading newspapers and visiting churchyards but, in the end, I had to use a more scientific way of establishing who his father was: DNA.

Yes, my father was a bastard. He was in no way unkind or unpleasant; indeed, he was a mild-mannered and genial man. Even so, he was an illegitimate child, for whom there is a plethora of names in Welsh, perhaps because there are so many like him in Wales. And yet my father was not a love-child.

He was raised in Heolgerrig, a village on the hill overlooking Merthyr Tydfil, by William Stephens, a policeman, and his wife Elizabeth. As a child, he spoke some Welsh, the language of the district. P.C. Stephens had a son, Billy, and two daughters, my Auntie Annie and Auntie Gwen, by his second wife, Rebecca *née* Giles, whose family owned the pottery in Rhymney. His first wife was Esther Hancock *née* Parrott; the composer Ian Parrott belonged to the same family. My parents led me to believe that Annie and Gwen were my father's half-sisters, but that wasn't strictly true. Anyway, it seemed a good idea to begin my search in Heolgerrig, or Pen-rhewl as the villagers called it. I managed to find an old man who could remember 'Dan the Bobby', the constable who came after him, but no one remembered my father. His birth certificate wasn't in the Registrar's office in town either.

From my father, with whom I tentatively broached the subject in October 1979, I learned that William Stephens had retired from the police force in 1919 when the boy would have been nine years old. The family went to live in Lower Ruspidge, near Cinderford, in the Forest of Dean, where Elizabeth Stephens had relatives. But about a fortnight later William died of lockjaw, a form of tetanus, after injuring himself while cutting firewood in the yard. My father heard of his father's death from a milkman on his way home from school: 'You better get on 'ome, old butty, your father's dead.' I went to Lower Ruspidge looking for someone who could remember Elizabeth Stephens, and to Devauden in Monmouthshire, William Stephens's home, but to no avail. About a year later Elizabeth brought my father back to Wales, and made her home in Nantgarw, and there she married William Christmas Llewellyn, an old flame of hers. My father was raised in Nantgarw and Dynea from then on by 'Ma and Pa Llewellyn'. Elizabeth died when I was one and William Llewellyn during the 'flu epidemic in the winter of 1950/1.

Where else could I search? I tried not to pester my father lest he suspect I was looking into the circumstances of his birth. Then, I had an idea that should have occurred to me at the outset. I wrote to the General Registrar requesting a copy of my father's birth certificate. When this document came from St Catherine's House in London about a week later, I saw my father's mother's name for the very first time: Annie Sophia Lloyd. But in the space where his father's name should have been, a blank. The old story, of course: *pater semper incertus, mater certissima est*. The mother's address was given as Blanebeddoe, Glescombe, Rads and the place of birth as The Green, Walton, near Old Radnor, Rads. Walton is a hamlet less than a mile from the border with England. I learned later that Annie Sophia's uncle had been a postman there. My father's date of birth was given as the 25th of February 1910. I was immediately suspicious because on that date his mother had been twenty years old: was this a coincidence? I think it must have been.

My father learned the circumstances of his birth in a most appalling way. Just before he married my mother in 1935, William Llewellyn's sister, Janet Dyke of Upper Boat, told my mother's mother as a way of getting at his wife, Elizabeth, with whom she'd fallen out. My grandmother went straight to my father and reported what she'd been told. My father, in turn, went to see Annie and Gwen in Merthyr to ask whether it was true, and they confirmed it was. My father was so upset that he spent a whole week in his bedroom, unable to speak or eat. The child had arrived in Heolgerrig at Christmas 1910, together with the sum of a hundred gold sovereigns, according to Annie and Gwen. His mother, Auntie Annie told me years later, was a tall, fair-haired woman who would visit the home of William and Elizabeth Stephens for two or three years thereafter, bringing with her a basket of butter and eggs from the country, except that as the child grew, she stopped coming and they never saw her again. I didn't know any of this in 1979, of course, and I didn't say a word to my father about what I'd seen on his birth certificate.

Nor did I know whether Annie Sophia Lloyd was still alive and so I had to tread very carefully. The next thing I did was go to Glascwm, a small village in the hills in the old hundred of Elfael a little to the north of Builth. I walked up from Hundred House and down into the little crease in the hills where the ruins of Blaen-bedw lay. The house had gone down, as they say in Radnorshire: the upper floor had disappeared and there were all kinds of agricultural materials and implements being stored on the ground floor. But the hearth was still intact and some of the window-frames had glass in them. A row of Charlie trees grew at the front of the house and a drover's road and small stream, the Twrch, ran past it and down to Glascwm. I took a cast-iron griddle from the grate as a souvenir of my visit.

In the village I went through the parish records and spoke to several old people who could remember Annie Lloyd, or Nancy Lloyd as she was known locally, including Mr and Mrs Stan Jones who kept the sub-post office and now owned Blaen-bedw. They told me Annie had had a 'by-blow' when she was about twenty but that no one in the village had known who the child's father was. She'd lived in Blaen-bedw with her brother, Hugh Lloyd, who also worked in the flour-mill at Hundred House until 1945. Annie had moved from the district immediately after the birth of her child and the villagers hadn't known where she'd gone. I also heard from Mr and Mrs Jones that someone had been in the village a few years previously asking about his mother and looking for a picture of her, but no one had been able to help him. That man was my father, almost certainly.

As I went through the registers of St David's Church in Glascwm, I discovered that Annie Lloyd, at the age of seventeen, had been in service at The Court, also known as The Yat, the village's 'big house'. I thought at once that her child, perhaps, had been fathered by one of the Vaughan family who lived in the house, and I went to the trouble of listing the twelve Vaughan children (all of whom had been given Latinate names like Septimus, Octavius and Decima) in an article which later appeared in the newsletter of the Kilvert Society. But this turned out to be a false trail, like so many over the years.

I now decided to take a different tack by looking for Hugh

Lloyd, in the hope he would lead me to his sister Annie, and this part of my search took almost a year. My task was complicated by the fact that Hugh had married three times and had four daughters by his first two wives. Every one had moved from the district. But by luck, and persistent enquiry, and a lot of detective work, I slowly began to make progress. One of Hugh's daughters, Dolly Lloyd, had died in Gladestry in 1944 and in the report of her funeral in the *Brecon and Radnor Express,* I found a list of mourners among whom was her aunt, Mrs A. Parsons of Leominster.

I began immediately to look for a woman of this name in and around Leominster, but in vain. The surname Parsons turned out to be a misprint for Passant. I learned as much in March 1981 in a report of Hugh Lloyd's funeral in *The Hereford Times,* where I saw a reference to a Mr Alfred Passant representing the late Mrs Passant, the deceased's sister. Among the wreaths there was one 'from Annie and Alf, Hanwood'. And that's how I tracked down my father's mother: Annie Sophia Lloyd had married Alfred Cornelius Passant and they'd lived at Great Hanwood, not far from Shrewsbury, from 1936.

I now had to find out whether they were still alive. At the crematorium in Shrewsbury I learned that Annie and Alfred had lived at 1 Vine Cottages, Great Hanwood, and that she had died on the 15th of April 1971 at the age of 81. If I'd been hoping to meet her, I was too late. I then decided to enlist the help of a solicitor in asking Alf Passant about his late wife. I had no idea of what their circumstances had been and so thought it prudent to go through a third party who was experienced in these matters. As I entered a solicitor's office in the centre of Shrewsbury I was taken aback to see Delwyn Williams, the former Tory M.P. for Montgomeryshire. He was more than ready to help me (for a small fee) and agreed to go to Great Hanwood to call on Alf Passant. He rang a few days later to say Alf was still living at Vine Cottages but knew nothing of a child.

I then took a while to think over the progress I'd made. I'd failed to find my father's mother while she was still alive but now that I knew she was dead I could hasten my search for more information about her. I sometimes wonder what would have happened had she been in the land of the living. Would I have been brave enough to contact her, and would my father have wanted to meet his mother, and would she have wanted to meet him? Fortunately, I'd been spared these considerations. I didn't attempt to imagine her motives or her emotions in giving her child away, for I knew nothing of her circumstances at the time, and above all, I didn't want to be judgemental. I took it for granted that she hadn't been in love with the child's father and she was too poor to keep him, but more than that it was impossible to know.

Perhaps I should have drawn my enquiries to a close now that I knew Annie Sophia was dead. But I was more determined than ever to find out more details about her and who the father of her child was. I wasted several months in 1981 trying to contact the children of Hugh Lloyd, namely Dilys Pickersgill, Maisie Harris and Kathleen Tait, in the hope they would remember something of their aunt, but they couldn't, or wouldn't help me. The only thing I learned from Mrs Tait, whom I visited in Oswestry, was that the family at Blaen-bedw had been poor, a fact that still caused her to feel great shame. Hugh Lloyd's third wife, Maude Owen, a native of Llandrindod and a graduate of Aberystwyth, who'd been the village schoolmistress at Glascwm, was dead and there were no children to the marriage.

There was nothing for it but to go and see Alf Passant, whom Annie had married in 1936 when she was 46 and he 36. It was a strange experience to sit at the bare hearth of 1 Vine Cottages, Great Hanwood, where my grandmother had lived for so long. I couldn't bring myself to tell Alf what the real purpose of my visit was; I called myself Roberts and talked for the most part about Glascwm. It was obvious that he didn't know about the child Annie had borne in 1910 and

I wasn't going to betray her secret. The marriage had been happy and Alf was quite prepared to talk about his late wife. Annie had been 'dangerous', he said, in the sense she could turn her hand to any work, especially with animals. Alf was a master builder whose firm had built the King's Hall in Aberystwyth and he had courted Annie for seventeen years. The reason why they hadn't married earlier than they did was that she was quite content with her life as a 'lady's companion' at a farm known as Weston, near Priestweston, not far from Church Stoke, again very close to the English border.

Alf Passant confirmed that his wife was from Glascwm and that her parents had died soon after her birth. This was true: Hugh and Martha Lloyd lie buried in the churchyard at Michaelchurch-on-Arrow. Martha was from a farm called Gwern-y-bwch, near Huntington, and her maiden name was Powell; it may be that she was related to the family of novelist Anthony Powell (pronounced Pole), who traced his origins to Traveley, a house near Brilley in the same district. I went to Michaelchurch-on-Arrow (the historian Griffith John Williams thought the Welsh name, Llanfihangel Dyffryn Arwy, the most euphonious of all placenames) to look for their grave with its inscription, 'Teach us to number our days that we may apply our hearts unto wisdom'. I have a photograph of Martha Lloyd in which she appears to bear a facial resemblance to my daughter Heledd. But what's more, Alf told me Annie, before moving to Shrewsbury, had been employed at Sheep House, a large farm about a mile or two outside the Hay. The farm was owned, he said, by a man called John Watkeys Jones, a well-known cattle breeder. Alf gave me two photographs of Annie in which both Ruth and I saw a strong likeness to my father and Heledd. This was the first time I'd seen a photo of my grandmother.

The next thing I had to do was find out as much as I could about John Watkeys Jones and Sheep House. Six or seven years were to pass while I visited people in the district hoping to find someone who could remember Annie

Lloyd. By good fortune I met Sheila Leitch of Glasbury, a prominent member of the Powys Family History Society and an accomplished genealogist. Together we must have spoken to well over a hundred people in hope of identifying men who'd been employed in the district in 1909/10. I kept a record of all these visits in what I came to think of as The Black Book of Blaen-bedw, which proved an invaluable way of collating the information I gathered. I drank many a cup of tea and ate dozens of small cakes while the people of the Borderlands welcomed the stranger who was enquiring about Annie Sophia Lloyd. I went up many narrow lanes and stood in many muddy yards, and was barked at by many a dog, as part of my field research. I learned not to press for answers at first but to chat casually of this and that with the hospitable people of Radnorshire before coming to the point. I enjoyed listening to them: 'Him be a cousin for we,' said one; when I asked another, 'Are you Mr Powell?' I got the guarded reply, 'If not him, who then?' or sometimes, 'Who's asking?' I learned a good deal about Radnorshire, the county not many people know much about, and that the old rhyme about the county being 'an old Englishwoman' is far from the truth.

Then, in February 1984, I went to meet a woman named Joan Whittaker in Mounton, near Chepstow. I'd seen a reference to her in a report of Annie Sophia's funeral where she was described as 'a very close friend'. It turned out she was a niece of Mrs Davies, the wife of Harry Davies, the owner of Weston in Priestweston. She had played many times with Lloydie, as she called her, and had remained in contact with her after she married Alf Passant. I called on Joan Whittaker on the pretext of enquiring about the Lloyd family of Glascwm, and using the name Roberts again – just in case.

I apologized for this deception on my second visit about a week later when I gave my real name and returned the photographs she'd lent me. It had dawned on her that I was a relative of Annie's because, she said, I bore a physical resemblance to her. She was happy to meet the grandson of 'my heroine', a woman who'd had a big influence on her while she was growing up. Joan Whittaker hadn't heard of any child but she knew Annie had had a sweetheart by the name of Joe whose picture she kept in her room, and she had a favourite cat to whom she'd given the same name. In the picture Joe wore a Glengarry cap and kilt. He'd died during the First World War, Lloydie had said. This detail coincided with what Auntie Gwen's daughter had told me back in 1962. Joan, an intelligent woman, wrote me a number of letters over the next twelve months, putting down everything she could remember about Lloydie. I was starting to get a fuller picture of the life and character of the girl from Glascwm and it was all duly recorded in the Black Book.

Joan had lots of stories about Lloydie. Clearly there'd been a close relationship between the two. One of the things she could remember was Lloydie saying, 'It's not always the bad girls who get caught'. The reason why she and Alf hadn't married sooner, Joan said, was that she was in a relationship with Harry Davies, owner of the farm where she worked; the farmer was known locally as 'The Stallion'. His wife wasn't willing to give him a divorce because she was a Catholic. Annie had left the farm for a year and the gossip was that she had borne a child by Harry Davies. When she announced her intention of marrying Alf Passant, Harry went beserk and threatened to shoot him. Shortly afterwards, he sold up and went to work as a bailiff on the estate of Sir William Fitzherbert in Tissington, Derbyshire. All this was confirmed by Bill Nicholas, one of the villagers in Priestweston.

In the same year I went with my brother Lloyd to see Roy Passant, Alf's brother, and his wife Mary in Shrewsbury. These fine people gave us a warm welcome but they knew nothing of Annie's ever having a child. Both were struck by the resemblance to Annie in photos I showed them of Heledd. Even so, they were unable to provide us with much information. Annie, it seems, had been a very reserved woman, according to Roy and Mary Passant, and she didn't often leave Great Hanwood. She'd been in their house, which was barely four miles from her home, only two or three times. There was a depth to her character, Mary Passant said, that she couldn't fathom. She could remember nothing about there being a child but she confirmed that Annie had left Weston for about a year during the 1930s, without explanation. Mary gave me Annie's copy of *Mrs Beeton's Cookery Book*, with her signature neatly written on the fly-leaf: Annie S. Lloyd. I was about to go to see Alf Passant again when I heard he'd died while clearing snow from his neighbour's front path. Before leaving the village I went to the churchyard to look for the grave of Annie and Alf. It was unmarked and there was no headstone but with the help of the vicar I located it and left a bunch of flowers on the upturned earth.

The time had come to change the direction of my enquiry and return to Glascwm. I called again on Mrs Jones in the sub-post office. She didn't know who the father of Annie's child was but suggested that her neighbour, Mrs Renée Harley-Davies, might know. When I told this woman the purpose of my visit I was astonished to hear her exclaim, 'Oh, you must be Mr Stephens's son!' My father had been in the village twice during the 1960s looking for a picture of his mother because, he said, he thought she might resemble my daughter Heledd; this was completely intuitive of him but spot on. Mrs Harley-Davies had written to Dilys Pickersgill, one of Hugh Lloyd's daughters, and she'd spoken to her sisters, but back came the answer, 'Why has he waited so long to look for his mother?' My father's response was to say he hadn't wanted to cause her any trouble, especially if she'd married. 'I could have hugged him for saying that,' said Mrs Harley-Davies. No one in the village could remember as far back as 1910. But, she said, she'd heard from her first husband's family, who were related to Florence Harley, Hugh Lloyd's wife, that a man I'm going to have to call X from here on, was the father of Annie's child. Everyone had been asking why Annie hadn't married the man who was courting her at the time, namely Billy Davies from the mill at Hundred House. No one knew for certain because Annie had been a very quiet woman, and Hugh, her brother, kept himself to himself, Mrs Harley-Davies informed me.

Now that I knew my father had been in Glascwm looking for his mother, I felt the time had come for me to tell him what I knew about her. The disquiet I'd felt while broaching the subject of his family from time to time arose from the fact that he'd misled me for so long. It was high time to clear the air and remove this obstacle in our relationship. First of all I told my mother and she agreed, in April 1984, that I should raise the matter with my father. I did so the same evening when Ruth and I went up to Trefforest. It came as a shock to my father that I knew. He held his face in his hands for a full ten minutes, after which he recovered and was ready to talk. Although he'd had a good home in Heolgerrig, he said, the knowledge that he was illegitimate and his mother had given him away to strangers had troubled him for fifty years. My mother had asked permission to tell us boys but he had always persuaded her not to do so. He'd been kept from talking about it by shame. 'It's been like a cancer in my head all these years,' he said; he was a man not given to hyperbole.

He also told us he'd changed his name in 1958 from Herbert Arthur Lloyd, his legal name, to Herbert Arthur Lloyd-Stephens, and had used this form for all official purposes ever since. It's strange to think I'm entitled to use a hyphen in my surname – just like Anglesey people! My father went on, unloading a number of things that had troubled him over the years. After buying a car in the 1960s, he'd gone up to Builth several times, walking the High Street on market day or sitting on the Gro by the river in the hope of seeing someone who looked like him, and he'd been to Old Radnor where he'd searched in vain for his mother's grave. I gave him the photos of Annie I'd obtained and, as he looked at them, he smiled – and that was the moment I knew I'd done the right thing. He said he felt a lot happier now that it was all out in the open. Our chat came to an end after I told him I loved him all the more because of the anguish he'd suffered. I felt it was high time I told him as much.

About a fortnight later Ruth and I took my parents to Michaelchurch-on-Arrow to see the grave of Hugh and Martha Lloyd, Annie Sophia's father and mother, and the plaque in memory of Hugh Lloyd the bone-setter, which bears the words:

> A talent rare by him possessed
> T'adjust the bones of the distressed;
> When ever called he ne'r refused
> But cheerfully his talent used.
> But now he lies beneath this tomb
> Till Jesus comes to adjust his own.

My father was pleased to know that he belonged to a long line of conjurors or bone-setters – among them Silver John – his chief delight (after the game of bowls and his dog Guto) was the St John's Ambulance Brigade which had acknowledged his proficiency in tending to his injured workmates on several occasions.

He also told how he'd been taken by William and Elizabeth Stephens to Maesycwmer in Monmouthshire when he was about twelve years old. There a tall, fair-haired woman had pressed him with questions about what he wanted to do after leaving school. This was almost certainly Annie Sophia, on a visit to her aunt and uncle, Sarah and Arthur Powell, the postman, who had been moved there from Walton, where my father had been born. Even so, my father had no interest in who his father might have been and he charged me not to make any further enquiries about him. I did his bidding while he was alive but he died suddenly in East Glamorgan Hospital on the 22nd of June 1984.

I was very glad I'd told him what I knew about his mother. Even so, I could have wished for a little more time in which to discuss the matter in more detail. I felt a lot closer to him during his last weeks and we were able to talk much more openly. I saw now that the burden he had borne for so long had made him introverted, cautious, tongue-tied, taciturn, and towards the end I felt great sympathy, no, great love for him.

I spent almost two more years trying to make a family-tree for the Lloyds. The late John Stratton of Llandrindod was a great help; his wife belonged to the same family. In John's opinion I bore a striking resemblance to Tom Lloyd, his wife's brother, who had been a blacksmith in Newchurch, Radnorshire, but that was not unusual: wherever I went I came across people who thought I looked like a Lloyd. It's easy enough to see a likeness between people whom you know to be related, but I heard this so often from strangers that there must be something about me that reminds them of the Lloyds. By the way, I was glad to see the other day a website entitled 'Lloyds of Baynham Hall' that's dedicated to the memory of John Stratton. My branch of the family, on the spear side but on the wrong side of the blanket, is now represented there.

The time had come to go looking for the father of Annie Sophia's child. In June 1986 I found Mrs Gwladys Worts, a sister for Billy Davies of the mill in Hundred House, the man who had been Annie's sweetheart. Mrs Worts was 88 years old and living at Disserth Mill not far from Builth. I went to see her in the hope of finding information about Billy but was surprised to hear Mrs Worts, a very alert and dignified old lady, starting to talk about Annie. She'd been employed, said Mrs Worts, on a farm known as Sheep House near the Hay. There, on the 17th / 18th of May 1909, while the farmer and his wife were in the May Fair, 'a waggoner had his way with her – what nowadays is called rape'. Mrs Worts didn't know the man's name. A few months later, Annie went home to Glascwm perhaps without realizing she was pregnant, and started working in the flour mill at Hundred House. When she didn't turn up for work one day Billy went looking for her and found her at her aunt's house in Walton, in bed with a new-born baby. When Annie's aunt assumed Billy to be the child's father, he rushed from the house in a rage and the relationship came to an abrupt end.

Hmmm. Was Mrs Worts telling a fib in an attempt to shield her brother? No, I don't think so. She was a very fine old lady, principled and kind-hearted, and was completely frank with me as far as I could tell. She was definitely of the opinion that Billy was not the child's father; if that had been true, she said, he would have married her, especially as his parents were fond of Annie and wanted them to marry. I was shown a photo of Billy and he bore no resemblance to my father whatsoever. But I was coming closer to solving the mystery.

Mrs Worts rang me in January 1987 to say perhaps she had been wrong to suggest a waggoner had fathered Annie's child. Perhaps it was the farmer, John Watkeys Jones, who'd been the father. This would have explained the fact, she said, that the baby arrived in Heolgerrig in December 1910 with a hundred sovereigns – a waggoner's wages for a year in those days. She described Annie as an honest, sensitive, hard-working woman who had been fond of animals. It was possible, she suggested, that she didn't want to cause trouble for the wife of John Watkeys Jones, who'd been kind to her. Mrs Worts knew the child had been given to a policeman and his wife in Merthyr. When William and Elizabeth Stephens had come to Sheep House to show the baby to his mother, Annie's first words were, 'Oh, he looks just like a Lloyd.' The advice I received from Mrs Worts was, 'Don't go on worrying about it, let it rest now.' She died a few months later.

But I couldn't let it rest. I now had to check out John Watkeys Jones and his family. I went to Sheep House, a fine building standing among the water-meadows of the Wye which can be glimpsed from the main road leading into the Hay. He had two sons, Elwyn and Eustace (Stacey), but they were children in 1910 and so could easily be struck off the list of suspects. At the house I had a very pleasant conversation with Sue Hudson, the daughter of Stacey Jones, who showed me photographs of the family. They were obviously well-to-do. But none of the men in the photos looked like my father, and I concluded at once that Mrs Worts's suggestion was wide of the mark. Who, then, were the waggoners working at Sheep House in 1909?

Before I set out to look for them I had some good luck. Alf Passant had shown me his marriage certificate where Annie Sophia Lloyd was given as living at 1 Mortimer Street in Leominster. I went there in June 1986 and spoke to the man living at that address, namely Edward Ralph Powell. He was the son of Arthur and Sarah Jane Powell, Annie's uncle and aunt, formerly of The Green in Walton where my father had been born in 1910. Eddie's father was the son of Margaret Powell of Huntington, the Grannie Powell who had raised Annie and her brother Hugh after the death of their parents. At 1 Mortimer Street Annie Sophia Lloyd had her home, the one from which she'd been married.

Eddie Powell was a strange man, but likeable enough. His only interest in life was messing about with wireless sets. The living room was full of them, and so were the kitchen, the bedrooms and the garden shed. Eddie could remember Annie's wedding-day in 1936, when he would have been 24, but he had no interest whatsoever in talking about her. In fact, he could talk only about radios: his hobby had become an obsession to the point of giving the impression that he was simple, though that wasn't true. Eccentric, more like it.

After listening to Eddie for about two hours, I was on the point of escaping from the house when he started going through a large sideboard and rummaging until he pulled out a huge album full of photographs and postcards. And now he began piling them up for me to inspect: postcards Annie had sent to her aunt and uncle, a few she'd received from other people, photos of her and of Martha Lloyd, her mother, and then, suddenly, a photo of a baby about ten months old – my father! What's more, this was the exact photo I'd seen at home in Trefforest. Across one corner someone had written 'Herbert Arthur Lloyd', and the date, 'December 1910'. I looked at it with open mouth. Clearly, his mother had given one of these photos to William and Elizabeth Stephens and kept the other for herself.

On my second visit to Eddie in September 1986 I had to listen to him rambling on about radios (he was a ham alright) before he gave me another dozen or so postcards. Most bore quite ordinary messages but one read: 'Sunday evening (Feb 7, 1910) the Mere Dear Nely just a line sorry I could not come up as I have been away we were all disappointed you did not come as they all expected you can you find my brother on the front will mark him with a x goodbye my dear one your Joe xxx.' The card was addressed to Annie at Blaen-bedw, Glascwm. On the other side of the card there was a group of soldiers in camp. Was this the Joe about whom Joan Whittaker had spoken of as Annie's sweetheart? Very likely. There was a photo of him in his Glengarry cap and kilt among the rest of the things in the album. Was this my father's father? Perhaps, but he didn't look at all like him. Why hadn't Joe known that Nely wasn't able to leave Blaen-bedw in February 1910, about a fortnight before the birth of her child? It's difficult to believe he would have complained about her not coming to see him if he'd been aware of her condition.

I had to find Joe in order to strike him off the list. It took two years of enquiry before I found him, and I had Sheila Leitch to thank for that. His full name was William Joseph Morgan and he'd been a gamekeeper on the estate of the Snead-Cox family in Eywood near Titley, between Presteigne and Kington on the Herefordshire side of the border. He was one of the twenty million who died in the Spanish 'flu epidemic of November 1918 at the age of 32, having served in the Machine Gun Corps, according to that dreadfully thorough work, *Soldiers who Died in the Great War*. On his grave in the

Catholic cemetery at Broxwood (the family employed only Catholics) were the words: 'The dearly loved son of Thomas and Mary Morgan, The Mere. My Jesus, mercy. R.I.P.' I stood quietly by the grave in the company of Sheila Leitch in June 1988.

The trail was now leading into the western counties of England. Having gone to the Army Archives in Hereford I spoke to about twenty people who claimed to be close or distant relatives of the Morgan family. Eventually I met Molly Bowden, Joe's niece, in Lyonshall. At the time of his death, she told me, Joe had a fiancée and she showed me a ring inscribed with the words 'From Willie to Ethel'. So, although Joe (Willie) had been courting Annie Lloyd in 1910, by 1918 he'd been engaged to someone else. It seemed unlikely that William Joseph Morgan was my father's father.

Even so, he has a part in the story. Years later, in 2006 to be precise, I received a phonecall from a woman named Margaret Scandrett living in Llandissil in Montgomeryshire. She told me she'd been reading my book *A Semester in Zion*, in which I gave details about Annie Lloyd, and that her late husband, Alan, had been her grandson. I was surprised to hear this and at first I thought she must be mistaken. But no, she was quite right. Annie had had another child, she said, a girl by the name of Muriel Gladys Lloyd, who was known as Laurie, and that had been in October 1911, although Margaret didn't know who the father was.

I went to visit Margaret Scandrett in Llandissil and let her see everything I'd collected in *The Black Book of Blaen-bedw*. I'm not going after this story here, lest the reader be confused by a narrative that's complicated enough as it is. But I have to say I shouldn't be at all surprised if Joe Morgan turns out to have been the father of Annie's second child, although I have no evidence to support this line of enquiry. If he was, it would be consistent with the version I'd heard from Auntie Gwen, that the father had died in the Great War, and with what Joan Whittaker told me about Annie keeping a photograph of Joe in his Glengarry and kilt, and calling her favourite cat Joe. It's more likely Annie had introduced these details into the story of my father, in order to put people off the track or they'd been mixed up in the re-telling. I haven't followed up this story nor the one about Annie leaving the farm in Priestweston for a while during the 1930s. These are projects I'm happy to leave for someone else!

I called at Sheep House again and spoke to Sue Hudson, Stacey Jones's daughter, who gave me an important piece of information: Margaret Jones, the wife of John Watkeys Jones, was known in the district for her good works and generosity to people in need. She was killed in a road accident at the gate of Sheep House in 1929. But this is the thing: having read about her funeral in the *Brecon and Radnor Express*, I learned that she came from Merthyr, and was the daughter of the Reverend Rees Evans and a sister to J. R. Evans who had taught History at Cyfarthfa School. Among those who'd sent wreaths was Annie Lloyd. I now understood, at last, how my father had come to be taken to Merthyr and how the baby had arrived with a hundred gold sovereigns: John Watkeys Jones, a wealthy man, and his wife, must have felt some responsibility for what had happened to Annie in their home during their absence on the 17th / 18th of May 1909 and had tried to help her in her difficulties. There is no proof of this, of course, but it seems to me more than likely.

I coursed several more hares during 1987. But by then I felt confident enough to give the name Blaen-bedw to our house in Whitchurch; this was one way of keeping the story of Annie and her child alive. Even so, I wasn't able to leave the matter there. After a break of a few months, I decided to renew my enquiries and this time more thoroughly, and to eliminate the ten men on my list one by one. Like every good detective, I wasn't going to leave a stone unturned. By now I'd collected a huge amount of material and The Black Book of Blaen-bedw had become a hefty file.

I began with the man named by Mrs Harley-Davies. X had

been a waggoner in the district of the Hay in 1910 and he was of the right age. I learned a good deal about him in a very short time because his family had been prominent Baptists. Some of his children were still alive and so I paid each a visit. Eventually, in July 2002, I found a man who was a son of X, an old farmer, a widower with no children, who was only too willing to talk about his father. I was struck at once by this man's resemblance to my father, and in the pictures he showed me the resemblance was even greater, and so I took the plunge and raised the matter with him. He didn't know of any child his father had had before marrying but he listened attentively to what I had to say. He agreed that I looked like his father and like him.

More importantly, on my second visit to his home, and after I'd assured him I wasn't after his money, he agreed to provide a sample of his saliva for the purposes of a DNA test. A fortnight later, the result came from Glasgow University's laboratories: positive. Hooray for the Y chromosome! There was no need to go after the other nine men on my list, fortunately. I'd proved who my father's father was at long last. I've decided not to name him here out of respect for his son, who's been of great help to me, and especially because his brothers and sisters know nothing about their father's child born out of wedlock. I'm still in contact with X's son and from time to time I go to have a chat and cup of tea at his fireside.

I had great satisfaction from the story's ending. I'd found my father's mother and now his father. Some twenty-two years had gone by since I began my enquiry but my efforts had borne fruit in the end. I tried not to think too much about why Annie Sophia hadn't kept her child. After all, there's a tradition in the countryside, especially in Radnorshire, of bringing up illegitimate children as members of the family. But she didn't have a family, except for Hugh Lloyd, and he hadn't shown much interest in her predicament. Nor have I given much thought to her life at Priestweston as the inamorata of Harry Lloyd and as Alf Passant's wife in Great Hanwood. But I can't help wondering whether she ever regretted giving her child away and had she ever thought about him? I very much hope so. For the grandmother I never knew I have only sympathy, and a feeling of loss, for my father's sake mainly, but I could have wished for better for them both.

My father worked for fifty years in the power station at Upper Boat. He was a hardworking and conscientious worker and never lost a shift at work, which was dirty, monotonous and dangerous. I see him now trudging on his old bike in fair weather and foul, down through the sandies of Cilhaul, and along the cinder path between river and railway, and coming home dog-tired but without complaint, after an eight-hour shift. Towards the end he suffered from the effects of asbestos dust in his lungs, which he'd contracted during the General Strike of 1926 when as a boy of 16 he'd been given the task of cleaning the lagging on the huge pipes that carried water to and from the cooling towers. He'd been trying to get compensation from the Electricity Board and a pitifully small sum arrived a few days after his funeral. I felt admiration for him but also gratitude for having given me higher education and the chance to experience a world of which he knew nothing. But I didn't have a chance to tell him as much while he was alive, and so I put it on record now.

The question remains why did I go to so much trouble to find my father's mother and father? Well, I began my search in the belief that my father would like to know, one day, who his parents were and to receive information about them. But after his death I wanted this information for my own sake. To paraphrase Alun Llywelyn-Williams, 'Wise is the man who knows his own dark yesterday'.

What's more, the story of my search for my father's parents spurred me into writing verse in Welsh, and for that I'm especially grateful.

7

Among Mormons

HAVING LEFT THE Arts Council during the summer of 1990, I intended earning a living as a freelance journalist, editor, translator, and literary agent. I set up a company called Combrógos (an early form of the word *Cymry*) and discovered there was plenty of work to keep me busy. By September I was contributing articles and news-stories to the *Western Mail* fairly regularly.

Then, quite suddenly, I was offered a term's work as a French teacher at the comprehensive school in Tonypandy, and although I hadn't expected to have chalk in my pockets ever again, unless I had to, accepted it happily enough. As Gwyn Jones, my old Professor in Aberystwyth, who'd been very supportive of me, once said, a teacher's job is an honourable and worthwhile one. I started in Tonypandy on the 12th of September 1990. The Head of Modern Languages was Jeff Powell, a former pupil of Pontypridd Boys' Grammar School, whom I didn't know before taking up the post.

The only cloud on the horizon at the time was the news that I was showing the first signs of having diabetes. The doggerel I wrote in my diary suggests I made light of this news:

What, still alive at fifty-two
And weighing more than eighteen stone?
Lose some weight, lad, if I were you,
And leave the *bara brith* alone.

To fats and sugars say goodbye,
Eat more carbohydrates, lad,
Give up puddings or you'll die,
On jam and marmalade declare jihad.

Life may be sweet but from now on
Guinness is a mortal sin,
Scrape the butter from your scone,
Or next you'll be on insulin.

Look your last on all things luscious,
Go easy on the currant cake,
Apple tarts may be delicious
But they are a big mistake.

Take my advice: diabetes kills,
You're too young to go to heaven,
Take those blue remembered pills
Or else you won't see fifty-seven.

Cut out chutney, cheese and chocolate,
The wines of Portugal and France,
Or you'll get a one-way ticket
To the isles of Coxsaike & Langerhans.

Take your blood-count every morning,
Then some strenuous exercise,
Let me give you this dire warning:
First it affects your feet and eyes,

Then, if you don't pay attention,
Hæmorrhage in heart and head;
Soon, I must not fail to mention,
You'll end up a statistic – dead.

Don't complain and never grouse, man,
Try to live a life that's savoury –
For there's life beyond the gravy,
And give up reading A. E. Housman.

But diabetes is no joke: my condition has got worse and by now I'm wholly dependent on a twice-daily injection of insulin as well as a fistful of tablets – I call them my Insulin Allsorts. It's best to laugh in the face of the Furies.

I enjoyed my term in Tonypandy, although teaching French to children who saw no point in speaking a second language was an 'ard 'eadin at times. Even so, the verbs and idioms came easily back to mind, thanks to Jack Reynolds, my old French teacher. I read a chapter or two of *La Peste*, the novel by Albert Camus, with the two girls taking French for A Level, something I hadn't been able to do in Ebbw Vale. One of the linguistic barbarisms I came across fairly often was Rhondda people's tendency to say things like 'I do go' and 'I do sing'. I was familiar with it in their English – indeed, some of the teachers used it. But it was difficult to accept *'Je fais aller'* and *'Je fais chanter'* and *'Je fais faire mes devoirs'* as French as it's spoken in France. When I mentioned this to one of my colleagues, he replied, 'Yeah, I know, mun, these old French verbs do do their 'ead in'; he was the English teacher. On the other hand, more than one class learned to give lusty renderings of *'La Marseillaise'*, *'Chagrin d'amour'*, *'Au clair de la lune'*, *'Ma Normandie'* and *'Dites-moi pourquoi, chère Mademoiselle'*.

I had no trouble from the pupils except on one occasion: an over-confident boy refused to come out in front of the class, so I went to get him, holding him with my forefinger in the vee of his jersey to help him to get up from his desk. He was a lad from London who thought he could behave just as he wished in school. He was very unpopular with his classmates and I heard some of them shouting, 'Go on, Sir, 'it 'im, 'e do talk funny, 'e's English!' In the end there was nothing for it but to send the boy to see the Headmaster, and shortly afterwards his father complained that I'd caused him GBH.

Fortunately, the Head knew about the behaviour of this pupil and did nothing about the complaint. The Head's name was Malcolm Jones, a former Physical Education teacher and one of the most genial men in the school. A native of Tonypandy and member of the Labour Party, like most of the staff, he knew every pupil by name and most of their families, as well. He was held in high esteem by his colleagues and I liked him too, particularly for his delicious malapropisms. For example, when Jeff Powell came back from Spain with a shield the boys had won at some sport of other, he was congratulated by Malcolm in Assembly on getting the trophy through the 'off licence' in Dover. But he also knew when to turn a blind eye to the misdemeanours of his staff. When some of us went over to Maerdy in the Rhondda Fach on the last morning of term, the 21st of December, to take part in the procession marking the closure of the last pit in the Rhondda, it was late afternoon before we came back to school, but Malcolm said nothing, fair play. It was a bitter-sweet experience to walk behind a brass band with the people of 'little Moscow' on that occasion.

I had a variety of jobs during the first half of 1991, mainly thanks to kind friends of mine. I was commissioned to do programme research by Euryn Ogwen of S4C. After the death of Dorothy Eagle, I prepared a new edition of *The Oxford Literary Guide to Great Britain and Ireland* for Oxford University Press, making sure it had more entries for places with literary associations in Wales. In March, courtesy of Ned Thomas, I went to Brussels, Barcelona, Paris, Amsterdam, Leuwarden and Aberystwyth to discuss the Mercator project and make a report for the European Commission. I spent three busy weeks as a French examiner (A Level) in the secondary schools of Monmouthshire and then, thanks to Geraint Talfan Davies, three months writing a memorandum for the BBC on ideas I'd culled from the archives. I was made a Life Member of Yr Academi Gymreig – the only person ever to receive this honour.

But best of all was an offer to teach at Brigham Young University in Provo, Utah. My friend Leslie Norris was responsible for the invitation. I flew to America at the end of August 1991, leaving Ruth and Huw at home; Lowri, Heledd and Brengain had started on their own careers. As is well-known, BYU is an institution that belongs to the Church of Jesus Christ of Latter-day Saints. Leslie and I were the only people on campus who were not Mormons. I accepted the invitation with alacrity, for the salary was very generous and I was to be given the title Visiting Professor. I knew every lecturer is a professor in the United States but I was to be a real Professor, with the status and some of the responsibilities to go with it. I'd be taking classes on only two days a week, that is to say, eight hours teaching, and the rest of my time was my own.

I spent the first few days at the Norris's home, where I made the acquaintance of Gwenno, a standard Welsh terrier, the most intelligent dog I've ever met. After I moved into my flat in Wymount Terrace I had a phonecall from the mother of Tiffany H. Joab who'd been the previous tenant: I knew this because her name was still on the door. Mrs Joab was anxious to know where her daughter was: 'How come she ain't called her mom?' I had the impression she suspected me of kidnapping her, or something even worse. I was unable to help and, despite her name, she lost patience with me, shouting over and over, 'Who are you and whadya doin' there?' A good question, I thought: who was I and what was I doing there? It deserved an answer. So I began keeping the diary that eventually became my book *A Semester in Zion*. I nearly dedicated it to Mrs Joab.

When I woke up next morning in Wymount Terrace there was a clear blue sky and a new world all around me. A humming-bird was feeding on the sticky buds of a pine growing at my window. The campus stretched over a thousand acres and mountains (altitude 11,750 feet) stood on all sides. There were about 27,000 students at BYU, from more than seventy countries, though I didn't see a black or Hispanic face in all the time I was there. As I began exploring the campus next day a pretty girl in a flowery dress rode past on a bike and singing, 'Oh, what a bootiful mornin'!', and I called after her 'That's a lovely song!' to which she replied, 'You bet!' I was going to enjoy my semester in Zion – perhaps.

The campus that first morning was swarming with freshers, the men in dark grey trousers, white shirts and a tie, the women in summery frocks and some wearing white socks as if on a film set in the 1950s. Leslie had warned me about the dress code but I was taken aback by a scene so deliciously retro. I saw nothing of the 'distressed look' that's so common among students at British universities. There were no graffiti on the walls and no rubbish anywhere, and the lawns and flowers were well-tended: no coffee, tea or tobacco in the shops and cafés, and no newspapers of any quality, either. BYU sends a lot of its right-wing graduates into the ranks of the CIA. The University's motto is 'The glory of God is intelligence' and its logo is a beehive denoting diligence. It was warm in the sunshine that morning and so I sat for a while under a eucalyptus tree listening to a band practising its music and marching. When one of the majorettes came over to ask me to suggest a piece of music, I said 'Shenandoah', and so they played one of my favourite songs. I enjoy listening to brass bands, especially when the instrumentalists are young and pert and willing to do my bidding.

In the corridors of the English Department, where I had an office with my name on the door, it always felt like a public school on Sunday afternoon with the headmaster keeping an eye on everyone's behaviour by means of closed-circuit television. I heard later that some of the teaching staff were hoping for 'tenure' (a full-time contract) and on their best behaviour. Even so, there were some colourful characters and mavericks such as Eugene England, a clever chap who was often in hot water with the Sanhedrin for writing that was considered unorthodox. But on the whole, everything and everyone was remarkably quiet and well-behaved.

I met that morning a professor by the name of William Shakespeare, who claimed to be a descendant of the dramatist's brother, and John Harris, a tall, handsome man who went around on crutches after being involved in an accident in an aeroplane he'd built himself. His forefathers had come to Utah from Wales, he told me, but he didn't show the slightest interest in the fact that I was Welsh. On condition that I listened to him telling yarns about his adventures in the army, we got on well throughout the Semester. One of the things we did to amuse ourselves was to play word-games. I would recite limericks and he introduced me to Tom Swifties: 'Send him down,' said the judge condescendingly; 'I am very partial to sweet pancakes,' he said surreptitiously; 'I shall go to Moab alone,' said Martha ruthlessly; that kind of thing, for hours on end. John was one of the better Mormon poets and most good poets like word-games.

I had my first shock during a conversation with him a few days later. One of his duties as a good Mormon, he told me, was to baptize the Hungarian nation, and he did this every Wednesday morning in the Temple, so that they might have the chance to go to the Mormon heaven. The crux of the ceremony, as far as I could gather, was that John would stand in a large basin of water with the dead person's name and dates on a plastic card … but he wasn't willing to go any further. *Omertà*. I was astonished by this piece of information but John accepted the responsibility without question. When I asked, not entirely seriously, whether he hoped to complete his task before he died – there are, after all, quite a few dead Magyars – he said his father and grandfather had done the same thing and he had sons and grandsons who would come after him. A kind of family industry, then, to save the Hungarian nation and allow them to enter the Mormon heaven.

Some while later I was introduced to Ron Dennis, Professor of Welsh and Portuguese, who told me immediately he was related to Captain Dan Jones, a Flintshire man and an early

Mormon. Ron spoke to me in Welsh about the Mormons – he'd learned enough to read newspapers of the period – but changed to English for discussion of other topics. Is there in the academic world, I wondered, any other university that has a Professor of Welsh and Portuguese on its staff?

Be that as it may, that's how I was introduced to the Mormon faith. I called on Leslie in his office that same day. He told me he had difficulty accepting what the Mormons believed but thought *The Book of Mormon*, on which the faith is founded, 'a good read' that was full of exciting events and colourful characters – rather like *Gone with the Wind* or *How Green Was My Valley*, he added with a grin. On the other hand, Leslie had great admiration for the Mormons, especially for their readiness to help their neighbours and the poor, and for their health service. The Norrises were both in poor health themselves (Leslie with sleep apnea) and set great store by being near a good hospital. The couple had lived in Utah for more than twenty years and the University had been uncommonly kind to Leslie, giving him a personal chair and just about every academic honour that was its to give. He was a familiar figure at cultural events in Provo and along the Valley of the Great Salt Lake. I heard him reading his work on several occasions and, it must be said, he could entertain and charm an audience like no other poet I knew. Now turning seventy, he talked endlessly about returning to Wales and buying a house in the Hay or the Vale of Glamorgan, but I could see he would never do so. He and his wife, Kitty, had put down roots in Utah, for the first time in their lives, perhaps.

In the shops and offices on campus I was often asked where I came from. Most had heard of Wales, perhaps because Welsh people had been among the first members of the Church and had played a prominent part in founding the Temple Choir in Salt Lake City. The conductor of the Choir while I was in Provo was a woman whose family came from Heolgerrig. I told a woman cashier that I came from Pontypridd and when she asked where that was, I said, mischievously, it was between Tonypandy and Merthyr Tydfil and not far from Llanfihangel Genau'r Glyn. Her only comment was that these names struck her as 'typically English', proving that an awareness of Wales was not all that developed in these parts.

If the Mormons didn't know much about Wales, I was determined to learn about the faith that had led them to the desert of Utah in 1847. So I began reading *The Book of Mormon*, which is considered, together with more than a hundred 'Revelations' and 'Covenants', as the Word of God. I read the Bible from cover to cover when I was a student, and so I had to try to read *The Book of Mormon* – or, at least, parts of it. Mark Twain referred to the *Book* as 'chloroform in print' and, with the book in my hands, I found myself nodding off more than once in my flat in Wymount Terrace.

The text of the *Book*, it is said, was discovered by Joseph Smith (1805–44) who had a 'vision' in 1823 that became the basis of the Mormon faith. When this roughneck, a professional conman, asked the two figures who appeared in his room – none other than God and Jesus – which of the churches in America was the True Church, he received the reply that they were all apostate and the activities of every one were 'anathema' in His view.

A few years later, when Smith would have been 22, he had another 'vision'. This time he said an angel by the name of Moroni told him to go to a hill called Cumorah near Palmyra on Lake Ontario, where Smith was living at the time. There he found a number of golden plates bearing words written in an unknown script he called 'reformed Egyptian' and guarded by a white salamander. Only he, Smith said, could read the plates, and then only with the help of a special pair of spectacles and two stones, the Urim and the Thummim – he'd read the Book of Exodus. This was said to have happened in 1827, a time when a number of new sects were sweeping the East Coast of America. Smith claimed to have translated the plates – he was, by the way, virtually illiterate – and then, conveniently enough, the angel came back to reclaim them. The text was published as *The Book of Mormon* in 1830. Moroni also told Smith that, since all other churches were apostate, he was to be head of the new church, which seemed fair enough since it was he who'd written its *Book*. The Melchizedek priesthood was bestowed on Joseph Smith and Oliver Cowdery by Saints Peter, James and John, and these two were given authority to organize the Church. The twelve 'apostles' who govern the Church today are direct successors to Smith and Cowdery.

This was the first time I'd come face-to-face with religious fundamentalism, apart from that which goes in the guise of Evangelicism and Catholicism in Wales, and I decided to meet it head-on, as it were, by trying to understand what the Mormons believed as best I could as an outsider, in order to understand the society in which I now found myself. That is why I'm going to give them so much attention in this book.

The Saints believe that the teachings of Christ, several centuries after His death, were corrupted and lost, and that *The Book of Mormon* (its sub-title is 'Another Testament of Jesus Christ'), every one of its 588 pages, restores His message. There are some similarities between the Bible and *The Book of Mormon* but the history recounted in the latter book is like no other. It tells a highly complicated story of how, in the year 600 BC, a small group of Hebrews escaped from their Babylonian captors and set off across the Indian Ocean, some continuing the journey across the Atlantic and landing in the Americas. There they established a great civilization with many a temple and city in it. But their endeavours were thwarted by a war between the light-skinned, virtuous Nephites and the dark-skinned, wicked Lamanites in which their cities were destroyed. After the Resurrection, Christ appeared in their midst. This is an important part of the rigmarole, I suppose: that Jesus once trod the soil of America.

For two hundred years after Christ's appearance, so the

story goes, the two tribes lived in harmony and prosperity. But as a result of schism and friction, sin returned among them and the people were split into two factions once again. Then, about AD 421, hostilities broke out afresh. Mormon was killed in a battle with the Lamanites but not before preserving the golden plates by burying them in the hill Cumorah as a witness to Christ's divinity 'in the latter days'. This was the text which Joseph Smith is said to have discovered in 1827. The Nephites were absorbed into other ethnic groups from Europe and Asia and became the forefathers of the Native American tribes of North and South America. The total absence of any archaeological or paleographic evidence for this baloney doesn't deter the Mormons from believing this arrant nonsense. I heard intelligent men telling the tale with conviction.

It came as no surprise to learn that the early Mormons had raised the hackles of their neighbours and all who came into contact with them; many were as hostile to their religious beliefs as they were to their practice of polygamy. It was said Smith had fifty wives and Brigham Young, who succeeded him after he was killed by a mob in Carthage in Illinois, had a similar number. After their leader's death about a thousand Mormons set off for the West, dragging their belongings in handcarts across the most mountainous terrain in North America. When they reached the Valley of the Great Salt Lake on the 24th of July 1847, they found a barren desert that was unpeopled – except by a tribe of Utes. According to the story, Young said, 'This is the place', and so Salt Lake City was built. Over the next twenty years, about 60,000 Mormons joined them. Their descendants were all around me as I wrote up my diary in the library. I searched in vain in the BYU library for copies of several famous books such as *Ulysses*, *The Grapes of Wrath*, and the poems of T. S. Eliot and Baudelaire. There wasn't a single book from Wales, with the exception of Leslie's. Hard to believe it, but BYU has a good academic reputation among the universities of the United States.

Whatever might be thought of the Mormons' religious beliefs, the story of their trek westward is quite heroic. Indeed, reading *The Mormon Experience*, a standard history by Leonard J. Arrington and Davis Bitton, I was reminded of the Welsh and their settlement in Patagonia: they were able to colonize the Chubut Valley because no one else wanted it, and the desert bloomed because of their tough character, hard work and persistence.

Joseph Smith was clearly a man of great energy and charisma. Some have considered him a rogue and others have looked upon him as a sort of demi-god. He was definitely an insatiable womanizer and something of a bully. Some anti-Mormon authors like his biographer Fawn McKay Brodie have portrayed him as a liar and the Saints as gullible, superstitious dupes, a people who were misled by unprincipled leaders. It's obvious a lot of poor people became Mormons in the hope of a new start on a new continent and chance to put down roots in a foreign, hostile land.

The Mormons believe their Zion will be built in America and, after the Second Coming, Christ will have His headquarters in Utah. Their aim, in the mean while, is to create the moral, social and political conditions that will form the basis for this longed-for event. The aim of a good Mormon, they say, is 'to be like Christ'. They couldn't understand me when I told them that to have great literature (such as the plays of Shakespeare) there must be sin, and one of my difficulties in class was to persuade them to say anything critical about their fictional characters or show how wrong-doers sometimes behave. Because their Church refuses to allow this aspect of writing, the Mormons don't have any really great literature. Their most important poet is May Swenson and she turned her back on the Church towards the end of her life. Clinton F. Larson, BYU's Laureate, was most certainly not an important poet. Mind you, the Mormons hadn't heard of any Welsh poet, with the exception of Dylan

Thomas, although one of my colleagues had heard of 'Horace Thomas', the poet from Aberdaron. In the programmes I watched in my flat I didn't see any violence or sex or hear any swearing; indeed, the most exciting film I saw was *Brideshead Revisited*, with the naughty bits cut out.

I watched a Mormon service from time to time, all three hours of it, and I went to a service in the Temple out of curiosity. During the proceedings, to my great surprise, I didn't hear a single reference to Joseph Smith or *The Book of Mormon*, and, indeed, everything was quite ordinary, except for the tears of a woman who was taking leave of one of her sons who was going overseas as a missionary. As I listened to them, the words of Byron came to mind: 'I stood among them but not of them in a shroud of thoughts which were not their thoughts.' But, like Alan Bennett, I didn't say anything.

The Cross on which Jesus died is nowhere to be seen in the Mormon temples, nor on their graves. They see no suffering or sacrifice in the death of Christ. They believe he was a prophet like Joseph Smith and both men have the same status in their credo. I found this hard to accept, as I am a great admirer of Jesus as a historical man whereas Smith was so clearly a blackguard. Only in the parts which have been translated 'correctly' is the Bible 'true', in their opinion, while *The Book of Mormon* is 'true' in its entirety. I heard this from one of my colleagues by the name of Cynthia Hallen over supper in the refectory one evening. She had been disowned by her family because of her conversion to Mormonism, poor woman.

In 1991, when I was in Provo, there were about six million Mormons, most of them in the United States, and their numbers continue to swell. The Church had assets worth $30 billion. Mormons who want to be considered 'members in good standing' must contribute about fifteen per cent of their income to the Church and also work for it as volunteers. The Mormons don't have their own language and while it's possible to speak of 'the Mormon people' there's no such thing as a Mormon nation. As in the case of the Jews, Mormonism is a religion which has created a people. They make up more than 60 per cent of the population of Utah and a lot live in Wyoming and Nevada too. Every Senator from Utah is a Mormon. They dominate the state's legal system, sit on the school boards, on the urban councils and the town halls. In short, the hand of the Church is to be seen in every aspect of public life. The comparison with the Soviet Union, where the Communist Party had its finger in every pie before the state broke up, struck me as particularly apposite. Islam is similar, like every religion that forbids the slightest disagreement and calls it heresy.

Not far from Wymount Terrace there was a Missionary Training Centre. Every male Mormon has to spend two years spreading the Church's message overseas, full-time and without remuneration. He receives barely three weeks' training in the MTC and is given orders to rely on the Holy Spirit for sustenance. These are the boys who knock on your door from time to time. The Melchizedek priesthood is not open to females, and women play a very inferior role in the life of the Church.

I often saw groups of young men in smart black suits and white shirts around the campus and found it easy to strike up conversations with them since they were always hoping for conversions. When I mentioned to two of them (they usually go around in pairs) that there's not a smidgen of evidence to support their belief that the Lamanites and Nephites built a great civilisation in North America and that Christ appeared in what is today New York State, I received the reply, 'Sir, it ain't been discovered yet.' It's difficult to argue with this sort of mindset except to remember the words of Benjamin Franklin (or was it Goya?): 'The sleep of reason produces monsters.' On the other hand, when I expressed some of my doubts to my students, one of them said, 'What you believe depends to a large extent on what you've been taught. We've been brought up to believe *The Book of Mormon* to be true and so we believe it is.' A good point, perhaps, and something to think about, but at the same time, whether or not intelligence is the gift of God, it must be used.

Noël Owen and his wife Pat hadn't been raised in the Mormon faith. He was a Welsh-speaker from Pen-y-bont-fawr in Montgomeryshire. As I walked into his office on campus, where he was Professor of Chemistry, I knew at once he was the brother of Ifor Owen, who lodged in the Sun Hotel in Aberystwyth. Noël, who'd been a lecturer in Bangor, told me he'd been converted to Mormonism on his own doorstep when a missionary had called at his home in Menai Bridge. Noël and Pat were quite pleasant, hospitable people but orthodox in the extreme. The Church could change, I was told, only through a 'revelation' among the Twelve Apostles who made up the all-powerful Sanhedrin. Every Mormon 'in good standing' accepts the authority of these old men (they are all in their nineties) without question. Noël and his wife were critical of the Anglican Church because of its failure, they said, to take a stand against the ordination of women. When I asked, very carefully, what their attitude to homosexuality was, they said they'd leave the Church if it were ever to be accepted, but they had no answer when I asked where they would go. The couple's eldest daughter could sing a few Welsh songs she'd learned in Anglesey but the other children didn't have a word of the language because they'd been raised in Utah.

One of the darkest episodes in Mormon history is the massacre at Mountain Meadows in south-west Utah in 1857. A band of non-Mormon settlers were killed while on their way to California. A tribe of Paiute were blamed at first but the real criminals were a group of Mormon militia whose leader, John D. Lee, Brigham Young's adopted son, was shot for his part in the killing. The young missionaries I spoke to in Provo hadn't heard of this incident, or so they told me, and nor did they know about *Salamander*, the book by Linda Sillitoe and Allen Roberts which gives an account of the murders that took place in Salt Lake City in the 1980s after Mark Hofmann, a master forger, had counterfeited hundreds of Mormon documents and sold them to the highest bidder, including the Church. It's difficult to believe Mormon missionaries hadn't heard of such things. I wonder whether any have been to see *The Book of Mormon*, the satirical musical that's been running in London these last three years. Ruth and I didn't see any when we went in 2013.

The truth is that there's such a thing as 'the blood covenant' in the Saints' culture by which a Mormon has the right, as long as God allows, to take revenge on those who trespass against him. On the way to Salt Lake City for the first time I saw the State Penitentiary, a grim building even with all its lights on by day and night. This is where Gary Gilmore was executed for killing two Mormons in 1976. He went to his death quite willingly, fully aware of 'the blood covenant', as described by Norman Mailer in his powerful book *The Executioner's Song*. After a year of legal argument, Gilmore was found guilty and, standing in front of the firing squad, shouted, 'Let's do it!' I also remembered Joe Hillstrom, leader of the Wobblies, the federation of unions and industrial workers who refused to fight in the First World War. Joe was executed in the Penitentiary after being found guilty on a trumped-up charge of killing a man in Salt Lake City. He's commemorated in the song 'The Ballad of Joe Hill' and as the bus drove past the prison I sang:

> I dreamt I saw Joe Hill last night, alive as you and me,
> Says I, But Joe you're ten years dead,
> I never died, says he, I never died says he.

Despite all this, there were five or six people in the English Department who were kind to me. I remember, for instance, Sally Taylor, a good poet, who invited me to her home, and Brian and Lorna Best who took me up into the Uinta mountains (altitude 7,500 feet) to visit the graves of their people. I also went for dinner to the home of Ron

Dennis and for supper with John and Susan Tanner, a very pleasant couple, and their five children. John, who was a Milton specialist, had visited the National Eisteddfod two years previously.

While I was in their house, John showed me seven rucksacks, each stuffed with tinned food and things like ropes, lamps, axes and sleeping bags. Provo, he explained, lay on a geological fault and earthquakes occurred from time to time. Before we began our meal, John thanked God for my presence in their home. I shut my eyes tight because the smallest children were watching me through their fingers. John also explained that the Church expects every family to hold an evening at home once a week and I think that's what they were doing that evening. As soon as I got back to Wymount Terrace I made myself a large cup of coffee from the jar I'd brought with me, and then another, as a rebellious act against the prevailing orthodoxy in Provo. I am a Dissenter by instinct.

A few days later I received a visit in my office on campus from a young woman who wanted to discuss her unhappiness with the Church in which she'd grown up. She wasn't willing to give me her name. I knew the students thought of me as a liberal, that is to say, someone who wasn't part of their conservative world and one who was willing to discuss their problems. She was critical of the Church because of the way it treated women, especially its emphasis on having to bear children in their early twenties. I'd heard that a number of my colleagues had six or seven children and one had twelve. When I asked my visitor the reason for this polyphiloprogenitivity she explained that the Mormon woman had a duty to provide physical receptacles for the spiritual children of God who came down from the planet Kolob, where God and his wife (yes, his wife) lived. I bridled at this and suggested a less fantastic explanation: it was important for a desert people in the early days of Mormonism to ensure there were plenty of people to work the land. I also suggested the Church's practice of polygamy could be explained in the same way: a small sect needs to grow and one way of growing is to have as many children as possible. But no, not at all, said this intelligent, quite sophisticated woman, that certainly wasn't the case.

Strangely enough, barely two hours later, I watched a television programme about polygamy. Although the Church prohibited it in 1890, as a condition of joining the American Union, the fundamentalist practice has survived to this day. During the lifetime of Joseph Smith, the Church's official teaching was monogamy. But when his brother Hyrum asked for heavenly guidance on the matter he received the 'revelation' that adultery was not a sin in God's eyes. Brigham Young went on: 'The only men who have the right to be gods are those who practise polygamy.' Handy things, 'revelations', sometimes. Although the Church has banned polygamy, it's estimated there are between 40,000 and 100,000 polygamists in Utah, Idaho, Nevada, Arizona and California who still practise it.

A few days later I had another visitor, this time a young man who wanted to discuss homosexuality. He wasn't gay, of course, but he had a friend who was – the old story I'd heard before on campus. I knew the Mormons proscribed both homosexuality and lesbianism and those who practised it had no place in their Church. I discussed sexuality with this student for about two hours, trying to explain as best I could the law and attitudes prevalent in the Yookay, and he listened earnestly.

Could these two visits within less than a week have been a coincidence? When I mentioned them to Leslie and Kitty, they advised me to be wary: it was possible the two students were *agents provocateurs* who were trying to ascertain what my opinion was on sexual matters so that they could report me to the University authorities. I was advised not to discuss sexual, political, religious and moral questions in my classes, too, and for the same reason. And this was supposed to be a university! I began to feel uncomfortable in such an environment.

The other thing that struck me as a very strange custom among the Saints was baptism of the dead. The Church teaches that the family relationship lasts beyond the grave and that every man is going to meet his wife, or wives, in the world to come. It's the duty of every Mormon 'in good standing' to trace his forefathers back at least four generations. As John Harris had explained, they baptise the dead in order to reserve a place for them in the Mormon heaven. One of the most poignant things I heard in Utah was that widows among the first arrivals who came over from Wales brought their husbands' best clothes with them in full expectation of meeting them in the next world – not the Christian heaven, but a heaven reserved for Mormons.

This is one of the reasons why they are so zealous about genealogy. They collect information from all kinds of sources, including gravestones and the National Library of Wales, so that the dead can be baptized. Indeed, there's something unhealthy in their zeal. Even so, I decided to take advantage of their obsession by visiting the huge archives at BYU to see what they had on my family. To my great surprise, the Lloyds of Glascwm were all listed: Annie Sophia Lloyd, her brother Hugh and their parents Hugh and Martha Lloyd of Michaelchurch-on-Arrow, together with all their relatives going as far back as 1760. Each and every one had been baptized in the Mormon manner and their marriages 'sealed for eternity'. When I asked the attendant what exactly this meant, he said they now had a chance of going to the Mormon heaven. He didn't flinch when I informed him that the Lloyds of Radnorshire had spent their lives here below as members of the Anglican Church, some of them as churchwardens. He went on to say about 200,000 people had been 'saved' by this means, including Buddha, the Popes, Shakespeare, Walt Whitman, Einstein, Freud, Anne Frank and Elvis Presley. 'So your folks sure are in good company,' he said with a grin.

This was the moment my attitude to the Church changed from curiosity and tolerance to contempt for the credulity of such people. In this respect, I must admit to be under Ruth's influence. Although she was brought up a Calvinistic Methodist, she is, like her parents, ecumenical in her attitude to other religions such as Islam, Hinduism and Roman Catholicism – though she has good reason to be very disapproving of the Evangelicals. I have no religious faith, at least not one I'm prepared to proclaim publicly, and I definitely don't believe in any world to come. Even so, I have a great interest in religions and I try to understand how people can be sure of what they believe. Ruth, on the other hand, can't stand the Mormon faith, seeing it as a blasphemous parody of Christianity – and in this she is right, of course. As for me, and in short, the more I learned about the Saints the more ridiculous they seemed. It's no wonder, each time the Church attempts to join the Christian community, all the other churches of America agree to exclude it.

In the mean while, I received news from Wales from time to time. One afternoon I was shocked to hear Ruth telling me my friend Michael Parnell had died at the age of 57 while on holiday in France with his wife Mary. On the afternoon of his funeral I walked up Provo Canyon to be on my own and remember Mike. When the trail petered out and I could go no further I saw a splendid panorama before me – the Rockies with snow on their caps and huge forests stretching in all directions, their leaves beginning to turn red and yellow and saffron. I recalled the happy times I'd had in Mike's company, most recently in Moscow and Kiev in 1989, and our friendship over the years. I was able to express my grief only by shouting as loud as I could – 'Mi-chael Par-nell' – before turning, as the echo reverberated around the canyon, to make my way back down to the Valley of the Great Salt Lake. I knew I wouldn't see my friend again, and that's how I chose to say goodbye.

Among other friends who wrote to me were Sam Adams, Don Dale-Jones and Bryan Martin Davies. From John Pikoulis

I heard I was being seriously considered for the post of editor of *The New Welsh Review*, to succeed Mike Parnell, and was likely to get the job. But a fortnight later he wrote again to say the Academi had appointed Robin Reeves. I was surprised by this news because I hadn't thought of Robin Reeves as a literary man and I would have preferred it if Herbert Williams, who was also on the short list, an experienced journalist and author of several books, had been appointed.

Fortunately, I had several chances to escape the Mormons for a while and drive out of Utah. I went on my own in a rented Chevrolet as far as Wyoming, Colorado, New Mexico, Nevada, Idaho, Oregon and Arizona. Ruth and Huw joined me for a fortnight in late September, so I had company on trips to see Dead Horse Point, Monument Valley, Four Corners and the Grand Canyon. We also saw our first game of American football and went to Sundance, the arts centre where Robert Redford lived with his Mormon wife. If I'd met Butch Cassidy I'd have asked for the truth about the murder of Llwyd ap Iwan in Patagonia in 1909, but I didn't have the chance. We saw a variety of wild animals such as deer, eagles, buffalos, vultures, elks, snakes and a huge skunk.

There was something memorable to see everywhere we went. At Four Corners, where the state lines of Utah, Colorado, New Mexico and Arizona meet, I fell into conversation about his native language with a young man who belonged to the Navajos. He informed me Navajo had a sound that didn't exist in any other language: *ll*, as in *lli*, the word for horse. When he challenged me to make the sound, I said 'Llanelli a Llangollen', but he thought I was making fun of him and the conversation ended abruptly. I noticed the flag fluttering on every stall, the Stars and Stripes, had a Native American's head in warpaint printed on it. We went through several small settlements where the Navajos lived in very poor-looking houses made of breezeblocks. In a grocer's shop our presence attracted a group of about forty youths who stared at us with less than polite courtesy. I wanted to tell them I'd always taken their side against the US Cavalry when playing in the Bute woods as a boy, but somehow I didn't have a chance. There were no American Indians on the BYU campus.

One day, out in the badlands of Utah, I came across a sleepy little place known as Wales. It was founded about 1854 by Welsh miners who'd discovered coal there. In the cemetery I saw scores of graves bearing the names Jones, Evans, Davies, Price, Rees, Thomas and Williams; the leaders of the first settlers were men from Merthyr called John E. Rees and John Price. There were *englynion* and Welsh inscriptions on most of the headstones, but no crosses. It's a wonder no Welsh television crew has been to make a programme about the place. I bought from an old lady two copies of a booklet entitled *Coalbed* (the place's original name), one to keep and one for the National Library.

The high point of the visit to Provo for Huw was meeting a conjuror who belonged to a company performing a play about Phineas T. Barnum, the circus impresario, and being given a ticket to see 'the greatest show on earth'; he even went up onto the stage to see a woman being sawed in half.

In Las Vegas, where I went alone in November, I visited all the famous places like Caesar's Palace, The Mirage and Excalibur. I also saw a sign with Tom Jones's name on it in bright lights and thought, 'Not bad for a boy from Trefforest'. This was the most vulgar place I'd ever been in, but as someone said, you must try everything once, except incest and folk dancing. It must be remembered, too, that the Mafia and the Mormon Church, in the early days, funded Las Vegas as a centre of prostitution and gambling. I wasn't inclined to prove or disprove the first of these assertions but, for the first time in my life, I decided I'd venture on the second. As I stood at one of the casino tables early in the morning the bloke in charge told me in a Welsh accent that he came from Tredegar in Monmouthshire. 'So what are Neil Kinnock's chances this time?' he asked. 'Pretty good,' I replied. I took his broad grin as a sign he was willing to fix things in my favour. So I put five dollars on a red number 10. I saw the wheel of fortune spin and spin and spin – and lost. I heard my Nan's voice in my head, 'Serve you right, you daft ha'porth!'

But my most determined attempt to escape Utah was my trip to Cupertino in California. Robert and Marilyn Bratman had seen something I'd published in *Planet* and through John Barnie, the editor, they tracked me down in Provo. Marilyn had been a librarian in Aberdare and her house was full of things reminding her of Wales; Robert, an American, was an obstretician with his own practice. I spent a most pleasant week with them, including a visit to San Francisco. On Thanksgiving Day a crowd of people calling themselves the Welsh Society of Southern California came to eat the turkey. Among the guests was David Vernon Thomas, another native of Trefforest, who was a nephew of E. R. Thomas, my old headmaster Piggy, and very like him in appearance. Everyone around the table expressed sympathy with me for having landed up in Utah rather than in what they called 'the real America'.

Another vivid memory is of meeting Lawrence Ferlinghetti, one of the beat poets I'd first read as a student in Aberystwyth. We had quite a long chat over supper in a trendy restaurant called Chez Moustache, in San Francisco, not far from his famous City Lights bookshop and publishing house. Among the topics we discussed was the poetry of Jacques Prévert and Émile Verhaeren. Ferlinghetti was the first to translate Prévert into English and wrote a thesis on Verhaeren, like I did, when he was studying at the Sorbonne, so we had plenty to talk about. After I'd returned to Provo he sent me a copy of his English translation of *Paroles*, Prévert's famous book, with his signature on the title-page. Inside he'd written the words *'Il ne faut pas laisser les intellectuels jouer avec les allumettes'*, as a response, I think, to my telling him about the burning of the bombing school at Penyberth in 1936. During my trip to San Francisco I stood up to my knees in the Pacific for the first and only time in my life.

I now had only ten days left of my semester in Zion. I'd had the chance of teaching at BYU for a full academic year but one semester was quite enough for me. If Ruth, Huw and Brengain hadn't come out to see me my *hiraeth* would have been all the greater. But now the end was in sight. More than a hundred people, including some of my colleagues in the English Department and a few of my students, came to hear me reading and talking about Wales. Afterwards I went over to the Department with the marks for the students in my classes. I gave an A grade to ten of them and a B to the rest, and a C to a few, among whom was a pleasant young man called Clint Graviet who'd written a number of passable cowboy ballads during the semester. But on the whole there were too many poems on numinous themes like The Soul, and Eternity, and The Truth – themes I'd warned the students to avoid. On one of the scripts a student had written, 'For this forrin guy, old, crazie but inteligant, who nows his stuff.' I took this as a sort of compliment, though I could have wished for better spelling.

After my last class the students applauded me and then we went out to take photos. Quite a few shook my hand and I asked them to let me know when their first books were published, but not one of them has done so. On my way along the corridor for the last time I looked in on John Harris in his office. He smiled when I said, like Huckleberry Finn, 'John, it's time to light out for the territory.' When he asked me what impression I had of BYU I gave him my honest opinion: the Saints had created a closed society, I replied, one that was more like a seminary than a university. I wasn't too fond of the Mormon character on account of what I took to be its vacancy of mind and credulity and the bland self-satisfaction of their belief that they are right and they alone. I preferred to love humankind in all its imperfection, I said. I didn't want to live in a community in which intelligent people must obey authority without asking questions or disagreeing occasionally. John smiled enigmatically and shook my hand warmly, but without a further word.

On my last evening in Provo I went with Leslie and his dog Gwenno along the bank of the river that runs through Orem and then, over supper, he told me a few stories that showed the Church and the Saints in an unfavourable light. One must suffice here. Shortly before I arrived in Provo, one of the Apostles, a Saint called Taft Benson, had had a 'revelation' to the effect that it was permissible to drink Coca Cola, the kind with no caffeine, after all. Soon afterwards there was a controversy when a newspaper in Salt Lake City discovered that the Church had invested in the company that made the drink. So it seemed that someone was keeping an eye on the Mormons, after all, and I was glad it was a newspaper. Journalists have a responsibility to keep tabs on people who believe that they, and they alone, are right.

On that note, I took my leave of Zion. I flew into Gatwick at eight in the morning on the 12th of December, after an eight-hour flight during which I'd had an opportunity of thinking over what I'd enjoyed in America and what I had not. On the whole, I was glad I'd accepted Leslie's invitation. I'd seen places and people unlike any others and learned something of how Americans (well, Mormons) thought and lived. Widening horizons is always good, I'd say.

But the first thing I did on the station in Reading was ring Ruth and, after telling her I'd made it across the Atlantic, I wrote Eifion Wyn's rhyme in my diary:

Mae'n werth troi'n alltud ambell dro
A mynd o Gymru fach ymhell,
Er mwyn cael dod i Gymru'n ôl
A medru caru Cymru'n well.

And soon afterwards, courtesy of British Rail, I was back on my own hearth in Heol Don, Whitchurch.

8

The Republic of Letters

AFTER UTAH, I intended earning my living as a freelance journalist, editor, researcher and supply teacher. I had an interview for the post of Director of the Bureau for Lesser Used Languages in Leuven in January 1992 and another for the job of Chief Executive of Plaid Cymru in September 1993, when Karl Davies was appointed. But I wasn't really looking for a full-time post, as I was doing quite well financially as a freelance.

Rather reluctantly, but to keep a promise I'd made to Leslie Norris, I wrote a *Culturegram*, a collection of facts about Wales, for the Missionary Training Centre in Provo. I had my last contacts with BYU when Sally Taylor and Eugene England came to stay a night or two during the summer of 1992 and when I adjudicated the English Department's poetry competition and gave the prize to John Harris.

I now resumed my work as an editor. My book of quotations about Wales and the Welsh was published by the University of Wales Press as *A Most Peculiar People*. I edited a series of polemical essays, which included Peter Lord's *The Aesthetics of Relevance*, *Cymru or Wales?* by R. S. Thomas, *Cardiff: Half-and-half a Capital* by Rhodri Morgan, *Language Regained* by Bobi Jones, *The Political Conundrum* by Clive Betts, *The Princeship of Wales* by Jan Morris and *The Democratic Challenge* by John Osmond. All these were meant to stimulate the Welsh into thinking afresh about their country after the fiasco of the devolution referendum of 1979, but the response was muted and there were hardly any reviews.

I also worked on a new edition of the *Companion* for the University of Wales Press, I compiled *A Rhondda Anthology* for Seren as a companion volume to *A Cardiff Anthology*, and I made a bibliography of the two literatures of Wales for the British Council. I began writing a weekly column for the *Western Mail* in March 1992 that ran for twelve years. I edited three hefty volumes of short stories by Rhys Davies and contributed 162 entries for *The Oxford Chronology of English Literature*. In March 1992 Vaughan Hughes made a programme about me for Ffilmiau'r Bont, a new experience for me. I translated long poems by Rhydwen Williams and Dyfnallt Morgan for *The Bloodaxe Book of Modern Welsh Poetry* edited by Menna Elfyn and John Rowlands.

The only freelance work that lasted more than a month was a spot of rummaging in the archives of BBC Wales under the supervision of Iris Cobbe. I managed to locate a number of programmes that the BBC could re-use, including quite a few tapes of Welsh poets reading their work in both languages. I also returned to teaching as a supply teacher, which I didn't enjoy much because the permanent staff in all the schools virtually ignored me, as was expected. Among the schools at which I taught were Llanishen Comprehensive and Coed-y-lan Comprehensive, my old school in Pontypridd. Dismal though the experience was, it was some consolation to get a cheque at the end of the month, so I made an effort.

I went to Turin in October 1994 with Tony and Margaret Curtis to deliver a lecture on the English-language literature of Wales in the university there. In the following month I went with Mererid Hopwood, Peter Stead, Heini Gruffudd and Rhys Williams to a small colloquium in Kiel in Germany. It was a great pleasure to hear Mererid discussing traditional Welsh metrics through the medium of her fluent German on that occasion. The trip was memorable for another reason, too. Left to our own devices for most of the time, the Welsh contingent went on a boat along the famous canal in thick mist: we could see nothing on either side, and nothing stern or aft, and the only amusement was in drinking schnapps in large quantities. I remember one evening in particular. While we were strolling through the town's backstreets, we came across a memorial to Max Planck, with the inscription E=hv. We stood before it for a while listening to the historian Peter Stead as he filled us in about the famous physicist's background. Although he was a genius and famous for his theory of quantum physics, said Peter, it wasn't generally known that Planck had two brothers who were mentally retarded dwarfs. 'Really?' I said. 'Oh yes,' said Peter. 'That's where the expression 'Thick as two short planks comes from.'' Boom boom!

But the most important event of 1994 as far as I was concerned was the death of my mother. She'd come to stay with us in Whitchurch a few months previously, while she was having chemotherapy at Felindre Hospital, which is just up the road from where we live. But lymphoma took her in the end. She was moved to St David's Hospital in Pontypridd, and there, in her home patch, she was happier. Ruth or I could visit her at least once a day and we found her in good spirits at the start, much appreciative of the nurses and the care they gave her. She looked forward to coming home and had started cutting recipes out of magazines. But I'd noticed a deterioration the day she didn't want to do her crossword, and after that the end came mercifully fast. I phoned the hospital on the Sunday morning to ask how she was and was told to go up immediately and be prepared for the worst. She died on the 4th of September 1994, before my brother and his wife could get back to the hospital they'd just left. This was the only time I'd seen someone die and heard the death-rattle.

There was a lot to do over the next few days. There

was no need to tell her neighbours because the word went round Trefforest like wildfire before I could put a notice in the *Pontypridd Observer*. I had to go and see the doctor, the registrar of deaths, the hospital, the chapel and the undertaker, filling in forms and collecting certificates as I went, before my mother's death was official. Then to the sub-post office, and the building society, to instruct them to close her pension and account, and back to the solicitor to discuss her will. My mother, an unassuming woman, would have been astounded by all the fuss.

Her funeral was held the following Wednesday at Glyn-taf, 'across the river' as the older inhabitants of Trefforest used to say as if the Taff were the Styx. The man who officiated was typical of his calling: I'd never heard so many euphemisms and circumlocutions. The chapel was full to overflowing and two hymns were sung, one in Welsh and the other in English. The minister was a Rhondda man who belonged to the old school, and he was a favourite of my mother's, his 'Amen!' frequent and delivered in a stentorian voice. If only I could have believed the half of what that good man had to say about the life everlasting.

Even so, I must admit I wasn't listening very attentively. Reading the order of service, in which my mother was described as a loving wife, mother, mother-in-law, grandmother and great-grandmother, the proof-reader in me was irritated to see my late father's name spelt incorrectly. On the other hand, the mistake was somehow a help in keeping my mind far enough away from Glyn-taf. I also recalled the rhyme that goes: 'Death for me will hold no terrors / for I have suffered from printer's errors', and strangely enough, despite the tears, I smiled. Nor did I wince as the minister pressed the hidden button and I saw my mother's coffin, crowned with our flowers, disappear from view, although I knew full well, having worked in the crematorium, what would happen next. No matter: I'd already said goodbye in a much more private way.

Then, over a cup of tea in the vestry at Castle Square where my parents were married and my mother had been a faithful member, the moment soon came when people began smiling again and talking about other things, and life resumed its equilibrium and the deceased started on the process of self-effacement which allows loved ones to rein in their grief and regain their places in the land of the living. It was difficult not to enjoy seeing old friends and neighbours again, even in such sad circumstances. A pleasure, too, to greet members of the chapel, warm-hearted, tidy women, their number dwindling with every year that passes. Some were anxious to share their memories of my mother, with whom they'd grown up, remembering for the most part her generous, neighbourly character. One went on and on, lachrymosely, about her long blond hair and starring role in a chapel production of *Pearl the Fisher Maid* back in the 1930s. The time had come to make our excuses and leave.

Trefforest was a cold, grey place next day. With the death of a second parent, the awareness of being an orphan is no less for occuring in middle age. As the old saying goes in Welsh, losing a mother is a blow from a sharp sword. Even so, I must say that I wasn't too upset on the day of her funeral, at least not in public. I didn't feel an overwhelming grief until I started on the melancholy task of going through my mother's things. Easy enough to deal with the small box where she kept documents like gas and electricity bills, her pension book and television licence, because she'd filed them neatly in their envelopes as she paid each. It was easy, too, to sort her clothes, with Ruth's help: I emptied her wardrobe quickly and rang Tenovus. Then I started clearing the cupboards, moving a pile of brown paper, knitting patterns and old greetings cards – things she tended to hoard lest they come in handy one day. The bereaved find some kind of comfort, I believe, in this act of kenosis.

But I had greater difficulty with the smaller items: the dishes, the cutlery, and so on, especially the older things I could remember from my childhood. The sugar basin, for example: my grandmother would let me dip my bread-and-butter into it when I was a small child; the nutcracker that came out only at Christmas; the large knife, its blade worn thin, that my grandfather used to carve the meat on Sundays; the little blue-and-white willow-pattern dish with the three Chinamen crossing a bridge in which my father had his Shredded Wheat; the brass candlesticks that had stood on the mantelpiece for years, outlasting my grandparents, and now my parents. Whatever else I threw out or gave away to neighbours over the next few days – there was a pile of stuff I was glad to be shot of – I had to keep the candlesticks. They stand on the mantelpiece in our house in Whitchurch to this day. I can't remember for the moment who said there is no reality except in things but it's quite true, in my experience. If you think I'm being too materialistic or too emotional, I'm sorry. I know, too, these things have no significance for anyone except me, and they'll be thrown out, probably, by my children and grandchildren in due course. But while there's breath in me, come what may, I shall cling to them with an affection that no one and nothing can break.

But I had to return to the land of the living. I spent some time with my friend Brian Morris (Lord Morris of Castlemorris in Pembrokeshire, to give him his full title). He invited me to visit the House of Lords, where I was introduced to Quentin Hogg, the chap who referred to members of *Cymdeithas yr Iaith Gymraeg* as 'baboons', and my handshake was of the limpest, too. Unexpectedly, Brian was interested in the work of Harri Webb and I'd promised to help him while he was writing about my friend for the *Writers of Wales* series.

I took Brian to see Harri at his flat in Cwm-bach. But the visit was a flop, unfortunately. Harri, who thought Brian 'a good chap', could be quite curt and even rude at times and on this occasion he was very loth to talk about his work. The only thing he was willing to talk about was the phrase, 'mosed in the chine', which is found in one of Shakespeare's plays, the main field of Brian's academic expertise. When in due course the monograph appeared and I gave Harri a copy, he took one look at it and flung it across the room. Such behaviour was typical of him: he was pretending he'd turned his back on the English language, that was, he said, 'a dead language'. The truth was he'd stopped writing altogether because of ill health.

By this time Harri had become a recluse. He saw no one, except me and Glyn Owen, the local Plaid man who looked after his cheque-book and credit cards, and the woman who cleaned his flat and prepared his meals. By July 1994 it was obvious that he wouldn't be leaving hospital and I was asked by his half-brother, Michael Webb, to remove anything of value from his flat. There wasn't much, as it happens, except for a few books, but I made a list of everything I took. There was no room in my car for the large oil painting by Kyffin Williams, so I left it hanging on the wall until such time as I could remove it. When I asked Harri what he wanted done with it he told me he wanted me to have it. But when I returned a week later the picture had gone. It was seen on the wall of a doctor's surgery in Cwm-bach a few weeks later, a neighbour told me. I asked Glyn Owen about the whereabouts of the painting but he said he knew nothing about it.

In August 1994 Harri made me literary executor of his will and gave me the rights on all his works. This was his last act in a friendship that had lasted since September 1962. I was given the copyright on the words of 'Colli Iaith', the song Heather Jones has popularized with her marvellous singing. I edited Harri's *Collected Poems* and selections of his literary and political journalism, in order to keep his Nationalist message in view for his compatriots. But Harri's two-fisted brand of romantic Nationalism is no longer in vogue and these books don't sell more than half a dozen copies a year.

Having asked to be moved to Swansea, since he was a 'Swansea Jack', Harri died in St David's Nursing Home on the last day of 1994. His funeral was held in St Mary's Church, Pennard, in Gower, on the 6th of January 1995 and he was buried in the churchyard in the same grave as his parents. Among those who attended his funeral were Gwilym Prys Davies, formerly of the Welsh Republican Movement, and representatives of Plaid Cymru, including Gwynfor Evans, and a number of Welsh writers. A fund was opened in memory of the poet by Nigel Jenkins, Sally Jones and me, and we organized a programme of readings. Strange to think there are now three poets in the churchyard at Pennard: Vernon Watkins, Harri Webb and Nigel Jenkins. It wasn't long afterwards that I arranged for the Rhys Davies Trust to put up a plaque in the foyer of the Public Library in Mountain Ash where Harri had worked after moving from Dowlais. As a last tribute to my friend, I put a line from the *Gododdin* as an epigraph to his *Collected Poems*: 'Beirdd byd barnant ŵr o galon.' (The poets of the people will say who is a man of courage.)

Harri had given me the larger part of his archive in 1989 and after his death I received the rest as his literary executor. The archive contained not only his poems in manuscript and typescript but a large assortment of other things he'd acquired since his childhood: birthday cards, school reports, memorabilia from his time at Oxford, his Navy medals, membership cards of the Labour Party, Plaid Cymru and Cymdeithas yr Iaith, files of correspondence, photograph albums, newspaper cuttings, memoranda, lectures, articles and reviews, radio and television scripts, and a large number of diaries he'd kept, on and off, since 1931. The archive was in complete disarray when I received it but over the next few years I managed to put it in something like chronological or thematic order. Reading his diaries was especially difficult because Harri's handwriting was so miniscule it was almost illegible. The whole lot is now in the National Library.

Gomer decided not to include three of Harri's poems

in his *Collected Poems*, in order to avoid the threat of libel, but I'm willing to publish one here now, namely 'Christmas 1966':

> Hooray for the festive season,
> Peace and goodwill to man,
> And a merry Christmas, Lord Robens,
> From the kids of Aberfan.

For those readers who are too young to remember the Aber-fan disaster of October 1966, when a coaltip slid into the Taff valley, killing 144 people, of whom 116 were children, I add the gloss: Lord Robens was Chairman of the National Coal Board at the time.

After Harri's death I didn't receive any more satirical poems through the post from someone calling himself John S. Billington. Written in the manner of E. J. Thribb in *Private Eye*, these verses make fun of some of the leading figures in the cultural life of Wales, including Peter Finch, Gillian Clarke, Dai Smith, Tony Curtis and John Pikoulis. Most were acerbic and some quite funny. Here is one of the least libellous:

> So. Its farewell then Ms Dora Mouley.
> You didnt last very long
> As Artistic Direktor of Swanseas Year of Litriture.
> My friend Dave says
> It was all the City Counsels fault
> Because basically their a bunch of illiterates.
> But I take the veiw that praps
> The whole caboodle was a nonstarter right from the start.
> After all,
> I ask you,
> Whoever heard of a litriture festival lasting a whole year?
> Anyway, Dora, the best of British,
> I hope this wont effect
> Your career as an arts administrator.
> (P.S. This poem would have been a sonnet but I couldn't get it to ryme.)

It's good to know that Harri, even from beyond the grave, is capable of raising people's hackles. At his best, he had a unique voice as a poet and he's greatly needed in the Wales of today.

I wrote a tribute to Harri that appeared in *The Independent* a few days after his death, and that's how I began writing obituaries of eminent Welsh people for the London press. I'd already written about John Ormond and Gwyn Williams, Trefenter, in *The Guardian*, but I preferred the *Indie's* style and I remain one of its regular contributors. This is how I wrote about Harri:

> A convivial man, noted for his iconoclastic wit and wide erudion, especially among the young and less abstemious of his compatriots, he earned and enjoyed the status of People's Poet, thinking of himself as belonging to the ancient tradition of the Welsh Bard, whose function it was to rally his people against the foe, whether the English invader or the servile, collaborating Welsh.

By the end of 1995 my obituaries of Glyn Jones, Lynette Roberts and Gwyn A. Williams had appeared in the same paper. Glyn died on the 10th of April 1995. He'd been a true friend to me and I'd helped him as best I could in various ways. Before he died he asked me to edit his *Collected Poems* and I had several conversations with him about his poems. In my obituary of him I wrote:

> Glyn's last years were marred by the amputation of his right arm, for a writer the ultimate indignity, but his interest in the republic of letters remained vital to the last. Among those who gathered at his bedside during his final illness none was untouched by the serenity of his temperament and his undiminished delight in the world he was about to leave.

Mercer Simpson wrote an introduction to the *Collected Poems*, published by the University of Wales Press in 1996.

Glyn had asked me to be his literary executor and left me the copyright on his literary estate for ten years until it was transferred to the Academi (now Literature Wales) in 2006. His ashes were buried in Llansteffan, the village of his forefathers and his favourite place in the whole world. The Rhys Davies Trust put up a plaque on the front wall of his house in Whitchurch, the first of a series the Trust has commissioned in association with the Academi. The second plaque was the one we put up on the house in Blaenclydach, where Rhys Davies was born.

I didn't know Lynette Roberts well, but I'd corresponded with her. I was more familiar with Gwyn A. Williams, whom I'd known since my undergraduate days and through working with him in Plaid Cymru, in which he was a member of the National Left. What's more, Gwyn was the partner of Ruth's friend Siân Lloyd (ex-Abertridwr) and we'd seen something of one another over the years. In my obituary I wrote:

> The image of Gwyn Williams which remains in the memory
> contains his pugnacious but engaging manner and the impish wit
> with which he expounded his theses about Wales and the Welsh. A
> small man, with a shock of white hair and the Iberian features that
> seem so typical of the valleys of south-east Wales, he developed a
> quirky but compulsive television style that had all the immediacy
> and eloquence of his writing, using the medium unapologetically
> to put over what he thought the Welsh people needed to know
> about their own past. But I am pretty sure that it is for his books
> he will be remembered. For many of my generation, who were
> undergraduates in the late 'Fifties and early 'Sixties, and who
> participated with him in the political campaigns of the 'Seventies
> and 'Eighties, he shares a place with that other great Welsh
> Socialist, Raymond Williams, as an important influence on the
> way we now think about our country and people.

At Gwyn's funeral in Narberth on the 22nd of November 1995 the 'Internationale'was sung *con brio* and I saw a number of people raising a clenched fist as a last salute to their comrade. Even so, I thought the shouts of 'Viva Gwyn!' from some of his closest friends were a bit over the top.

It's significant, perhaps, that I began writing obituaries soon after the death of my mother and my friends Harri, Glyn and Gwyn. But an obituary isn't about death, mark you. Rather, it celebrates a person's character and achievements in all their variety. The obituarist's function is to praise the dead and comfort the living, and to convey information about the deceased's life. There's nothing morbid about writing or reading an obituary. The only thing that's really important is *de mortuis nil nisi bonum*: one doesn't speak ill of the dead – unless, of course, the deceased was in charge of a Nazi concentration camp or a Soviet gulag, and there haven't been many of those in Wales. Everything else should be ruled by common sense and good taste. The obituarist shouldn't draw attention to himself; you have only to read the obits by Tam Dalyell in *The Independent* to see what I have in mind.

In a good obituary anything that might cause discomfort to the bereaved should be avoided. Even so, for even the most humble life it's possible to find circumlocutions that cast a light on the personality and behaviour of the dead person. Phrases such as 'He was good company late at night' can suggest he was voluble in his cups, and 'She was an attractive woman who turned many a head' can mean she had scores of lovers; 'He never married' is factually accurate but can also arouse curiosity and conjecture. Skeletons in the cupboard, or sexual preferences, or marital scandal, are not revealed unless relevant to the facts of the dead person's life, and only then when the family gives permission. Even so, such references can add a pinch of salt to an obituary and save it from resembling the tributes that are sometimes delivered over coffins by clergymen who weren't acquainted with the deceased, so the obituarist must tread warily. You know you've managed to sum up a person's life correctly when his relatives, friends or colleagues ring or write to express their appreciation – which is recompense enough.

The obituary has another, less personal, function. To read 'the big four' – *The Times*, *The Daily Telegraph*, *The Guardian* and *The Independent* – is to be informed about a wide range of subjects and a variety of people who have contributed to the civilization of humankind. It's a pity the *Western Mail*, our 'national newspaper', doesn't fulfil the same function. A key part of my purpose in contributing obits to the London press is to try to convey something about Wales and its society to the world beyond our borders.

Some of my friends have asked me from time to time how it's decided who in Wales merits an obituary in *The Independent*. In the first place, I must have known the person, if not very well then at least well enough to be able to write with confidence. Only once or twice have I written about someone I didn't know, and then at the request of their family. Secondly, the person must have made a significant contribution to life in Wales and third, the question must be asked, 'Will this person be remembered?' Or, in other words, 'Why does this person deserve to be remembered?' Above all, the person must be of interest to readers who didn't know him or her in life. Collecting biographical facts is much easier than answering questions like these. Fortunately, *The Indie* is always willing to publish my pieces and by now I've had some two hundred in its pages; a third collection is in preparation. The paper is even willing for me to write about people who are still in the land of the living, to keep in its files.

In 2005 the National Eisteddfod offered a prize for an obituary 'in the style of a quality newspaper' and I sent in, under the pseudonym Taphos (the Greek for 'grave') an obit of myself. The adjudicator, Menna Baines, thought the entry by Taphos, and two others, were the three best in the competition but she wasn't entirely happy with it because she could have wished for a little more about personality alongside the factual biographical information. And I'd deliberately not said too much about myself! She saw nothing wrong in the fact the person was still alive, bearing in mind that newspapers were in the habit of commissioning obits in advance, fair play. She added, kindly enough, that Meic Stephens was 'a man with years ahead of him in which to go on contributing to the literature and culture of Wales'. Be that as it may, the prize was not awarded. This was a rap across my knuckles. It's good to note that the magazine *Barn*, under the editorship of Menna Baines and Vaughan Hughes, now has a policy of publishing three or four obituaries every month. Perhaps I shall rejig the one I wrote for the competition and send it to the *Indie, mutatis mutandis*, against the time it's needed. I must add that as an adjudicator of the obituary competition at the National Eisteddfod of 2009 I was disappointed by the general standard of the entries.

I was still in mourning for the death of my mother when I had an unexpected offer from Tony Curtis to do some teaching at the University of Glamorgan, and I started there on the 6th of October 1994. The job was meant to be part-time but soon I was teaching more hours than anyone in the Humanities Faculty: twenty hours a week, including classes in Modern Fiction, Journalism, and Literature and Politics in Wales in the 20th Century, and each one of these suited me well. I also took evening classes in Bridgend, Blaenllechau in the Rhondda, and Bedwas, and I taught graduates for a year in the Centre for Journalism Studies and the Welsh for Adults course at Cardiff University.

Walking into one class on my first day at Glamorgan, to my astonishment, there was Marilyn Bratman, formerly of Cupertino, beaming at me from the front row. The Bratmans had left their very comfortable life in California and moved back to Aberdare. Marilyn was one of my best students and in due course she took a good degree – on her own merits, I should add. She and Robert now live in Llwydcoed and we see one another occasionally.

It was quite a strange experience to be teaching at the University of Glamorgan in Trefforest. I had come back to where I started from, as it were. Although I was very proud to think the University was in my home village, this wasn't the place I remembered from my boyhood. The post-industrial village hadn't become used to its new function as a university quarter. I saw immediately that its dilapidated state could be attributed to the presence of thousands of students who had no respect for the place. There was litter in the streets, graffiti on walls, music blaring late at night, drunkenness, burglaries, cannabis-growing and several instances of violence against women. Many families had moved out to places like Church Village because Trefforest was no longer a place in which to bring up children. Hundreds of houses had been bought by absentee landlords as financial investments. As a result, many houses stood empty during the summer months and university holidays. Only old people were left and the community had been destroyed altogether. Of the eighty-odd houses in Meadow Street, most had been let to students. The situation became even worse after the opening of the Atrium in Cardiff, because many students prefer to live and study in the capital, thus contributing to the rundown aspect of Trefforest where even more houses remain empty throughout the year.

As I walked around campus for the first time I felt a twinge of guilt when remembering what damage my stones had caused to the windows of Tŷ Fforest in times gone by. But in a short while, and to make amends for the hooliganism of my youth, I persuaded my friend Dai Smith, the Deputy Vice-Chancellor, to rename the old building Tŷ Crawshay after that rapscallion Francis Crawshay, and to put up a portrait of him on a wall inside the building, and I felt a bit better for having done so. The agenbite of inwit!

The year 2000 was *annus mirabilis* for me. I was awarded an honorary MA by the University of Wales and then the senior degree of DLitt by publication. I remember meeting Seamus Heaney and Bryn Terfel on the first of these two occasions and went up onto the stage in Aberystwyth to shake hands with Elystan Morgan, Derec Llwyd Morgan and

Gruffydd Aled Williams on the second. When the University of Glamorgan gave me a personal chair in 2001 I was allowed to call myself Professor of Welsh Writing in English. I took great pleasure in informing my colleagues that I was one of the few Professors in the Yookay, as far as I knew, who could see from campus the house where they'd been born.

When I came to deliver my inaugural lecture I chose as my subject, naturally enough, the industrial history of my square mile, concentrating on the key role played by the Crawshays in the development of Trefforest. The title of my lecture was 'Pontypridd, a town with no history but one hell of a past'. It was heart-warming, that evening, to see so many local people in the audience, the largest number ever for an event of this kind, or so I was told. To show my gratitude for the generosity of the University, and to mark its tenth anniversary, I edited, with Dai Smith, a collection of essays under the title *A University and its Community* that was published by the University of Wales Press.

By this time I'd published more books, and my production rate was a boon to the University of Glamorgan in its annual application for funds. Among them were translations of works by Saunders Lewis, Gwynfor Evans and Islwyn Ffowc Elis, as well as a book about the Basques translated from the French. But all these were lead balloons as far as sales were concerned. Take *Shadow of the Sickle*, my translation of *Cysgod y Cryman*. This is one of the Welsh books which have sold in large numbers over the years, perhaps as well as any book ever published by Gomer. Even so, fewer than a thousand copies of the English translation have been sold, and even fewer of its sequel, *Return to Lleifior*. It's hard to understand why anyone goes to the trouble of translating Welsh classics into English if the publisher is unable to sell them. The inertia of Welsh publishers which I'd tried to stimulate when I was at the Arts Council, and against which I thundered in an article entitled 'A Ridiculous Mouse' in *Planet* (134, April / May 1999), still exists. I am speaking from experience: I've published books with a dozen publishers in all and there's not much difference between them, as far as I can see. Considering the hundreds of thousands of pounds that go to publishers and the Books Council every year, this is very disappointing. I see the time coming when Welsh books will have to be given away – not a bad idea when you think about it.

I have fond memories of some of my colleagues in the Humanities Faculty at Glamorgan. Jane Aaron, who was responsible for teaching courses on the cultural history of Wales, a fluent Welsh-speaker, and a sensible and very capable woman, did me more than one good turn. Tony Curtis was one of the stars in the English Department, a good poet and critic and a very busy man, especially when buying and selling paintings by Welsh artists, his chief delight. There were many stories about Tony's difficulties with his students but, somehow or other, he was able to talk himself out of every tight corner by using his fluency and charming manner. The running joke at staff meetings was that he was often unable to attend because he was having 'stress management therapy'. No one dared to ask what this entailed until he revealed that he was playing golf on the proposed date. Tony was always good company; he made me laugh and I'm very grateful to him for offering me a place on Glamorgan's staff.

Among the lecturers I remember Sheenagh Pugh, an able poet but a very eccentric and moody woman who recently went to live in the Shetlands; Chris Meredith, an accomplished writer and excellent teacher; Jeremy Hooker, an English poet who's made a notable contribution to the English-language literature of Wales; Rob Middlehurst and John Young, highly respected on account of their skills as teachers; and Jeff and Diana Wallace (not related), both fine scholars. Helen Phillips, an expert on Robin Hood, was kind to me and I had more than one chat with Adrian Price from the Welsh Department, a brother of Adam Price, the ex-M.P., before he moved to Cardiff. In the farewell dinner held in the

Coedymwstwr Hotel in 2006 I had an opportunity to thank the University for giving me a berth for the last twelve years and my colleagues for their kindness. I presented each with a book and was given a piece of artwork by Toby Petersen, the artist-craftsman.

I enjoyed my contact with the students. I persuaded some of them to start a literary magazine that we called *Daps*. In one of the editorial meetings I heard a rumour about a secret chamber under the floor of Tŷ Crawshay, and I went to see it. It was shaped like an igloo and built of red bricks. In the middle there was a block of smooth grey stone and around the perimeter a low seat or shelf. There was no window but there was a small grating in the roof through which a woman, child or slim man could gain access to one of the main rooms in the building. I saw no date or any mark that suggested what the chamber might be for. There were numerous theories: a secret room used by Francis Crawshay when communing with spirits; a hiding place for his friend Dr William Price when he was on the run from the police after the Chartist march on Newport; an ice-house; and so on. I appealed for information and wrote to CADW, the body responsible for ancient monuments, but I received no explanation that made sense and the purpose of the chamber remains a mystery to this day.

The academic standard of Glamorgan students was not particularly high, with some exceptions, and although the University tried hard to be a university after years of being a Polytechnic, its degrees were not very impressive in the world of academia, or so I was told. Some wag had suggested it should adopt a new motto, 'Degrees Я Us', since the University offered so many courses in obscure subjects. Almost no one failed examinations. In my experience, it wasn't a matter of low intelligence on the part of most students but a lack of knowledge of anything other than pop music and sport and television programmes. They didn't understand references to a wide range of subjects – the Bible, the Classics, Shakespeare, Dickens, contemporary literature, or any aspect of European history in the twentieth century – a serious lack, in my view, in students who were studying Journalism and English Literature. A journalist, I told them, should know a little about a lot and be able to write correct English. Above all, he or she should read newspapers. Very few of them had read a quality paper and I had to try hard before they would read a daily paper. I did my best to establish Journalism as a degree subject at Glamorgan, which it now is at the University of South Wales.

I was daunted in one third-year class when I tried to explain the difference between 'who' and 'whom'. I gave them the anecdote about Lenin defining Marxism with the words 'who whom?'. He meant, of course, who exploits whom, or who governs whom, but the class didn't understand what I was driving at and, in desperation, I asked a woman student, 'You do know who Lenin was, don't you?' Came the answer, 'Yeah, one of the Beatles'. Making matters worse, most knew nothing about the history and culture of the towns where they'd been brought up. Every year I met students from Rhymni who'd never heard of Idris Davies, students from Aberdare who knew nothing about Alun Lewis, students from the Rhondda who'd never heard of the riots of 1910, and students from Merthyr who'd never read a word by Jack Jones or heard of the Merthyr Rising of 1831. I put the blame on the schools. The empty spaces between the ears of these young people reflected the poverty of their environment and inadequate schooling.

It came as a shock to discover the handicaps under which some students were labouring. One morning I was discussing the sonnet form with a class of first-year students and gave them, as an illustration, Shakespeare's poem beginning 'Shall I compare thee to a summer's day?' I asked one student to read it and he began, 'Thee to life gives this and this lives long so,' continuing all the way up to 'Day summer's a to thee compare I shall.' I was taken aback that he'd managed to read the poem backwards. So I asked him to read it again and he did so, as before. I thought he was trying to be funny, but on enquiring at the office I learned he suffered from Asperger's Syndrome, of which I'd never heard at the time.

I made strenuous efforts to awaken an interest in the students' cultural backgrounds, taking ten minutes off before each class to chat about anything that came into my head or was in the news: the history of the English language, the Spanish Civil War, Al Capone, the Suffragettes, the first man on the moon, Edith Cavell, the Depression, the part played by Japan in the Second World War, Albert Einstein, Stockholm Syndrome, Mabon (William Abraham), Germaine Greer, Ned Kelly, the situation in Northern Ireland, and so on. But once again my heart sank when one student told me, 'I do enjoy your classes, Meic, especially when you waffle.' Despite all this, when I retired they presented me with a tankard inscribed with the words, 'To Meic Stephens, the best lecturer ever, from the Class of 2006'. I knew this to be an exaggeration, but I must have done something right, after all – apart from waffling. Some of my students still come to see me occasionally: as I write I'm expecting a visit from Tom Anderson and Barrie Llewelyn. I also see Ali Yassine from time to time and we chat in Welsh. I remember Ali arriving in class one morning and apologising profusely for being late. *'Popeth yn iawn, Ali, steddwch i lawr,'* I said – 'Alright, Ali, sit down.' A few weeks later another student said to me, 'We didn't know you could speak Yemeni, Meic.' Ali is a well-known broadcaster on BBC Cymru and his voice is often heard speaking Welsh during matches in the Millennium Stadium.

Among the people who were given honours by the University while I was there were Leslie Norris, Philip Madoc, and Kyffin Williams. The last of these, who was receiving an honorary DLitt, made the biggest impression on the congregation. I recall one of his anecdotes well. He'd been out painting in the fields of Anglesey and, while sheltering under a hedge, an old woman happened to come by, leading a sheep on a piece of twine. In order to greet her in his usual sociable manner, Kyffin asked, 'What's the name of your sheep?', to which she gave the rather sour reply, 'Sioned.' 'Oh,' said Kyffin, determined to keep the conversation going, 'Sioned Jones, is it?' 'Oh no,' said the old woman, 'Sioned Parry Jones.' I don't know how many people in the hall understood the joke but it struck me as very funny at the time.

My friend Rhydwen Williams died on the 5th of August 1997. Like many others, I was particularly fond of Rhydwen and had spent many evenings in his company. We once went to Dublin together to read Welsh poetry to members of the Wolfe Tone Society among whom we had a memorable few days. But it's the small things about him I remember now. When I introduced him to my mother, he said, 'Mrs Stephens, if I'd known there were such good-looking women in Libanus, Trefforest, I'd have preached there more often.' I also saw an example of his generosity and childlike attitude to money. We were walking down a street in Cardiff one morning in the 1980s when a little boy ran out of his house and fell flat on his face in front of us. My instinct was to put him back on his feet and make sure he was alright. But my friend took a pound note from his pocket and gave it to the boy. The great heart of Glamorgan beat in Rhydwen's breast.

On the other hand, his friends, including me, had to collect money for him more than once. He had several bursaries from the Arts Council and I once managed to wring a grant for him out of the Royal Literary Fund – quite an achievement, believe me. One of the most amusing stories about Rhyd was the one in which he was on trial before the Pontypridd Magistrates' Court for failing to pay insurance stamps as a freelance writer. He pleaded that he didn't know about stamps. 'Come, come, Mr Williams, everyone knows about stamps,' said the Clerk of the Court, a fellow named Jordan. 'Sir,' replied Rhydwen loftily, 'philately was never one of my hobbies.' Then the chairman of the bench said something to the effect 'If I were you, Mr Williams, I wouldn't cross the Clerk of this Court.' 'Sir,' said the defendant, 'I have no more intention of crossing the Clerk of this Court than I have of crossing the river that bears his name.' He was fined £200 and ordered to pay costs.

This is part of what I wrote about Rhydwen in *The Independent*:

> Of a rebellious nature, he was often in trouble with his denomination on account of his pacifism, political Nationalism, unorthodox religious views, and bohemian lifestyle. He had a fondness for good wine, expensive restaurants, fast cars, the theatre and good company into old age, and his profligate attitude to money was legendary. But the call to the Christian ministry had always been strong in him and, blessed with good looks and a voice that were compared with Richard Burton's, he became a powerful preacher and a gifted reader of poetry on the Welsh Home Service of the BBC.

A General Election was held on the 1st of May 1997. The result was the long-expected victory of the Labour Party; in Wales the party won 34 seats, Plaid Cymru four, the Liberals two and the Tories none; yes, the Tories none. Ron Davies became the Secretary State for Wales with a commitment to establishing an Assembly – but after a referendum. I played a small part as a foot soldier in the Yes campaign by canvassing and attending meetings in which No-sayers like Llew Smith were speaking; I was fond of heckling him. But I didn't do much for the Yes cause; by 1997 I'd become a sort of *Mitläufer* with Plaid although I still contributed to its coffers. But shortly before the referendum held on the 18th of September 1997 I went out distributing leaflets and attending public meetings. In my diary on the night before the count I wrote, '*Fe awn i ennill patshyn bach o dir / y sydd heb elw ond yn ei enw ef.*' ('We go to gain a little patch of ground / that hath in it no profit but the name.') That was my attempt to raise my spirits by turning two of Hamlet's lines into Welsh.

Ruth and I were at the Park Hotel in Cardiff as the results came in. Late that evening, tired out after a busy week, we were on our way home, expecting confirmation of a defeat, when we heard on the car radio that the Yes campaign had won – by a whisker. We just had to return to the hotel to join in the celebrations. The night was made all the more memorable when the actress Eiry Thomas kissed me! This was an experience akin to Gwynfor's victory in July 1966. At last, Wales was starting out on its journey! George Thomas, one of devolution's most implacable enemies, died a few days later, mourned by few.

In 1998 my friend Sam Adams edited a *Festschrift* in celebration of my sixtieth birthday. A number of my friends contributed to *Seeing Wales Whole*, among whom were Emyr Humphreys, John Harris, Don Dale-Jones, James A. Davies, R. Gerallt Jones, M. Wynn Thomas, Tony Curtis and Sam himself. To their essays was added a selected list of my publications down to Christmas 1997 and about 125 people subscribed to the book which was published by the University of Wales Press. In his introduction Sam wrote:

> Meic's capacity for work is extraordinary. When he is not teaching, he is usually to be found in his study, surrounded by reference works, or among his collection of Anglo-Welsh books and magazines, which is rivalled only by that of the National Library... His vision, he has told me, is of a society 'in which the English-speaking Welsh play a full part in the life of the nation', and of a concept of nationhood that is 'inclusive, progressive, out-going, forward-looking and liberal, part of the modern world'. The contributors to this book, and the many subscribers, friends and admirers, will join me in saying Amen to that, and wishing Meic many more productive years.

My heart missed a beat when I received this generous tribute and I allowed myself to think the attempt to involve the English-speaking Welsh in the life of the nation had begun to succeed. After all, without the support of the people of Gwent and Glamorgan the referendum result (with a majority of 6,721) in September 1997 wouldn't have been enough to ensure a Yes vote. Clearly, those of us who'd tried to attract English-speakers to their country's cause had had some effect on the result.

I sensed that something was stirring that could be significant and so I decided to put my shoulder to the wheel once more. I was accepted as one of Plaid's list candidates in the south-east for the first election to the Assembly on the 6th of May 1999, albeit in seventh place. I didn't have a red canary's hope of being elected but I was glad to have a small part in the campaign nevertheless. Plaid Cymru won 17 seats, Labour 28, the Tories 9 and the Liberal Democrats 6.

Gwyn Jones died in December 1999. He'd played an important part in my life, as the Professor of English at Aberystwyth who had redirected me to the French Department, as an author and editor whose example I would emulate, as Chairman of the Welsh Committee of the Arts Council, as first Chairman of the *Companion's* management board, and as a friend thereafter. I wrote his obituary for *The Independent* which began:

> Gwyn Jones, the writer and Viking scholar, sometimes gave the impression that had he not been a Welshman, he might have been a character out of the Icelandic sagas – Eirik the Red, perhaps, who may have discovered Greenland, or the legendary Olav Tryggvason, or Snorri Sturluson, the chronicler of the Kings of Norway, or any other Norseman who had lived up to the Heroic Ideal. For him, physical prowess, unremitting effort, honourable conduct, a dignified manner, a command of lofty language, and courage in adversity were the manly attributes he most admired, and he had them in abundance.

In July 2000 Ruth and I went to Lorient in Brittany, where I enjoyed living for a few weeks at the expense of the municipal council as a writer in residence. As it happened, the *Festival Folklorique* was taking place at the same time, but dressing up and dancing in the streets held little appeal for me. I took an opportunity of meeting my old friend Per Denez and discussing with him the cultural and political situations in Brittany and Wales; Per died while I was writing this book. We also went to Quimper to see Marie-Thérèse Lemaire, daughter of the woman who'd been at Liverpool University with Ruth's mother in the 1920s. I also had to go and see the *École Normale* where I spent the academic year 1959/60. But it's a mistake to revisit places and expect them to be the same forty years on. Everything had changed, no one remembered me and I was even refused permission to go inside the building to see my old room. *Eheu fugaces labuntur anni...* A much happier occasion was the family reunion held in Bala when more than 500 people – descendants of Dafydd Tomos (1720–1804) of Tanbwlch, Cwm Cynllwyd, Ruth's great-great-great-great-great-grandfather – gathered to celebrate their connection.

In 2003 I addressed the Culture Committee of the National Assembly and delivered a lecture on the orthography of Breton in a seminar at the University of Glamorgan. In May 2005 I went to the Czech Republic to deliver a lecture on Welsh literature. I met Vlad'ka and Leoš Šatava and some of their students, all of whom spoke such impeccable English that it was difficult to believe they were not English. Ruth and I also went to Dublin, one of my favourite cities, where once again I was astonished at the wit of the citizenry. I saw two men loading a lorry with heavy boxes: 'You lift, I'll grunt,' one said to the other. Dubliners have a talent for referring to some of the statues that enhance the city like this: Molly Malone is 'the tart with a cart', Anna Livia Plurabelle (the Liffey) 'the floozie in the jacuzzi', James Joyce 'the prick with the stick', the Monument of Light 'the stiffy by the Liffey' and Oscar Wilde 'the queer with a leer'. If only the Welsh could coin nicknames for some of the people whose likenesses stand in our parks and in our streets. But there we are: Cardiff is not Dublin.

213

I didn't do much for Plaid Cymru, I must admit, except for making financial contributions and attending public meetings and distributing leaflets in Cardiff North, Pontypridd and Merthyr. Ruth was much more active than I was: she's always been a staunch supporter and worked at one time in the party's head office. But I decided to return to political life after seeing, fairly close-up, the state of the Valleys and their people. Most of the students at the University of Glamorgan were working-class and came from the Valleys. Their cultural poverty came as a bit of a shock and disappointment to me. Clearly, these were young people who'd been deprived of every educational and social advantage. They had little understanding of political ideas and so were incapable of changing their world. At my last class on the 4th of May 2006 no one turned up (an old tradition) and so I didn't have to give my farewell speech, fortunately.

I am a civic nationalist, I suppose, in the sense that I want to see Wales win full status as a self-governing nation, but as I belong to the Democratic Left, I want to help improve our people's cultural and economic state as a step towards that end. I stood outside the Assembly on the day it opened, the 26th of May 1999, with a mixture of feelings beating in my breast. I was proud to have done my bit in establishing it but I wasn't at all confident it would improve the economic condition of people's lives until it has the levers of power that a proper Parliament needs. I voted for the coalition between Plaid Cymru and the Labour Party in 2007. Even so, I didn't see much that contradicted Antonio Gramsci when he referred to political action as *'Pessimo da inteligencia, ottismo da volante'* – 'Pessimism of the intellect, optimism of the will'.

9

The Wooden Spoon

I SOON REALIZED there wasn't much chance of my becoming politically active again. The cause is supported in Cardiff North by only a handful of Plaid people and they do very little for the voters here, it must be said. Every time I've proposed doing something practical in the community, even small things such as picking up litter in the streets, they aren't even prepared to consider it. How can political parties expect their candidates to be elected if they haven't done anything for the community? The branch meetings are dull affairs and seldom do I attend them, leaving it to Ruth, who is much more enthusiastic than I. The members are fine people, mind you, but they belong to Plaid Cymru for reasons mainly to do with the Welsh language. Holding a garden party once a year isn't the same as entering the political arena, in my book.

The number of votes cast for our candidates in Cardiff North has always been small. In the council election of May 2012 the Plaid candidate, Ben Foday, a pleasant enough chap from Sierra Leone long resident in the city but with no connection with the constituency whatsoever, polled 1,850 votes – the lowest percentage of any Plaid candidate in the whole of Wales – and that was no surprise. Of the 150 members said to be living in Cardiff North there wasn't one prepared to stand as a candidate and only about a dozen were brave enough to show their support by putting placards up in their gardens. Not a single Plaid leaflet came through our door and our candidate's name didn't appear in the local paper even once.

Plaid Cymru took a heavy blow when it lost seats in the Assembly elections of 2011, especially in Llanelli and Aberconwy, and failed to win Caerffili. It was dispiriting to see people like Alun Davies, of whom I have a low opinion, being elected while Ron Davies, Nerys Evans, Chris Franks and Helen Mary Jones were unsuccessful. But it was good to see Elin Jones, Leanne Wood, Alun Ffred Jones, Rhodri Glyn Thomas, Bethan Jenkins, Simon Thomas, and Jocelyn Davies back in the chamber, and Lindsay Whittle and Llŷr Huws Gruffydd joining them. I was delighted to hear that Leanne Wood and Bethan Jenkins had stayed away from the Assembly's opening ceremony because the Queen would be present.

Even so, Plaid didn't win a single seat in Glamorgan or Gwent this time – indeed, its vote in most of industrial south Wales, where economic and social deprivation is at its worst, remained much the same as before. There must be something wrong with the party's policies and tactics if it's unable to appeal to voters in these parts, and I find that very disappointing, I must confess. The same was true of the elections in May 2013: our candidates in Whitchurch got about 600 votes each. Perhaps it's only in countries with comparatively buoyant economies such as Scotland, the Basque Country and Catalonia that autonomist movements can succeed. Wales has had the stuffing knocked out of it, economically speaking, for nearly a hundred years and that is bound to have an effect on the psyche of its people – that's what we're up against.

It's true Plaid Cymru has come a long way since 1958, when I first became a member, and we've gained substantial ground in the last decade or so, but we haven't broken through in the post-industrial areas where the majority of our people live. I voted for Leanne Wood, a left-winger who lives in her native Rhondda, to follow Ieuan Wyn Jones as the party's leader and

I wish her well. She has added cubits to her stature in recent months and is showing signs of becoming the forthright leader the party needs. There was some consolation in Jill Evans's return to the European Parliament in May 2014.

Above all, we have to break the chains that bind the Welsh people's spirit and minds, and that's part of the writer's function. Easy, of course, to list the shortcomings. Perhaps I'm in the wrong party but I can't turn my back on Plaid Cymru altogether and the English parties hold no appeal for me. I still carry the Plaid membership card and wear the *triban* (not the new badge) in my lapel.

Some pundits believe a greater degree of self-government will come to Wales as a consequence of what happens in Scotland – and England, perhaps. While I was naturally disappointed by the result of the Referendum on Scottish Independence in September 2014, I take heart that something good may come of it for Wales. If so, and if the Labour Party plays its part, instead of shilly-shallying every step of the way, many Plaid people would be prepared to support Carwyn Jones, I think. But it's far from clear that will happen while Labour has a majority in the National Assembly. I was not alone in thinking the First Minister's intervention on behalf of the No side in the Referendum disgraceful. I see in today's *Western Mail* that he is calling for Home Rule for Wales! *On verra*. The old problem I first detected in the 1960s remains: *Delenda est Carthago*. I was pleased to hear Plaid's campaign at the General Election of May 2015 would be led by Dafydd Wigley, who seems to me at least as good a leader as Alex Salmond, both of whom I admire greatly. But little good it did the party. Plaid kept its three seats but failed to win the seats it had targeted. More people voted for UKIP than for Plaid Cymru. Our candidate was an able woman but she lives in Caernarfon and polled only 2,301 votes (4.5 per cent).

To return to the year 2000, I had to find some other way of burning energy. Even so, I'm not certain why I began writing poetry in Welsh. I'd written a small number of poems in English and they'd appeared in *Triad* (1963), *Exiles All* (1973) and *Ponies, Twynyrodyn* (1997). But only infrequently had the Muse come calling since then; indeed, Ceridwen had remained at arm's length throughout the 1980s while I was with the Arts Council and the 1990s when I had to earn a living as a freelance. What's more, I'd grown tired of having to read so much of other people's work as editor, critic, and arts apparatchik, and I'd more or less lost a taste for the tang of poetry.

Even so, there was plenty of prose to keep me busy at the turn of the century. I translated thirty short stories by young Welsh writers under the title *A White Afternoon*, and fifty essays published as *Illuminations*, both of which appeared in 1998. I wrote *The Literary Pilgrim in Wales* (2000), edited *Decoding the Hare* (2001), a critical study of Rhys Davies, and selections of prose and verse by a dozen authors for the Corgi series (2003–5). I also translated *A History of Llanegryn* (2002) by William Davies at the request of his son, Gwilym Prys Davies, one of the best local histories in the Welsh language, and *The Plum Tree* (2004), a volume of stories by John Gwilym Jones. My 'journal with memoirs', *A Semester in Zion* appeared in 2003. I began writing entries on eminent Welsh people for *The New Oxford Dictionary of National Biography*, work that continues to the present. I've tried to persuade Welsh publishers to commission a Who's Who in Wales, but without success.

The only time I'd tried writing poetry in Welsh before 2000 was by imitating other poets, especially Americans such as Carl Sandburg and Edgar Lee Masters, the author of *The Spoon River Anthology*. I had more success with a poem by Conrad Aiken (1889–1973), 'Tetélestai', one of my favourite poems in English. Strangely enough, it's a religious poem, very complex and mysterious. The word *tetélestai* means 'it is finished' in Greek: it's said this was one of Christ's last seven words on the Cross (although I've always thought He spoke

Aramaic). Theologians among my readers will know that classical proofs of the existence of God include the 'teleolegal' proof which refers to God's order in the universe; the apostle John considered the death of Christ as part of that order (John 19:30). Anyway, with help from T. James Jones, the husband of Manon Rhys, one of the editors of *Taliesin*, I made a Welsh version of this powerful poem and, in due course, it appeared in the magazine (109, Summer 2000); I'm grateful to Jim for putting me on the road in this way. This is how the original poem begins:

> How shall we praise the magnificence of the dead,
> The great man humbled, the haughty brought to dust?
> Is there a horn we should not blow as proudly
> For the meanest of us all, who creeps his days,
> Guarding his heart from blows, to die obscurely?

Despite my admiration for the Americans and French poets such as Émile Verhaeren and Jules Laforgue – I learned how to write the long line from both – I'd also been reading Welsh poets, and as my grasp of the literary language grew firmer, I started to enjoy their work. When someone asks whether I prefer T. H. Parry-Williams, R. Williams Parry, Waldo Williams or D. Gwenallt Jones, I'm always in two minds because all four mean a lot to me. At the same time I enjoyed reading younger poets such as R. Gerallt Jones, Dafydd Rowlands, Rhydwen Williams, Bryan Martin Davies, Gwyn Thomas and Derec Llwyd Morgan. In English I'd been reading Seamus Heaney, Philip Larkin, A. L. Rowse, Tony Harrison, W. H. Auden, and Louis MacNeice, among others. I'd also been rereading Wordsworth's *Prelude*.

But when I came to write my first poem in Welsh, '*Gwreiddiau*' (Roots), the poet I'd been reading most often was Alun Llywelyn-Williams. I didn't really know him and on the few occasions I was in his company we never talked about poetry, although one of his daughters, Luned, is the wife of

David Meredith, Ruth's brother. But I'm a great admirer of his verse, because it keeps a fine balance between the personal and the impersonal, which I try to maintain in mine, too. I don't like verse that is too egotistical and raw emotion, for me, is something to be held in check. The Parnassian Muse has been an ideal of mine since I was a boy studying Leconte de Lisle at grammar school, and the exterior world is as interesting to me as the interior. Only in an autobiography is an author allowed to display his innards, as Kate Roberts once put it, by speaking about himself all the time!

Come to think of it, the greatest spur to start writing verse in Welsh, if I understand aright, was the experience of searching for Annie Sophia Lloyd and her child's father in the hills of Elfael. The circumstances of my father's birth must have been churning in my subconscious, causing a tension that had to be relieved somehow or other; the experience of looking for Annie had lifted a latch. Be that as it may, I felt liberated as I put Welsh words on the screen, an act for me not unlike spreading thick oils on canvas with a palette knife that Kyffin Williams talked about in connection with his epilepsy. A few days after starting to write 'Gwreiddiau' the sun came out, quite literally, while I was walking on the Garth in the pale sunshine of late September. I'd better state here that I've never had a supernatural experience, but as I walked on the summit that day I felt sure that life was good and to be enjoyed in all its variety, and to be celebrated. My father's story grabbed me by the scruff of the neck.

I wrote 'Gwreiddiau' (all 200 lines of it) in the autumn of 2002 and the first part of 2003, before I saw that this was the subject set for the Crown competition at the National Eisteddfod in the following August. After showing a draft to my friend Bryan Martin Davies, I resolved to send my poem in under the pseudonym Hwnco manco (Him over there). I didn't know what to expect from the adjudicators but I wasn't disappointed by their remarks. Gerwyn Williams thought my use of dialect was 'one of the artistic achievements of this competition'. Nesta Wyn Jones was a bit less appreciative but said, '... this is an able and powerful poet'; Cyril Jones was much more enthusiastic and of the two poets he thought worthy of the Crown *Hwnco manco* was one. But the prize went to Mererid Hopwood.

I was grateful for the adjudicators' comments. But I couldn't agree with the emphasis they put on avoiding prose when writing verse. The line between 'prose' and 'verse' is a fine one and I was willing to tread it without too much bother. This is a weakness in the view of some conservative critics, and as a consequence, the poetry that appeals to Eisteddfod adjudicators tends to be 'poetic', often full of flowery imagery and archaic vocabulary, just as in medieval times when many poets deliberately used such devices to keep outsiders from understanding their work. My aim is to employ 'the language of the people in the mouth of the scholar' (though I don't know the source of that expression) and this means, sometimes, that my lines strike an adjudicator as 'prose'. As long as the line throbs with emotion, rather like an underground cable carrying electricity, I don't care. I use the speaking voice when I write a poem because the difference between the spoken and written language is growing ever wider – one of the major problems for the Welsh-learner. Since Cyril Jones praised '*Gwreiddiau*' in 2003 we've been friends and I've learned a lot while listening to his sound views and discussing them with this Gamaliel.

My poem '*Gwreiddiau*', which used a certain amount of dialect from south-east and mid-Wales, was published in *Barddas* (274, Autumn 2003). It was about this time I realized that there's a lot of prejudice against dialect among the more conservative of Welsh poets and critics. One of the arch-priests of traditional, standard Welsh as it is written rather than spoken wrote something to the effect, 'Woe betide us if we ever give the Crown or Chair for a poem in dialect.' Fie on such a reactionary view! I wanted to express my experience of industrial Wales and not the life of the countryside like so many poets writing in Welsh today. Indeed, I was fed up with their pretty lyrics and countless *englynion* lamenting the demise of the Welsh language in the rural communities where they have let incomers buy everything up. There's something utterly predictable and guilt-laden in most of their work, in my opinion, and I deplore 'the poetry voice' in which they habitually read it.

Although I haven't won the Crown, I've come very near it on at least two occasions. In 2005 I submitted a sequence taking the title *'Cerddi R'yfelwr Bychan'* (The little soldier's poems), which was about growing up in Trefforest during the 1940s. One of the adjudicators, Derec Llwyd Morgan, was particularly taken with them and called my sequence 'a notable contribution to the Welsh literature of the Second World War'. The Crown was won by Christine James and my poems appeared in *Taliesin* (126, Winter 2005).

I didn't really expect to win with my sequence *'Cerddi 'Whant y Cnawd'* (Call of the flesh poems) which I submitted in 2006 but was pleasantly surprised to see it placed high in the second division. The poems are about a young lad's sexual awakening and remember, with gratitude, the girls and women who had a hand in the process. They come very near bawdy but are redeemed, I hope, by the serious points they make about politics and society. I can give only one example here (in translation): looking back at my time in Brittany, I wrote:

> Whenever I feel a bit downhearted
> And having had my fill of Tony Blair,
> I remember Marc'harid ar Bihan
> Stark-naked on her mattress in Quimper.

Of the three adjudicators, it was Nesta Wyn Jones who seemed to be most tickled by the bawdiness of the sequence. If I'd been awarded the Crown there would have been ructions among the Sanhedrin and the *Western Mail* would have had enough copy to last several months.

I soon became aware of the orthographical problems that arise when trying to write verse in dialect. There's no dictionary of dialect in Welsh, though the splendid Dictionary edited by Bruce Griffiths and Dafydd Glyn Jones is a big help with regional variations. I made a special study of what other writers had done, such as J. J. Williams, Myfyr Wyn, Islwyn Williams, Dyfnallt Morgan, and, in our own day, Mihangel Morgan, all of whom use Gwentian, the dialect of the south-east. I learned a lot from Mary Wiliam's booklet, *Blas ar Iaith Blaenau'r Cymoedd*, her study of the Welsh spoken in the district of Tafarnau'r Bach that's based on her MA research. As she records, the dialect was once spoken by more than a million people from Bryn-mawr as far as Cwm Amman in the west and northwards as far as the Brecon Beacons. It began to lose ground with the move to standardize the language in the early twentieth century by removing dialectical variations, so that by today the children of Gwent and upland Glamorgan hardly ever hear the dialect that came naturally to their forefathers' lips. It's incongruous to hear them say *'fo'* and *'rwan'* and *'llefrith'*, instead of *'fe'*, *'nawr'* and *'llaeth'*, but that's what they've been taught in school.

I can't say exactly why I've written so much verse in the Gwentian. My grandmother came from the Rhymni Valley and my father from Heolgerrig, two bastions of the dialect, and for that reason I think there may be something atavistic in my fondness for it. I'm certain I was entranced by hearing Harri Webb speaking to the people of Dowlais in the 1960s. And when I think of Wales, it's places like Heolgerrig and Dowlais that first spring to mind. Be that as it may, I don't want to know more, lest my grasp of the dialect begin to slacken in my memory and leave only 'standard' Welsh behind. If that were to happen, an important part of me would be wiped away. By using dialect, 'I get a grip on my own personality,' as T. H. Parry-Williams once said about himself. Although I speak it only with other dialect speakers, I find that when I write verse it's the Gwentian – its phonology, vocabulary and syntax – that comes first to mind. I used it extensively when writing my autobiography, *Cofnodion* (2012).

I came even closer to winning the Crown in 2009 with a small collection of poems on the subject '*Yn y gwaed*' (In the blood), but this time it was as a result of what I can only think was an oversight on the part of the Eisteddfod that I wasn't awarded the prize. Using the pseudonym *Fferegs* (the old name for the territory that later became Radnorshire), I sent in a sequence of seven poems, each one referring to my father. My entry was put in the first division by M. Wynn Thomas, who compared the poems with the sonnets in Tony Harrison's book *The School of Eloquence*; I considered this high praise because I have great admiration for that poet. A second adjudicator, Dafydd John Pritchard, was of the view that my sequence was 'one of the most powerful in the competition and... the poems certainly deserve the Crown.' The third adjudicator, John Gruffydd Jones, wrote: 'We are in the presence here of a very talented poet... and I'd award the Crown to *Fferegs*.'

But I was dismayed to read the response by Wynn Thomas:

> In the past it was made clear from time to time by the rules of the Crown competition that a *pryddest* or sequence of poems that used *cynghanedd* or the traditional metres would not be acceptable. And that was quite right, in my opinion, lest the Crown poems come to resemble the Chair poems and the free metres disappear from the land. But in the absence of a clear directive to that end, the entry by Moelwyn must be accepted.

I don't want to make too much of this but I was astonished that an adjudicator as perceptive and experienced as Wynn could take such a view. After the Eisteddfod was over, he told me, rather wanly, that he hadn't known who *Fferegs* was, despite the fact that my poems had told exactly the same story as those by *Hwnco manco* in 2003.

The disappointment of not being awarded the Crown in 2009 was enough to put up with. But when I heard the winner, Ceri Wyn Jones, had won the prize with a sequence of poems written in the strict metres my disappointment morphed into something else. I should explain here, perhaps, for readers not familiar with competitions at the National Eisteddfod, that the Crown is given for verse in the free metres, while the Chair is reserved for poets writing in the strict metres, that is in *cynghanedd*. This is a custom that goes backs more than a hundred years and everyone understands and accepts it. My sequence was judged to be the best in the free metres but the poems by Ceri Wyn Jones were thought to be even better. In the view of many, he'd gone 'against the grain', as Dafydd John Pritchard put it. It seems there'd been an oversight on the part of the Eisteddfod, which had asked for 'a poem or sequence of poems' instead of simply stipulating that the poems should not be in *cynghanedd*. Ceri Wyn Jones had spotted the erroneous wording and, rather cynically, I thought, as did many others, had seen his chance to send his strict-metre poems in. There was no word from the Eisteddfod. The only observation to appear in print that showed a smidgen of sympathy for me was that of Vaughan Hughes in *Barn:*

> In the mean while, consider for a moment what happened to Meic Stephens this year. He was placed second in the Crown competition and for the third time. (His pseudonym was *Fferegs*.) But this time he has to live with the disappointment of knowing that, in the opinion of two out of the three adjudicators, he was the best poet in the free metres at the National Eisteddfod in Bala. But it wasn't he who was crowned. And the Crown is meant for poets in the free metres, for heaven's sake.

In the year following, the set subject in the Crown competition was 'Newid' ('Change'). T. James Jones and Mererid Hopwood were the adjudicators; a third, Iwan Llwyd, had died before the Eisteddfod took place but had expressed a view. Jim Jones particularly liked my poem 'y gair olaf', which I'd written in memory of my friend B. S. Johnson; I've made this English version for the purposes of this book:

slowly bit by bit
one's body changes

a moment ago a hair or two
last night a bit of dry skin
a nail this morning tomorrow a tooth perhaps
and from time to time the name of a neighbour
or the title of a book or even
the conditional mood of *avoir* and *être*
in the past tense
goes beyond recall

dysnomic aphesia
Oh what lovely words

slowly bit by bit
the body decomposes
like a sack full of rubbish
at the back of the garage

bit by bit
one dies

unless you are prepared
like my friend Bryan
a true writer

unless you are prepared
to lock the door on the beauty of the world
and lie in a warm bath

unless you are prepared
to swallow half a bottle of whisky
and a fistful of aspirins

unless you are prepared
in all seriousness with no going back
to put a razor to your wrists

unless you are prepared
to write on the wall
in your own blood

this is my last word

Jim thought this the best single poem in the competition. He was willing to award the Crown to *Coeca* (my pseudonym) or to another poet; the other two adjudicators chose the work of the other poet, namely Glenys Mair Glyn Roberts.

Coeca's poems appeared in *Taliesin* (141, Christmas 2010). Someone hiding behind a pseudonym in *Y Cymro* asked, 'Would Dic Jones ever have won the Chair if he'd written in dialect?' The old prejudice was still alive and well: the Gogs and Cardis don't have dialects, only Hwntws! Even so, my heart was warmed in the spring of 2011 when Ifor ap Glyn made a programme about *Y Wenhwyseg* and put on a televised reading in the Pop Factory in Porth. Two of my poems were read by Elin Jones and Gaynor Morgan Rees in authentic accents and the talented actress Shelley Rees read excerpts in dialect by other writers. Most poems in dialect deal with homely or humorous rather than serious subjects; I've tried to correct this as far as the Gwentian is concerned. I had some satisfaction from winning the prize of £200 at the National Eisteddfod of 2013 for a collection of words and phrases found in *Y Wenhwyseg*. The wooden spoon!

But I don't know whether I shall ever again compete for the Crown; who knows? I've had praise enough as it is – and a few brickbats. But although it's useful to have the opinion of Eisteddfod adjudicators, a poet shouldn't worry too much about what they have to say. So I shall go on writing poems anyway. Even so, I feel sometimes that I've left it too late to start writing verse in Welsh and to grow to my full stature as a poet. What's more, I don't write the kind of verse that appeals to those who were brought up in rural, Welsh-speaking Wales: I am still an outsider in their eyes. But I'm glad to have written, in the space of just ten years, a number of poems that some people like. I'd thought of calling the book of mine that was published by Barddas last summer *Cerddi'r Llwy Bren* (The wooden spoon poems), but in the end it took the title *Wilia*, the word for 'to speak' in Gwentian. The book contains 77 of the hundred or so poems I've written in Welsh since 2003. I was chuffed to hear that it had been one of three short-listed for the 2015 Book of the Year – not the only book of mine to receive this accolade.

10

Cultivating my Own Garden

HAVING RETIRED FROM the University of Glamorgan in 2006, I had enough leisure for the first time in many years – a chance to be a private person at last! But I don't like being idle and just had to find things to do rather than hanging around the house all day like a proper Rodney, as my grandmother used to say of my grandfather in the years of his retirement.

For a start, I was unable to give up my habit of editing books. It's one way of putting off the day when the Vimto and faggots will be served. My capacious anthology *Poetry 1900–2000* appeared in the Library of Wales in 2007, my ninth and last attempt to demonstrate the range and quality of English-language verse produced in Wales. In the year following my edition of Leslie Norris's *Complete Poems* was published, together with a selection of my obituaries from *The Independent*. I also agreed to serve as an external examiner for Bangor University's English Department for a three-year term, but that apart, I severed my connection with the groves of Academe. This stint came to an end in June 2011 when Ruth and I flew in a small 'plane from Valley in Anglesey to Rhoose in the Vale of Glamorgan and saw the beautiful land of Wales from the air.

The Academi put on an evening at St Fagans in celebration of my seventieth birthday in 2008. The speakers were Wynn Thomas, Gwerfyl Pierce Jones, R. Brinley Jones, Tom

Anderson, Dafydd Elis-Thomas, Herbert Williams, Sam Adams, Dai Smith, Tony Curtis and Chris Meredith; Heather Jones sang '*Colli Iaith*' and our son Huw played some of my favourite music, including excerpts from *Má Vlast*. I chose Smetana's music again when I had the pleasure of being interviewed by Beti George, as well as '*Le temps des cérises*' sung by Yves Montand, Gwenallt reading his mighty poem '*Y Meirwon*' and the traditional song 'Finnegan's Wake' sung by the Dubliners.

Since then I've published two short novels, *Yeah, Dai Dando* (2008) and *A Bard for Highgrove: a Likely Story* (2010). The first of these is about a twenty-five-year-old man brought up on an estate not unlike Glyn-coch in Pontypridd who works for the Gwalia Building Society in Cardiff. The story is told mainly in dialogue but also by stream of consciousness and an internal voice that Dai uses to talk to the author; it also employs Youfspeak, complete with glottal stops and Australian question intonation (also known as Uptalk) from start to finish. The novel portrays an English-speaking Welshman from a poor background whose interests are limited to rugby, drinking, and women. But then he meets Eleri Vaughan Jones, an attractive young woman from the Welsh-speaking middle class and a member of Plaid Cymru, and his ideas about what it means to be Welsh are turned on end. He also has to come to terms with the experience of meeting Fred Peregrine, an old bloke from the Rhondda who represents the radical Wales for which he yearns; the old timer troubles his conscience after drowning in the Taff after spending a night on Dai's sofa.

The novel plays with the idea of '*chwedleua*' which means 'to tell stories' and, in Gwentian form, '*wilia*', 'to speak'; we all tell stories, so to what extent do we tell the truth? At the end Dai is left standing on the grey bridge in Llandaf and looking down into the dark waters of the river. Once again I had more than one enquiry about my mental well-being after the book appeared, and I had to point out that a novel is fiction, not autobiography, and the story about poor Dai is entirely made up. Some of my friends have urged me to write a sequel but the book has sold barely 450 copies and has now been pulped and so I don't see much point in continuing the story.

While the novel about Dai was meant to be comic and serious by turns, *A Bard for Highgrove* is a farce from start to finish, a sort of extended joke and an opportunity to satirize His Royal Highness the Prince of Wales and deliver a few home truths about contemporary Wales. The Prince gets it into his head that he should appoint a household poet to help him make his Princeship and his home in the Cotswolds more 'Welsh'. But the poet appointed to this illustrious post, Cerys Gifford Huws, a young woman from Fishguard, has other ideas. Bit by bit she turns Charles Windsor into a sort of renegade Welsh Nationalist who insists on having bilingual signs not only in Highgrove but throughout the Yookay. Furthermore, he uses his influence to get Welsh on the schools syllabus in England: 'The Welsh have had to put up with such things for centuries,' he says. 'Now let's see how the English like a taste of their own medicine.'

In the mean while, Welsh Nationalism grows apace. At the second referendum held in March 2017 the country follows Scotland's example and votes in favour of Independence, and by 2020 Charles, who's become very unpopular among the English, relinquishes his claim to the throne, stops fiddling with his cufflinks and goes to live in Gregynog (since the University of Wales no longer exists). The Queen dies and William and Kate are crowned. More importantly, Wales wins the status of a self-governing republic within the Celtic Federation. In the book's last scene the Windsors – more than fifty of them in their fancy dress, all swords and ostrich feathers – come out on the balcony of Buckingham Palace. When gunfire is heard from the direction of the Mall, it puts some people in mind of what happened to the Romanovs in Ekaterinaburg in 1918, and that's how the novel ends – with the monarchy's future in jeopardy. Nothing more needs to be said here, I hope, to suggest my contempt for the institution of monarchy and, in particular, the Windsors and their hangers-on in Wales. I've probably been too kind to them. Certainly, I've blown my chances of ever being offered an MBE, and I was so much looking forward to refusing that high honour.

I am asked from time to time who it was I had in mind when writing about the chief characters in *A Bard for Highgrove*. Who, for example, is Cerys Gifford Huws, and the poets Adam Wyndham Hamlyn, Rosie Spode, Clint Bellis, Gronow Gittins and Elfael Protheroe, and who are Sir Peredur Rice-Boothby, the Prince's Private Secretary, and his wife the Hon. Jane Ankaret Heleth Letitia Fortinbras-Pryce? And who is Jack Yorath, the Professor who is Chairman of so many public committees? And who is the historian Dan Jarvis and the politician Lord Dyfed Goodfellow and the journalist Luther Jones, and so on? Well, readers will have to go on guessing what the answers to these questions may be, I'm sorry. After all, an autobiography can't be expected to reveal everything!

But I'm willing to confess that while writing about the poet Adam Wyndham Hamlyn I had Alan Llwyd in mind. This arose out of Alan's response to a review I'd written of his anthology *Out of the Fire of Hell: Welsh Experience of the Great War 1914–1918 in Prose and Verse* in the magazine *Planet* (191, October / November 2008). Having praised the selection and referred to Alan as 'a most knowledgeable and industrious editor', I dared to suggest he'd tended to choose poems and prose extracts that were out of copyright and this had skewed his selection to some extent. I'd also expected to see something by Kate Roberts, Gwenallt Jones and E. H. Jones, author of *The Road to En-dor*, for example, and I raised an eyebrow at the inclusion of English writers such as Ivor Gurney and T. E. Lawrence. But when I happened to ring Alan a few months later to ask his advice about something or other, he refused to speak to me because of 'that bad review' and put the phone down.

I was taken aback because we'd been on quite good terms since the 1970s when I'd been very much in favour of creating *Cymdeithas Gerdd Dafod* and appointing Alan as its chief officer; I'd struggled hard since 1983, against the wishes of some members of the Literature Committee, to keep him in post. He also knew I admired his poetry and his industry as editor and publisher. But obviously, I hadn't praised him enough. I know it was petty of me to satirize him in the novel as Adam Wyndham Hamlyn, editor of the magazine *Awena* (Muses) who moonlights as the inventor of a machine for the manufacture of verse in the strict metres. But that was my way of paying him back for his discourtesy. Alan's decision to stand down as editor of *Barddas* in June 2011 was long overdue, for he'd been in the post far too long. Since then he's published three excellent biographies of Kate Roberts, Robert Williams-Parry and Waldo Williams, but still suffers from paranoia, so they say.

The story of the publication of *A Bard for Highgrove* by Cambria Books in December 2010 is a most unfortunate one. The magazine went to the wall about a month later with substantial debts. This was a heavy blow for Henry and Frances Jones-Davies, the publisher and editor, for they'd been funding *Cambria* out of their own pockets since its launch in 1997. Nevertheless, the magazine was resurrected in 2011, in the hope of securing sufficient funding to carry on. But unfortunately the Books Council wasn't willing to offer grant-aid to the literary pages. I felt thoroughly browned off with the Books Council for its failure to fund the magazine, especially as the decision was taken on the recommendation of a Panel none of whose members had experience of editing or publishing a magazine. *Cambria* was one of the best-looking journals in Wales. As literary editor since 2003 I'd managed to choose a variety of poems, stories, articles and reviews for publication. Thousands of readers were disappointed to hear that this patriotic publication had been put in the hands of the Receiver. Meetings were held in our house with the aim of discussing whether it was possible to breathe new life into the magazine with the help of investors. Among those who tried to help were David Petersen, Eurfyl ap Gwilym, Howard Potter, Clive Betts and Alan Jobbins. But we could see no way of putting it back on a more secure footing and so the magazine became intermittent. A glimmer of hope appeared in the spring of 2014 when office space was provided by Trinity St David's and so it limped on, held together by the remarkable determination of Frances Jones-Davies not to let it fold. But the final blow came in January 2015 when the Books Council again refused to offer the magazine a subsidy. She and Henry are delightful people: she comes from a distinguished Norfolk family that counts Elizabeth Fry among its members and he's related to T. E. Ellis, the Gladstonian Liberal Member for Merioneth and leader of Cymru Fydd until his untimely death in 1899. They are both committed to the cultural life of Wales in sundry ways, of which *Cambria* was a shining example.

As a consequence of the magazine's financial difficulties, Cambria Books, its publishing arm, was unable to distribute *A Bard for Highgrove* and so I undertook to sell my book through my own efforts. I didn't want to hand over stock to the Books Centre in Aberystwyth because that would have meant losing 55 per cent of the retail price, another policy that needs changing if small publishers are to flourish in Wales. Even so, within two months I managed to sell 350 copies, which isn't too bad for English-language fiction in Wales. But it meant I had to approach relatives, friends, neighbours, former colleagues and old ladies on bus-stops in order to get rid of copies. And fair play, only one or two refused to buy, so that we got our money back and broke even. I had a good response from those who bought the book, too, especially the Republicans among them, and a favourable review in *Taliesin* from Rhun ap Iorwerth, who now represents Ynys Môn in the National Assembly: 'he is not an amateurish writer, but a prodigous one who is prepared to take up the cudgels against the system. In his latest novel there's hardly one institution, and very few national figures in Wales, who are spared his satirical knife... (He is even ready to take a bullet or two himself)'. Even so, despite the plaudits, I didn't win the prize for the Book of the Year and in that I wasn't disappointed, either. I didn't win again in 2013 when two of my books – *Welsh Lives* and *Cofnodion* – made the final short-lists in the non-fiction categories. But my luck changed in 2014 when my biography of Rhys Davies, *A Writer's Life*, came top of the pile. Ah, nobody likes my best work!

Over the years the Rhys Davies Trust has been helping the English-language literature of Wales as much as it can. Lewis Davies, our patron, died at the age of 98 in December 2011, leaving us his entire estate, including his substantial savings and investments. Sam Adams and I, as executors of his will, together with our wives, had the task of clearing out his flat in Lewes and arranging his funeral. The Trustees are now Dai Smith, Sam Adams and Peter Finch, and I'm still Secretary.

I don't belong to any club or society in Cardiff but I was honoured in 2003 to become President of the Tonyrefail branch of the University of the Third Age. This was arranged by Hywel Gillard, a most cultured and literate man, who died last September. He even collected postcards of famous writers, and we used to swop cards every now and then. I gave up collecting stamps in 2000 for a particular reason. Marie-Thérèse Castay, a French woman who speaks fluent Welsh, retired from her post in the English Department at the University of Toulouse and I didn't think it fair to expect her to send me the latest French issues every month, though she was happy enough to do so and to receive from me copies of recent Welsh books. To fill a gap in my life, as it were, I decided to collect literary postcards instead and I now have more than a thousand of them – all collectors like swanking. The 64 cards depicting Welsh writers recently published by Literature Wales are welcome additions to my collection. Yes, I'm a deltiologist – now there's a new word for the sesquipedalians among you! Collecting postcards is an innocent and pointless hobby, as I keep reminding Ruth, and this is the only one I have. And yet I hear you whisper, 'Not everyone goes barmy in the same way.' Quite right, too.

I don't go out much these days, mainly because of my wobbly legs. As the years go by I find it more and more difficult to stand on the same spot for more than a minute or two and I can't walk more than twenty yards, even with the aid of a stick. A stroll along the prom in Penarth or around the shelves of Tesco Extra is about as much as I can manage. I missed the National Eisteddfod last year for the first time since 1956. Because I'm unsteady on my feet someone referred to me recently as 'a bear on roller-skates' (E. E. Cummings, I think.) I shall have to give up my salsa lessons soon, too. What's more, I'm beginning to forget people's names – the dysnomic aphasia mentioned in my poem about Bryan Johnson. I remember a very eminent Welshman, now himself in the yellow leaf and sere, once warning me that this would happen: 'You'll know when you're getting old, Meic, when you start peeing on your shoes and forgetting people's names.' Quite right, too, as far as the second of these is concerned.

Although I have no truck with Facebook and Twitter, I manage to keep in touch with scores of people by means of email and I'm quite comfortable sitting at my computer or lap-top. Fortunately, I've always been content to stay at home. We've been very happy living in 10 Heol Don. It's a fine Edwardian house of generous proportions and some charming features, and we've furnished it with antiques, mainly in Welsh oak. As an old timer in the backwoods of Utah said when I asked him what he did all day, 'Sometimes Ah sets and thinks and sometimes Ah just sets'. In fine weather there's nothing better than sitting in the garden with the Red Dragon flag fluttering overhead and a newspaper or book to read. I remember the advertisement for beer that used to be on television years ago in which a bloke wearing a Hawaii shirt and sunglasses stands at the bar and someone asks him, 'Where yew goin' for yewer 'olidays, Dai?' and gets the reply, delivered with lip-smacking satisfaction as Dai downs his pint, 'Nowhere!'

Even so, *la vie est belle*. I have the love of a good woman and delight in our children and grandchildren. I don't yearn for anything, as Parry-Williams said. Since I don't believe in a world to come, this life, with all its myriad quiddities, is to be enjoyed and appreciated to the full. We're not foodies, Ruth and I, but we relish simple, nourishing fare such as faggots and peas and the occasional glass of Vimto. Friends, neighbours and relatives come for supper from time to time and we enjoy the company and chat. We helped to organize a barbecue in our garden last June at which we raised more than a thousand pounds as a contribution towards the cost of sending Nannon, one of our granddaughters, to Patagonia. At the same time, we try to remember the world's unfortunates and contribute to Oxfam, Amnesty and Save the Children. And I still laugh in the face of the Furies.

Cardiff is a fine place to live. It's fast growing into a proper capital city, with shops, schools and cultural and leisure facilities of the first rank. We don't know everyone who lives in Heol Don – the people of suburbia aren't all that neighbourly – or every Welsh-speaker who has settled in the area. But we live to a large extent through the medium of Welsh. Most Welsh-speakers in Cardiff are people from somewhere else, of course, and yet, although I moved here from Trefforest, a good seven miles up the Valley, I don't feel I'm one of them. I feel very much at home in Cardiff, and so does Ruth. We don't intend moving west or north like so many of our friends. So it's natural that we consider ourselves to be citizens rather than displaced villagers or country people, leaving those who yearn for the Welsh-speaking districts to try to help solve their problems – by living there.

I try not to worry too much about the fate of Wales these

days. I let others work for it in full expectation that our country will win a larger degree of self-government in due course. As Harri Webb once said, Wales is walking backwards towards independence and everyone is calling it something else. There's still fire in my belly and my fuse is sometimes still lamentably short. I can lose my moss over a lot that happens here, especially when I see the servility of the Welsh and the mindset of those Welsh-speakers who bring up their children through the medium of English, and make excuses for it, and I deplore those who accept medals from the Queen, especially writers, as if this flummery were necessary or important. Nor do I approve of the patriots who belong to English political parties. But the country that existed when I was a lad has changed irrevocably and for the better. Even so, I feel that the present state of affairs is far from satisfactory – 'half and half and nothing quite right', as Parry-Williams put it. I sense that something game-changing is going to happen in the not-so-distant future. I may not see it but it will come, and the English-speaking Welsh will play a vital role. In the mean while, there's plenty to do, both politically and culturally, in 'this world of Wales' and I wish those who face these tasks every success. I'm very proud to have put my shoulder to the wheel.

For my part, I cultivate my own garden nowadays – not literally (Ruth is the horticulturalist in our house) but in Voltaire's sense. I get up around half-past eight every morning and read the papers for an hour before setting about whatever I have on the stocks. We take the *Western Mail* (it's hard to give up that bad habit), *The Independent*, *The Guardian* on Saturday and *The Observer* on Sunday. It's sad we Welsh have to depend so much on the English press. On Fridays Ruth buys *Y Cymro* from Siop y Felin in the village, as everyone calls the main shopping street of Whitchurch, so that we can read the news in Welsh, and *Golwg* from time to time, but they are very limited in scope. There's much more substance in the monthly *Barn*. We have supported *Y Dinesydd*, the community newspaper for Welsh-speakers in Cardiff, since its inception in 1973. The radio is always on in the kitchen and we watch the BBC News, *Newsnight* and *Question Time*, but on the whole, I think of television as 'chewing gum for the eyes' – apart from the occasional play or documentary. Among the programmes I dislike most are those about food, holidays, buying houses, tennis and hymn-singing. I try to avoid Welsh comedians because they're so feeble. The only Welsh-language programmes I watch regularly are the news bulletins, *Y Byd ar Bedwar, Heno, CF99* and *Pawb a'i Farn*. Programmes made for S4C these days are pretty poor on the whole, especially those in English.

I sometimes click on to the BBC Cymru news site and, less often, *Golwg 360*. It's a great pity *Y Byd* didn't come into existence, because the snippets we get on the websites don't come close to fulfilling the function of a newspaper in the opinion of those of us who know the true function of journalism, whatever paltry excuses have been made by our mutton-headed politicians, including some from Plaid Cymru. It was a good reason for not renewing my membership of Plaid for a while on account of its failure to keep its promise to fund a daily newspaper in Welsh. What point is there in belonging to a party that doesn't keep its promises?

Like Montaigne, I shut myself in my study to avoid the infectious barbarism of the age. It's been a privilege to serve the literature of my country and my books still give me pleasure by reminding me of the treasures of Welsh literature. Like most inveterate book-worms, I keep my rarest and most valuable books in a glazed, mahogany case beyond the reach of direct light, dust and the little ones' sticky fingers. I learned this lesson about thirty years ago when a pipe burst in the central heating system in one of the bedrooms: the water came downstairs through the coving and seeped over an open shelf and ruined my Golden Cockerel edition of *The Mabinogion*, the magisterial edition by Thomas Jones and Gwyn Jones.

By the time I discovered the damage the water had begun to dry, leaving a nasty stain on the red leather spine of this noble tome. I groan to remember the disaster to this day. All the same, even books that are kept with care can suffer from mites, dampness, and a kind of fungus that feeds on the leather, the paper and the glue. They also rub against each other if they are too tight on the shelf, and their pages acquire brown blotches similar to those often seen on the hands of old people like me. One of the things I like doing from time to time, especially in the idle days between Christmas and the New Year, is to examine every book to make sure it's in satisfactory condition. I can relax while doing this for hours at a stretch. At heart, I am a librarian *manqué*!

Be that as it may, I start with my Gregynog editions, among which are a number from the early days of the Press between the two world wars. Here are the books by Ceiriog, Owen M. Edwards, T. Gwynn Jones, Edward Thomas, W. H. Davies and Henry Vaughan which booksellers tend to consider are the least desirable in monetary terms, on account of their plain design, I suppose. I don't care. I don't worry too much about what books are worth and I reserve an honourable place for them on my shelves. Nearby I keep my *peithynen* – the oaken frame with spindle rods bearing a series of *englynion* written in the alphabet devised by Iolo Morganwg early in the nineteenth century, one of my greatest treasures.

Among the books printed at Gregynog in its new dispensation, I buy only those by Welsh authors, of whom there are now a substantial number: R. S. Thomas, Alun Lewis, Ann Griffiths, Williams Pantycelyn, Dylan Thomas, John Ormond, Morgan Rhys, Waldo Williams, Kate Roberts, Williams Parry, Saunders Lewis, and others. Every copy of my selection from Kilvert's Diary, *The Curate of Clyro*, was sold soon after its publication in 1983 and it now appears in catalogues at six times its original price. I bought four copies, one for each of my children, and they are still in my bookcase.

I'd better note here that I buy only the ordinary editions of Gregynog books, and not the special bindings. If I were to spend a lot of money on a piece of art I'd prefer to buy a picture rather than a book that shows only its spine to the world. Furthermore, I don't buy the more esoteric books the Press publishes from time to time and which tend to reflect only the tastes of members of the management board. Gwasg Gregynog nowadays resembles the band of gentlemen who belong to the Roxburghe Club, their choice of titles reflecting only their own interests and without wider appeal; it's no wonder so many of their recent titles have sold so poorly.

There are other valuable books on my shelves apart from the Gregynogs. From the Golden Cockerel I have *The Green Island* by Gwyn Jones (with his friend Jack Jones's signature on the fly-leaf) and *The Saga of Llywarch the Old* by Glyn Jones and T. J. Morgan. I also have a copy of the anthology *Gorchestion Beirdd Cymru*, with the names of Samuel Johnson and John Jones, Blaencwm, Ruth's great-great-great-great-grandfather, in the list of subscribers. Since the editor, Rhys Jones of Y Blaenau, belonged to Ruth's family and I was given the book by my friend Glyn Jones, I treasure it. I paid for a new binding in quarter leather a few years ago, and remember the binder, an Englishman in a shop in Bath, pulling my leg about 'the long words you have in your language' – until I informed him that '*gorchestion*', in his language, means 'masterpieces'.

From the same period comes my leather-bound edition of the poems of Dafydd ap Gwilym published at the expense of Owain Myfyr in 1789. This was the first time Dafydd's poems had appeared in a printed book and so the volume was a milestone in the history of Welsh scholarship. The preface begins like this: 'Of Dafydd ap Gwilym, whofe Poems are now for the firft time offered to the public, few memorials have furvived to the present day; in the lapfe of four hundred years moft of the incidents of his life have been forgotten.' This book was a prefent from my efteemed friend Harri Webb.

It stands alongside *Llewelyn: a tale of Cambria*, published by the Military Orphans Press in Calcutta in 1838. Having bought it for a shilling in Cardiff market, I took ten years to discover who the author of this long, patriotic poem was: Grace Buchanan Stevens, daughter of the Laird of Auchenbreck in Scotland. It must be very rare because there isn't a copy in the British Library. The second edition is dedicated to Lady Llanover but I don't know what the relationship between the two ladies was. Llywelyn ap Gruffydd appears in the poem not as a rebel against the English king but as a Welsh national hero; quite right, too.

On the shelves where I keep copies of books signed by their authors, there are some by Hugh MacDiarmid, David Jones, Sorley MacLean, and Seamus Heaney – giants of the twentieth century. But the one that gives me most pleasure is a copy of the booklet by R. S. Thomas, *An Acre of Land*, and on its fly-leaf the words 'Gwenallt, R. S. Thomas 1952'; it's hard to say how much this unique item is 'worth'. At its side stands a copy of *Y Mynach a'r Sant*, poems bound as one volume in 1928, and the words '*I Nelws, Gwenallt*' written inside; it's touching to see his wife's pet-name in the hand of the poet himself.

I must stop: it doesn't do for a man to swank too much about his valuable books; that's about as naff as showing neighbours your holiday snaps or inviting them to leaf through your stamp album. After all, collecting books should be one of life's private pleasures. Woe betide if I turn into a Lord Kenyon!

Although I spend time with my books, I spend much more in my study and at my desk where my computer sits together with everything else that's necessary for someone who tries to write. Usually, I keep office hours, working on until nine in the evening if the words are appearing on the screen without too much trouble. That's where I am at the moment, trying to finish this book. Above my desk there's a piece of calligraphy by Jonathan Adams, Sam's son, based on the poem '*Pa beth yw dyn?*' by Waldo Williams and a photo of my father at work in the power station at Upper Boat; I like to see the image of a turbine generating energy when my head starts drooping.

There are three desks in my study: one to hold the computer, one where I keep the books I am currently reading (I don't like reading in bed), and one for envelopes, stamps, letters, reference books, and contacts book. At my back are the oaken shelves I was given by the widow of Jack Jones which hold the files in which I try to keep copies of everything of mine that appears in print. Correspondence and the Rhys Davies Trust accounts book are on one shelf and copies of poems, stories, articles, reviews and cuttings on another. A large file contains my obituaries, an ever-growing file since there's no let-up in the rate at which eminent Welsh people pass beyond the veil. Yes, I'm a tidy boy, and the state of my study reflects the fact that I spent more than twenty years as a bureaucrat. It was therefore easy to choose a title for the original Welsh version of this book, *Cofnodion* (Minutes), since I've tried to record some of the main events in my life on its pages, and I hope the English title serves just as well.

I keep my reference books on the walls of my study. The *Oxford Companions* are almost all here. They sit on shelves with other books such as the *Shorter Oxford Dictionary*, the Academi's *English-Welsh Dictionary*, the *Dictionary of Welsh Biography*, the *Dictionary of National Biography*, Brewer's *Dictionary of Phrase and Fable*, Roget's *Thesaurus*, the *Princeton Encyclopedia of Poetry and Poetics*, *Yr Odliadur* (rhyming dictionary), *Enwau Afonydd a Nentydd Cymru* (R. J. Thomas's study of river names), five or six foreign-language dictionaries (including *le Grand Robert*), Cruden's *Concordance to the Bible*, *A Dictionary of the Place-names of Wales* compiled by Hywel Wyn Owen and Richard Morgan, *Llyfryddiaeth yr Iaith Gymraeg*, the two volumes of *Llyfryddiaeth Llenyddiaeth Gymraeg*, *The Oxford Dictionary for Writers and Editors*, and a number of other useful books. I know it's possible to call up a huge amount of the information contained in these books by clicking Google nowadays, but it's an incomparable pleasure to open these handsome works and spend hours browsing them.

I derive the same pleasure from magazines. Although I wasn't able to read Welsh when the first number of *Taliesin* appeared in 1961, I've read every one of the subsequent numbers thoroughly, as part of my attempt to master the literary language. This is the only magazine I've kept in its entirety, although there are longish runs of *Y Genhinen, Tir Newydd, Y Fflam, The Welsh History Review, Y Faner Newydd, Barddas, Tu Chwith* and *Y Casglwr* on my shelves, too. I gave away hundreds of copies of *Barn* the other day because I needed the shelf-space.

Of course, I specialize in the English-language literature of Wales. So here are Keidrych Rhys's *Wales*, Gwyn Jones's *The Welsh Review*, Raymond Garlick's *Dock Leaves*, Roland Mathias's *The Anglo-Welsh Review, Poetry Wales, Planet* edited by Ned Thomas and later John Barnie, *Arcade, The New Welsh Review* and *Cambria*. I've always thought periodicals to be indicators of a literature's health and I try to support them as best I can. Having said that, I've recently grown tired of the *New Welsh Review* and started to feel the same about *Poetry Wales*. Indeed, I've cancelled my subscription to the former and will do the same for the latter unless it improves soon; I have no interest in magazines that neglect the literature of Wales in their attempts to appear 'international' – a woefully misused word. Writers who think themselves 'international' usually turn out to be monoglot provincials. If I want to read poetry in foreign languages, or translations, I know where to find it. The proper function of *Poetry Wales* should be to care for poetry in or from or about Wales.

But back to the study. How many books do I own? Hard to say, as I've never counted them. But too many, that's for sure. I've tried to stop buying books via Amazon. There are so many in our house I have to keep them in the parlour (from Jane Aaron to William Williams), in the sun lounge (Welsh books before 1960), in the living-room (books Ruth and I are reading from day to day), in the lounge or front room as I still call it (history, politics, English, Irish, Scottish and American writers) and in the five bedrooms (art and Russian, French, German, Italian and Spanish writers). Of course, I know where everything is and can put my hand on any book in a jiffy. From time to time as I reach for a book on a high shelf I remember the composer Charles-Valentin Alkan, who was killed in 1888 when an enormous bookcase fell on top of him.

I also sometimes think of what will be the fate of my books and pictures after my day. I was brought up in a home that had virtually no books in it. Collecting them has doubtless been for me a kind of compensation for having been raised on a hearth where the only reading matter were the *South Wales Echo*, *John Bull* and *Old Moore's Almanack* – if I could get to them before my grandfather began to make spills for his pipe.

Our children can hardly be expected to read my copies of poetry in the Romance languages, or English-language poets from Auden to Yeats. They live in the digital age and the book has lost much of its appeal: the internet and world wide web and all the electronic devices like iPad, Facebook, YouTube, wi-fi, Skype, Twitter and Kindle rule their lives; I had to ask one of them the other day what exactly an App is. But I'm quite sure they will be glad to have our pictures. They include examples of work by Ernie Zobole, Ceri Richards, David Jones, John Elwyn, Alfred Janes, Will Roberts, Kyffin Williams, John Petts, Robert Macdonald, Brenda Chamberlain, Robert Hunter, Claudia Williams, William Brown, John Piper, David Woodford, Mary Lloyd Jones, Josef Herman, Eleri Mills, Nina Hamnett, Robert Colquhoun, Clive Hicks-Jenkins, David Carpanini, William Selwyn, Feliks Topolski, Anthony Evans, John Uzzell Edwards, Chris Griffin and James Donovan, as well as a few Russian ikons and antiquarian maps.

So I shall have to get rid of many of my books while I'm still on my feet. But where? In the Hay you get only pennies for second-hand books these days and only Ystwyth Books in Aberystwyth is likely to offer anything like a fair price. So this is my chance to load the car and sell a pile of books and spend the money on a slap-up meal for two in Gannets. We shall have the pleasure afterwards of sitting on the prom in what was once Ruth's hometown and where I bought books as an impecunious student, a long time ago; and on the way home I shall regret parting with so many of my old friends.

Even so, perhaps I'm being a bit hard on my children. All four have been brought up Welsh-speaking. They went to Ysgol Gyfun Glantaf, an excellent school, and the three girls studied for their degrees through the medium of Welsh in Bangor and now earn a living by using it in their work. All three, and our son Huw, are pretty cultured and literate, it must be said.

Huw Meredydd didn't want to go to Bangor like his sisters, mother, father and grandfather, although a place awaited him. Having grown from being a wizard and conjuror who earned pocket money by performing at birthday parties around Cardiff, starting when he was nine, he decided he wanted to be a professional broadcaster. Before he was seventeen he had a voluntary job in Rookwood Hospital where he learned to be a disc jockey and discovered he had a gift of the gab. Soon afterwards, and after having got his A Levels in Welsh, Drama and Media Studies, he had an offer to present a music programme on BBC 1. By now he presents radio and television programmes in Welsh and English and is a familiar face on S4C as well. He's also one of the founders of Sŵn, the popular music festival in Cardiff. In May 2011 the Open University gave him an honorary doctorate for his contribution to culture and education, and the University of Glamorgan and Bangor University have made him an honorary Fellow. Two years ago he married Sara Davies, a delightful young woman from Tregaron who had a job in the European Parliament when they first met.

Our eldest daughter, Lowri Angharad, has three children, namely Martha Glain and the twins Begw Angharad and Elis Rhys, and they live in Llanllechid near Bethesda, a mile or so from Margaret, Ruth's sister, who lives on the square in Rachub. Lowri, who has a degree in Welsh, is a producer with the television company Rondo and her husband, Gareth Evans, who comes from Bethesda, is an Assistant Head of Ysgol Syr Hugh Owen in Caernarfon.

Heledd Melangell also has a degree in Welsh. She recently left her secondment as temporary Head of Ysgol Bodringallt in the Rhondda to resume the deputy headship of Ysgol Gymraeg Pont Siôn Norton in Pontypridd. She has two children, Gwenno Angharad and Gethin Emrys; she recently bought a house in Whitchurch, five minutes from where we live.

Brengain Gwenllian, who has a degree in Drama and Sociology, has retrained as a primary schoolteacher. She's married to Aron Evans, who makes animated films and whose father is the painter Anthony Evans who also lives, with his wife Glenys, in Whitchurch. Brengain has five children: Elan Meredydd, Rhiannon Wyn, Gwern Arthur, Luned Rhys and Menna Llwyd; they too live very near us in Whitchurch. Elan is studying Drama at Cardiff and Nannon Welsh and Drama at Aberystwyth.

So we have ten grandchildren and every one has Welsh as a first language – as is evident when they come to Blaen-bedw for Sunday lunch and rampage around the house and garden afterwards. Not every Welsh-learner can swank as much – not every native Welsh-speaker either. I hope I haven't bragged too much or been too self-satisfied in this book (common faults of most autobiographers) and that I shall be excused for saying I feel the better part of pride in the fact that all our grandchildren are Welsh-speakers.

They will know so much more about Wales for having two languages and a better understanding of other cultures.

One of my pleasures these days is listening to them chatting in Welsh around the table when they come for a meal at Blaen-bedw. Whatever else I've achieved over the years (and I blush to think how little my contribution has been), the future belongs to them and their contemporaries, and from now on theirs is the world too, and this small part of it that's called Cymru. May they grow up to be worthy citizens of both and so be as happy as their Bampa has been (most of the time). I'm content to think that in these bright and articulate children, and their descendants, I shall have all the life everlasting that I desire. And now I hear them raising their voices and telling this old codger to be quiet and let them have their say. Quite right, too.

Also by the author:

M e i c   S t e p h e n s

Welsh*lives*
Gone but not forgotten

75 obituaries of eminent people

£12.95

Also from Y Lolfa:

£9.95

Looking up
England's
Arsehole

The Patriotic Poems and Boozy Ballads of

Harri Webb

Edited by Meic Stephens

£5.95

My Shoulder to the Wheel is just one of a
whole range of publications from Y Lolfa.
For a full list of books currently in print, send
now for your free copy of our new full-colour
catalogue. Or simply surf into our website

www.ylolfa.com

for secure on-line ordering.

Talybont Ceredigion Cymru SY24 5HE
e-mail ylolfa@ylolfa.com
website www.ylolfa.com
phone (01970) 832 304
fax 832 782